The Great Bronze Age of China

A Symposium

The Great Bronze Age of China
A Symposium

George Kuwayama, Editor

Los Angeles County Museum of Art

Distributed by University of Washington Press, Seattle and London

Library of Congress Cataloging in Publication Data
Main entry under title:
The Great Bronze Age of China: A Symposium

Held May 23–24, 1981.
Bibliography: p.
Contents: The origin of Shang and the problem of Xia
in Chinese archaeology / K.C. Chang—Some Anyang royal
bronzes / Louisa G. Fitzgerald Huber—Western Zhou
history reconstructed from bronze inscriptions / David
S. Nivison—[etc.]
1. Bronzes, Chinese—To 221 B.C.—Congresses.
2. China—Antiquities—Congresses. 3. China—History—
To 221 B.C.—Congresses. I. Kuwayama, George.
II. Los Angeles County Museum of Art.
NK7983.22.G73   1983   730'.0931   83–9393
ISBN 0–87587–113–5

Published by the
Los Angeles County Museum of Art
5905 Wilshire Boulevard
Los Angeles, California 90036

Edited by Sarah Handler and Erwin Rosen
Art Direction and Design by Michelle Gauthé

Text set in Times Roman typefaces
by Petersen Publishing Company, Los Angeles
Electronic pagination by Jack Cooke

Printed in an edition of 2,000 copies
on Westvaco 70# Sterling Gloss Book
by Franklin Press, San Bernardino, California

COVER: *Rubbing* (taken from the Bo Ju li)
Excavated from Tomb M 251 at Liulihe, Fangshan, Beijing
late 11th–early 10th century B.C.
h: 13 in.
Beijing Cultural Relics Bureau

The Great Bronze Age of China symposium was held
at the Los Angeles County Museum of Art, May 23–24, 1981.

Contents

6

Foreword

The rich cultural artifacts of China's Bronze Age are testaments to the artistic achievement and technical virtuosity of China's ancient civilization. *The Great Bronze Age of China* exhibition, organized by The Metropolitan Museum of Art, featured Bronze Age ritual vessels, jades, and life-sized terracotta warrior figures from the tomb of China's first emperor, Qin Shihuangdi—all unearthed within the last decade.

The Los Angeles County Museum of Art was among the participants in this exhibition, which marked an important cultural exchange between the People's Republic of China and the United States. Circulated to four other American museums, the exhibition was shown in Los Angeles from April 1 to June 10, 1981.

In conjunction with this exhibition, the Museum was able to bring renowned scholars specializing in China's Bronze Age culture to Los Angeles to participate in a two-day symposium. The project, endowed by a generous grant from the National Endowment for the Humanities, provided a unique opportunity for the Southern California community to share in current research in this field. Now, with the support of the Museum's Far Eastern Art Council and Petersen Publishing Company, Los Angeles, we take great pleasure in publishing the papers generated by that symposium. We are proud to be able to offer this fine collection of innovative scholarly research to the public.

Earl A. Powell III
Director

Acknowledgments

China is the oldest continuing civilization in the world and its cultural achievements over seven millennia are without peer. The flurry of archaeological activity in China within the last few decades has revolutionized our knowledge of ancient China. The enormous amount of new material, much of it magnificent like the impressive bronzes from Lady Fu Hao's tomb or the funerary army of Qin Shihuangdi, offers rich substance for analysis and interpretation.

On May 23 and 24, 1981, a symposium was held at the Los Angeles County Museum of Art in connection with *The Great Bronze Age of China: An Exhibition from the People's Republic of China*. America's most eminent scholars of Chinese art, archaeology, philology, history, and technology were invited to participate. Their profound insights into the many facets of China's Bronze Age civilization in the light of these recent discoveries are published in this volume. On behalf of our Museum I would like to thank the writers listed on the contents page for their splendid efforts and brilliant contributions.

This publication would not have been possible without the encouragement and tangible support of a large number of people. The members of the Far Eastern Art Council of the Los Angeles County Museum of Art have underwritten the costs of editing and production, and the Petersen Publishing Company has generously provided its professional services gratis to enable us to produce this volume. Special thanks go to Frederick R. Waingrow, the company's president, and to Jean Kissell, Production Coordinator, for their kind assistance. Clarity and readability of these papers have been enhanced by the editing of Sarah Handler and Erwin Rosen, while the handsome graphic design was created by Michelle Gauthé. Finally, my deepest appreciation goes to Leslee Leong and Jane Burrell of the Far Eastern Art Department for their assistance.

G. Kuwayama

Notes to the Reader

Chinese terms and names in the following symposium papers are rendered in pinyin *except for those of Louisa Huber and David Nivison, which are in Wade-Giles. Bibliographic references are romanized according to the system practiced at the time of publication. Chinese and Japanese names are printed in traditional fashion with the family name preceding the given name without a comma.*

The Origin of Shang and the Problem of Xia in Chinese Archaeology

K.C. Chang

Professor of Anthropology

Harvard University

THE SHANG CIVILIZATION of the Zhengzhou and Yinxu (Anyang) phases (from approximately 1650 to 1100 B.C.) is now relatively well known according to archaeological and (for Yinxu) inscriptional data, but its earlier developments and ultimate origins are still clouded by insufficient evidence on the one hand, and by entanglements with the issue of Xia civilization on the other. Ongoing research in early Shang and Xia archaeology is so active and productive that no attempt to summarize the pertinent literature can achieve real currency in a volume of symposium papers. At the same time, useful purpose can be served by a review of the fundamental concepts involved in the pertinent issues.

The Natural Setting

It is important first of all to ask about the conditions of land, coasts, waters, climate, and vegetation of North China during the third and the second millennia B.C., not only because the distribution and the wealth of natural resources were crucial considerations in any study of the rise of ancient civilizations, but also in view of the very marked changes of natural conditions during this period that presumably were pertinent to the distribution and movement of ancient peoples.

Many palaeogeographers are convinced that in geological times much of the alluvial plain of eastern North China (now drained by the Yellow and Huai Rivers) was submerged under water, which in fact separated the central Shandong highlands, then an island, from the western part of North China.[1] This belief is based on two sets of facts. First, geological studies along the coastline of the Gulf of Chihli (or the Bay of Bohai) have shown that the sea level began to rise since the end of the last glaciation at about ten to twelve thousand years ago, reaching its present condition at about 7000 B.P., and kept rising until 6–7 meters higher than the present level at 5000–6000 B.P., which is at the precise threshold of the period of our concern. After that, the sea level fluctuated at least three times, at 4500–4000 B.P., 3000–2500 B.C., and 1000 B.P., before the current line was reached.[2] When the sea level was high, most of eastern Hebei, central and eastern Henan east of the 50-meter contour line that follows approximately the Beijing-Hankou railway, and northeastern Anhui were submerged. The second set of facts has to do with the deposition of silt by the Yellow River after the river flowed out of the western highlands near the city of Zhengzhou. It is believed that most if not all of the silts deposited in eastern North China, where they have made up the alluvial plain, have been deposited within the last few thousand years. These deposits, coupled with the lowering of sea water level, produced the dry land that bridged the western highlands with Shandong.

These facts are not questioned, but some specific details are particularly relevant to the issues at hand. These can be summed up in two questions: At precisely what time periods did the dry land form or begin to form? And what was the climatic and biogeographic condition that prevailed on the land surface after it had formed? The alluvial plain area of North China is poorly understood geologically and archaeologically, because the Yellow River has continued to deposit its silts over the plains surface, putting under very thick cover much of the remains that were left on the land surface and could have been studied. But these questions are crucial, for without some answers we cannot even visualize the topographic and biogeographic stage on which our Xia and Shang peoples

10

had acted.

Regarding the date of the formation of dry land between Shandong island and the western highlands, we have already mentioned the chronology of the coastline changes: The highest sea water level occurred during the fourth millennium B.C. However, we do not know the precise coastline in the area of Henan, and in any event by the third millennium B.C., the sea water had begun to recede. There was, therefore, dry land in the area in question by the time Xia and Shang peoples and their near ancestors came upon the stage. Moreover, on the basis of a conjectured rate of silt deposition from the Yellow River, Ding Su, a geographer writing in the late 1940s, had speculated that by 5500 B.C. the alluvium of the Yellow River had begun to reach Shandong, connecting up the latter landmass with western North China, and by 2300 B.C., the time of Xia dynasty, the vast plain of the lower Yellow River and the upper Huai had formed.[3]

As to the natural conditions of this newly formed land, we are fairly certain that during the third and the second millennia B.C. the lowland of North China was vast, flat, and marshy, with a climate both warmer and more moist than the same area is at present. Even though eastern Henan and westernmost Shandong are covered with very thick silt deposits (at places as much as seven or eight meters) which makes the study of ancient soils here difficult, a number of peat deposits have been found in the central Hebei plain, indicating the presence of lakes and marshes that had long dried up.[4] A long pollen profile taken from the peat deposit at the southern tip of Liaodong peninsula, which faces Shandong across the mouth of the Gulf of Chihli, shows that from 6000–3000 B.C. the climate there as indicated by the prevailing vegetation was 3°–5° C. higher than the present average, and that from 3000–500 B.C. the climate was still 2°–4° C. higher than the present.[5] Other lines of evidence, including zooarchaeological and textual, strongly corroborate the above pattern, namely that of a warmer and more moist climate, heavier vegetation cover, and more marshes, ponds, and lakes in North China during the third and second millennium B.C. than at the present time.[6]

"Xia" and "Shang" Defined

Xia and Shang were two of the dynasties that are said to have ruled in North China, but when different scholars talked about the "origins" of Xia and Shang they often had the origins of different things in mind, and the ensuing confusion is actually a more serious obstacle to understanding the issues at hand than even paucity of data.[7] When we consider the origins of Xia and Shang, it is necessary first to define the latter names so that we are clear about the precise entities whose origins we are discussing.

Since we know quite a bit more about Shang than we do about Xia, let us begin with Shang. It is customary to refer to Shang as a dynastic period, the time during which the ruling house of the Shang dynasty "reigned" in the North China political stage. In this sense we can use the phrase "Shang period," even

though we cannot precisely place it chronologically. Traditionally, Chinese historians date the dynastic reign to 1766–1122 B.C., but contemporary Shang scholars are agreed on only one thing: this date is probably inaccurate.

Within the Shang time period, the word Shang is used in several other senses, one very broad, others strict and narrow. In its broad sense, Shang refers to the civilization of the Shang period and all its components. The Shang civilization is characterized by distinctive and identifiable features in its architecture, bronze vessels and weapons, horse chariots, pottery, jades, wood- and bone-carvings, oracle bones, lacquerware, stone sculpture, and burial customs. When we see an archaeological find bearing some diagnostic features of the Shang civilization, we have no hesitation in calling the find a Shang site or a Shang object, no matter where the find is located. It so happens that the Shang civilization defined in such stylistic terms is found to occur in a large part of China, from northern Hebei to southern Hunan, from central Shandong to central Shaanxi. It is legitimate to say that the name Shang may be used to refer to the whole high civilization that is archaeologically found throughout China. Thus, in its broad sense "Shang" is a synonym of the Chinese civilization of the Shang period.

On the other hand, the word Shang is also used in several narrower senses: a political dynasty built by the royal house of a particular clan; a subculture specifically associated with, and generated by, the dynastic elite; and a political state imposed on a specific but shifting territory. These we may abbreviate as the Shang dynasty, Shang subculture, and Shang state. Their definitions are rather self-evident, although the precise differences between the Shang subculture and the rest of Shang civilization have not been carefully studied. There is an obvious distinction in bronzes between those from Anyang and some of those from Anhui, for example, and these have been referred to as "metropolitan" and "regional."[8] The contrast implied by these terms ought to be that internal to a state, but the distinction in question is actually more likely to be that between different states. It is safer for now to apply the term "Shang subculture" to the stylistically distinctive cultural entity confined geographically to within the Shang state, ruled by the Shang dynasty, which includes, in today's provincial terms, most of Henan, western Shandong, southern Hebei, northwestern Anhui, and northern Hubei.

It may be useful to point out that of the five senses of the name Shang—Shang period, Shang civilization, Shang dynasty, Shang subculture, and Shang state—"Shang dynasty" appears to be the primary sense in terms of ancient Chinese ethnosemantics, while all the others are derivative. First there was the political dynasty of the Zi clan, called Shang by their Zhou conquerors. The dynasty ruled the Shang state and was responsible for the formation of a distinctive elite Shang subculture. The Shang subculture was, of course, a part of the ancient Chinese civilization, which is referred to as Shang civilization because it flourished during the Shang period, i.e., the period when the Shang dynasty reigned in its own state, probably the dominant state of China at the time. The concept of "Shang people" can also be understood as the group of people who followed the Shang dynasty's rule and assumed the Shang subculture; many of them were probably the lower members of the same clan from which the Shang dynasty rose or from their affiliated clans.

When we discuss the origins of the Shang, which of the Shang definitions do we have in mind? Realistically there are two possibilities. One is the origin of Shang civilization, meaning the Chinese civilization of the Shang period; the other is the specific origins of the Shang dynasty and the Shang subculture associated with it. When most people talk about the Shang origins, they probably have the second aspect in mind.

All of the above definitions of the Shang can be applied to the Xia in the abstract. According to textual history there was a Xia dynasty, which reigned during the Xia period (c. 2200–17th century B.C.) in a Xia state located in southern Shanxi, southern Hebei, and northwestern Henan. Zhou texts refer to a Xia subculture that contrasts with the Shang and Zhou subcultures. The archaeological study of the Xia, thus, centers on two related issues: an archaeological definition of the Xia subculture, and an archaeological exploration of the Chinese civilization during the Xia period.

Archaeology of North China During the Third and Second Millennium B.C.

The known Shang civilization is well exemplified by the archaeological finds at Zhengzhou and Yinxu. The issue of the origins of the Shang subculture can be pursued as follows: Take stock of the archaeological data in North China dating to the third and the second millennium B.C. prior to the Zhengzhou phase, beginning approximately 1650 B.C. Classify these data into cultural groups and place them chronologically and geographically. Identify these groups with Shang, Xia, and other subcultures. This procedure is logically simple, but is as yet inadequate for conclusive statements. Let us examine the extent to which statements are now possible with regard to the pertinent issues.

During the third and the early second millennium B.C., in the area of Henan, Shandong, and southern Hebei, there were the following archaeological cultures that are radiocarbon-dated:

1. Dawenkou Culture: Along the edges of Shandong highlands and the eastern Shandong plain.[9]

2. Shandong Longshan Culture: Approximately the same area of distribution as the above, but generally later in time.[10]

3. Henan Longshan Culture: Divided into at least three regional phases: central-western Henan, northern Henan (and southern Hebei), and eastern Henan.[11]

4. Erlitou Culture: In the same area as the central-western Henan Longshan but later in time.[12]

The chronological placement of these four cultures

according to available radiocarbon dates is shown in Chart 1.[13]

Chart 1 can be simplified into the following diagram of the time-space placement of the four major cultures of North China:

C.–W. Henan	N. Henan/ S. Hebei	E. Henan	E. Shandong/ S. Liaodong	B.C.
Zhengzhou	Zhengzhou	Zhengzhou		1500
				1600
				1700
Erlitou	? (1)	? (2)	Longshan	1800
				1900
				2000
				2100
				2200
C.–W. Henan Longshan	N. Henan Longshan	E. Henan Longshan		2300
				2400
				2500
				2600
				2700
				2800
		Dawenkou		2900
				3000

From this diagram, it is clear that the Zhengzhou phase of Shang civilization was probably derived from a Shang subculture represented by [a] Erlitou, [b] ? (1), [c] ? (2), or Dawenkou/Shandong Longshan, or any combination of the above. Let us examine each of the several possibilities in turn.

Erlitou Culture

First brought to light in 1954 at the Yucun site in Dengfeng, Henan, Erlitou is the first culture in China to yield a fortified town, palatial structures, ritual bronze vessels and bronze weapons, and evidence of human sacrifice. Since all of these also characterized the Shang, in the early 1960s and much of the 1970s a number of archaeologists came to regard Erlitou as "Early Shang," serving as the link between the Henan Longshan Culture and the Shang civilization of the Zhengzhou phase.[14] Bo, the first capital city of the Shang dynasty, is sometimes said by historians to be located near Luoyang, which happens to be the center of the Erlitou Culture.

At least two things, however, stand in the way of calling Erlitou Early Shang and thus the solution to the problem of Shang origins. On the one hand, there is much in Shang that is not found in Erlitou but is found in Dawenkou, suggesting that the ancestor-descendent relationship between Erlitou and Shang is far from exclusive. On the other hand, the temporal and geographic distributions of Erlitou match almost exactly those of Xia, according to textual statements. Beginning in the mid-1970s a growing number of archaeologists came to regard Erlitou as the archaeological manifestation of the Xia subculture and perhaps the core of the Xia state,[15] but there is lingering uncertainty with regard to the later strata at the Erlitou

Chart 1

Central-Western Henan			N. Henan-S. Hebei			Eastern Henan			E. Shandong and S. Liaodong			B.C.
												1500
			BK75007	Zhengzhou	1520±160							
			ZK177	Zhengzhou	1590±140							
			ZK178	Zhengzhou	1620±140							
ZK286	Erlitou	1625±130										
									ZK364-0	Longshan	1783±110	
ZK280	Erlitou	1900±130							ZK361-0	Dawenkou	1879±115	
ZK825	Erlitou	1911±110										
ZK212	Erlitou	1920±115										2000
									ZK363-0	Longshan	2006±115	
ZK353	Erlitou	2007±185										
ZK349	Longshan	2007±165										
									ZK321	Longshan	2035±115	
									ZK391-0	Dawenkou	2038±190	
									ZK362-0	Dawenkou	2070±160	
			ZK771	Longshan	2130±160							
			ZK441	Longshan	2135±165							
			ZK442	Longshan	2230±160							
			ZK443	Longshan	2230±165							
						ZK763	Longshan	2260±130				
ZK386	Longshan	2293±150				ZK866	Longshan	2290±140				
			ZK745	Longshan	2325±145				ZK317	Dawenkou	2340±195	
ZK680	Erlitou	2356±190	ZK133	Longshan	2340±140							
ZK31-1	Erlitou	2388±150										
ZK126	Longshan	2390±145	ZK769	Longshan	2390±140	ZK458	Longshan	2390±130	ZK390-0	Longshan	2390±170	
						ZK456	Longshan	2420±145				
			ZK770	Longshan	2450±140	ZK541, 457	Longshan	2450±175	ZK78	Longshan	2465±145	2500
			ZK200	Longshan	2515±145	ZK457	Longshan	2515±140				
									ZK415	Longshan	2575±135	
			ZK570	Longshan	2577±125							
			ZK740, 756	Longshan	2580±145							
			ZK823	Longshan	2610±140				ZK413	Longshan	2640±135	
									ZK479	Dawenkou	2700±180	
			ZK824	Longshan	2765±135							
									ZK470	Dawenkou	2860±150	
						ZK739	Longshan	2950±200				
												3000

site, which seem to date from a later stage than the Xia Dynasty. This results in the curious phenomenon of breaking the cultural continuum at Erlitou (in four strata) into two subcultures, Xia in the earlier phase and Shang in the later phase.[16] Even if the late dating of the upper strata holds up in future data, the Erlitou sequence as a whole should obviously be regarded as the continuum of the Xia subculture, with its later stages surviving into the Shang period.

The exact nature of the Erlitou Culture is the major part of the so-called Xia problem in contemporary Chinese archaeology.[17] The presence of archaeological markers for a highly stratified society and aristocratic power center—primarily fortified town walls, palaces, bronze vessels and weapons, and human sacrifice—qualify the Erlitou for the Xia dynasty, and the geographical and chronological coincidence between archaeology and textual history is highly persuasive in the same direction. But until written evidence is found to tie the Erlitou aristocracy with the legendary Xia dynasty—a prospect whose materialization is uncertain because of our ignorance of the media of Xia inscriptions—this will probably remain a problem in Chinese archaeology for years to come.

Question Mark No. 1 (North Henan-South Hebei, 2150–1650)

This space in the chart is marked with a question mark because of a lack of radiocarbon-dated sites. Actually there is a likelihood that an early-looking Shang culture, earlier than the Zhengzhou phase, occurred here during the interval of 2150–1650, as represented by the "early Shang" layers at Jiangou in Handan[18] and the Xiaqihuan in Ci Xian,[19] both in Southern Hebei. The "early Shang" description here has been based largely on pottery types, but at these sites no ritual vessels of bronze or major aristocratic centers have been located. We need absolute dates to confirm the chronological position of this culture, and we need additional excavations to enable better understanding of the nature of the society here, although this culture does seem to serve as bridging the Northern Henan Longshan and the later Zhengzhou phase of Shang in a stylistic sense.

Southern Hebei, along the southern slopes of the Taihang mountains and the coastal plains, has always been a legendary area of Early Shang and predynastic Shang activities.[20] Wang Hai, an important predynastic ancestor of the Shang royal house, had left some legends in Hebei, and some of the early dynastic capitals could be located in the southern part of the province also.[21] Zou Heng, of Peking University and an important scholar writing prolifically on the issue of Xia and early Shang, believes that the Shang subculture originated in southern Hebei and adjacent areas.[22] We should certainly look at this area very carefully as it yields additional achaeological finds.

Question Mark No. 2 (Eastern Henan and Westernmost Shandong)

This area is the least archaeologically explored; there are many Longshan sites located on natural and artificial mounds (locally called *gudui,* "ancient mounds" or "solitary mounds"), but very few remains from the early historical periods have been located here in the plains. This is the famous (or infamous) Yellow River flooding region ("Huang fan qu") and the ground is covered with many meters of silt deposited during the many centuries in China's historical period when the Yellow River meandered its course from Zhengzhou eastward. This same area, however, is where Shang (Shang dynasty's sacred citadel) and Bo (the capital city of Tang, Shang dynasty's founding king) are believed located. As early as 1936, Li Jingdan of the Institute of History and Philology, Academia Sinica, came to the Shangqiu area to look for evidence of Shang's ancestors, but he described the seven to eight meters of silt an insurmountable obstacle in his quest.[23] Thirty-some years later, archaeologists at the Luoyang Archaeology Station of the Institute of Archaeology came to the Shangqiu area for the same purpose, but they were no more successful.[24]

It is certainly unfair to point to a *terra incognita* as the most likely area of the origins of the Shang subculture, but all things do point to it. Shang and Bo were here, as we just mentioned. The Kongsang region, the Region of the Hallow Mulberry—the legendary home of Yi Yin, Tang's prime minister—is located in this area. Oracle bone inscriptions refer to Shang as a sacred ancestral shrine where kings made reports to cover their most important military moves; Dong Zuobin has convincingly shown that Shang was indeed located near modern Shangqiu. My own prediction is that an important Early Shang culture will someday be found here.

The Dawenkou and Longshan Regions of Shandong

The Shandong Longshan Culture persisted into time periods contemporary with Zhengzhou and Yinxu Shang; at least some of them were probably the archaeological manifestation of the Yi people in the oracle bone inscriptions and the historical texts. The Dawenkou Culture, probably directly ancestral to Shandong Longshan, is characterized by a number of important cultural features also characteristic of the Shang civilization of Zhengzhou and Yinxu. These include burial customs such as rich furnishings, wooden burial chambers, and the earthen ledge for grave goods; the ritual use of turtle shells; animal motifs in art; and white pottery.[25] One strongly feels the possibility of important input into the Shang subculture from Dawenkou. If an Early Shang was indeed the dominant culture of eastern Henan and adjacent regions, its closeness to the Dawenkou Culture would in no way be unusual or difficult.

Notes

1. Li Ssu-kuang, *Chung-kuo Ti-shih Pien-ch'ien Hsiao-shih* [A short history of landform changes in China], Shanghai: Commercial Press, 1930; Ting Su, "Hua-pei Ti-hsing-shih yü Shang-Yin ti Li-shih" [Topographic history of North China and the history of Shang-Yin dynasty], *Bulletin of the Institute of Ethnology, Academia Sinica,* Taipei, vol. 20, 1965, pp. 155–62.

2. Guo Xudong, "Wan Gengxinshi Yilai Zhongguo Haipingmian di Bianhua" [Sea-level changes in China since late Pleistocene], *Scientia Geologia Sinica,* vol. 4, 1979, pp. 330–40.

3. Ting Su, "Hua-pei Ti-hsing-shih yü Shang-Yin ti Li-shih"; *Chung-Kuo Ti-hsing* [Chinese topography], Taipei: Chinese Cultural Publication Commission, 1954.

4. K.C. Chang, *The Archaeology of Ancient China,* New Haven and London: Yale University Press, 1977, p. 32.

5. Chen Chenghui, Lu Yanchou, and Shen Chengde, "Liaoning Sheng Nanbu Yiwan Nian Lai Ziranhuanjing di Yanbian" [Changes in the natural environment in southern Liaoning in the past ten thousand years], *Scientia Sinica,* vol. 6, 1977, pp. 603–14.

6. K.C. Chang, *Archaeology of Ancient China,* pp. 31–35; *Shang Civilization,* New Haven and London: Yale University Press, 1980, pp. 136–41.

7. For much of the discussion in this section, consult *Shang Civilization* (see n. 6).

8. Virginia Kane, "The Independent Bronze Industries in the South of China Contemporary with the Shang and Western Chou Dynasties," *Archives of Asian Art,* vol. 28, 1974–75, p. 78.

9. Archaeology Program, Department of History, Shandong University, *Dawenkou Wenhua Taolun Wen Ji* [Essays on the Dawenkou Culture], Jinan: Qilu Xueshe, 1979.

10. Shandong Provincial Museum, "Sanshi Nian Lai Shandong Sheng Wenwu Kaogu Kongzuo" [Cultural relics work and archaeology in Shandong in the last thirty years], in *Wenwu Kaogu Kongzuo Sanshi Nian* [Thirty years of cultural relics work and archaeology], Beijing: Wenwu Press, 1979, pp. 186–97.

11. Li Yangsong, "Cong Henan Longshan Wenhua di Jige Leixing Tan Xia Wenhua di Ruogan Wenti" [Some issues of the Xia civilization viewed from the classification of Henan Longshan Cultures], in *Proceedings of the First Annual Meeting of the Archaeological Society of China,* Beijing: Wenwu Press, 1980, pp. 32–49.

12. Sun Hua, "Guanyü Erlitou Wenhua" [On the Erlitou Culture], *Kaogu,* vol. 6, 1980, pp. 521–25.

13. For radiocarbon dates prior to 1977, see Xia Nai, "Tan Shisi Ceding Niandai he Zhongguo Shiqian Kaoguxue" [Carbon-14 dates and the prehistoric archaeology of China], *Kaogu,* vol. 4, 1977, pp. 217–32. For additional dates after 1977, see *Kaogu* and *Wenwu,* 1978–81.

14. This thesis is still prevalent in K.C. Chang, *Archaeology of Ancient China.*

15. T'ung Chu-ch'en, "Ts'ung Erh-li-t'ou Lei-hsing Wen-hua Shih Lun Chung-kuo ti Kuo-chia Ch'i-yüan Wen-t'i" [The issue of the origin of the state in China as seen from a discussion on the origin of the Erlitou-type culture], *Wenwu,* vol. 6, 1975, pp. 29–33; K.C. Chang, "Yin-Shang Wen-ming Ch'i-yüan Yen-chiu Shang ti Yi-ko Kuan-chien Wen-t'i" [A key question in the study of the origins of Yin-Shang civilization], in *Essays Pre-*

sented to Mr. Shen Kang-po on His Eightieth Birthday, pp. 151–70, Taipei: Lien-ching Press, 1976; Yü Po, "Kuo-jia Wen-wu Chü Tsai Teng-feng Chao-K'ai Kao-ch'eng I-chih Fa-chüeh Hsien-ch'ang Hui" [A conference held at the site of Kao-ch'eng, Teng-feng, under the auspices of the National Cultural Relics Bureau], *Honan Wenpo T'ung-hsün,* vol. 1, 1978, pp. 22–24.

16. See a summary of various hypotheses in Hsia Nai (Xia Nai), "T'an-t'an T'an-t'ao Hsia Wen-hua ti Chi-ke Wen-ti" [On several issues in the investigation of the Hsia culture], *Honan Wenpo T'ung-hsün,* vol. 1, 1978, pp. 32–33.

17. There are numerous writings on the Xia problem in Chinese archaeology. The following are among the notable: Tsou Heng, "Kuan-yü T'an-so Hsia Wen-hua ti T'u-ching" [On the approaches to an exploration of the Hsia culture], *Honan Wenpo T'ung-hsün,* vol. 1, 1978, pp. 34–35; Wu Ju-tso, "Kuan-yü Hsia Wen-hua Chi-ch'i Lai-yüan ti Ch'u-pu T'an-so" [Preliminary explorations into the Hsia culture and its origins], *Wenwu,* vol. 9, 1978, pp. 70–73; An Jinhuai, "Yü Xi Xiadai Wenhua Chu-tan" [Preliminary explorations of the Xia culture in western Henan], *Zhongguo Lishi Bowuguan Guankan,* vol. 1, 1979, pp. 24–28; Li Xiandeng, "Guanyü Tansuo Xia Wenhua di Ruogan Wenti" [On some issues in the exploration of the Xia culture], *Zhongguo Lishi Bowuguan Guankan,* vol. 2, 1980, pp. 29–34; Wu Ruzuo, "Xia Wenhua Chulun" [A preliminary discussion on the Xia culture], *Zhongguo Shi Yanjiu,* vol. 2, 1979, pp. 132–41; Zou Heng, *Xia Shang Zhou Kaoguxue Lunwenji* [Essays in the archaeology of the Xia, Shang, and Zhou], Peking: Wenwu Press, 1980.

18. "1957-nien Han-tan Fa-chüeh Chien-pao" [Brief report of the excavations in Han-Tan in 1957], *Kaogu,* vol. 10, 1959, pp. 531–36; "Hopei Han-tan Chien-kou-ts'un Ku-i-chih Fa-chüeh Chien-pao" [Brief report of the excavation of the ancient site at Chien-kou-ts'un in Han-tan, Hopei], *Kaogu,* vol. 4, 1961, pp. 197–202.

19. "Cixian Xiaqihuan Yizhi Fajue Baogao" [Report of the excavations of the Xiaqihuan site in Cixian], *Kaogu Xuebao,* vol. 2, 1979, pp. 185–214.

20. Chin Ching-fang, "Shang Wen-hua Ch'i-yüan yü Wo-kuo Bei-fang Shuo" [On the hypothesis of the Shang's origins in the north of China], *Chung-hua Wen-shih Lun-ts'ung,* vol. 7, 1978, pp. 65–70, Shanghai: Ku-chi Press.

21. Yan Yiping, "Xiaqihuan Yizhi Wei Pan Geng Qian Yin Qian Gudu Zhi Tuice" [Speculation on the Xiaqihuan site as old capital of Shang prior to Pan Geng's removal to Yin], *Zhongguo Wenzi,* n.s., no. 2, 1980, pp. 239–55.

22. Zou Heng, *Xia Shang Zhou Kaoguxue Lunwenji.*

23. Li Ching-tan, "Yü-tung Shang-ch'iu Yung-ch'eng Tiao-ch'a Chi Tsao-lü-t'ai Hei-ku-tui Ts'ao-ch'iao San Ch'u Hsiao Fa-chüeh" [The surveys in Shang-ch'iu and Yung-ch'eng and the minor excavations at Taso-lü-tai, Hei-ku-tai, and Ts'ao-ch'iao in eastern Honan], *Chinese Journal of Archaeology,* vol. 2, 1947, pp. 88–120.

24. "1977-nien Honan Yung-ch'eng Wang-yü-fang Yi-chih Fa-chüeh Kai-kuang" [A general description of the excavation of the Wang-yü-fang site in Yung-ch'eng, Honan, in 1977], *Kaogu,* vol. 1, 1978, pp. 35–40.

25. K.C. Chang, "Yin-Shang Wen-ming Ch'i-yüan Yen-chiu Shang ti Yi-ko Kuan-chien Wen-t'i."

Some Anyang Royal Bronzes:
Remarks on Shang Bronze Decor

Louisa G. Fitzgerald Huber

Harvard University

MEASURED BY THE ACHIEVEMENTS of Bronze Age
art at large, the sacrificial vessels of Shang China
stand unequaled, particularly with regard to their decoration. Yet, of the various forms of Chinese art
throughout the ages, Shang bronzes, even more so
than those of the ensuing Chou dynasty, remain even
today one of the least approachable. Our understanding of these bronzes is limited not least by our ignorance of what meaning the images or designs on these
vessels may have had, or what meanings may have
accrued to them with the passage of time.

The only written records contemporary with the
bronzes themselves—the divination texts inscribed on
turtle shells or ox scapulae—seem to provide us with
no information on these matters. These inscriptions
record prognostications about the affairs of state, the
likely success of a military campaign, the auspicious-
ness of founding new settlements, the well-being of
members of the ruling family, and also about the sacrifices to the ancestors. But mention is seldom made
of the bronze vessels to be used in these sacrifices,
and questions regarding major casting events are also
rare. Although there occur in these texts references
both to the supreme god Shang Ti and to the spirits
of nature—as well as to the influential spirits of the
former kings, their consorts, and ministers—there is
evidently no mention of any spiritual being or creature that could be directly associated with the animallike images seen on the bronzes.[1] These lacunae are
indeed puzzling, yet they would seem to suggest two
things: the relative autonomy of the bronze workshops, and—a matter that cannot be sufficiently
stressed—the independence of the artist in making the
designs.

As the evolutionary sequence of bronze decor established by Max Loehr[2] makes clear, the business of the

Shang artist was not to render in appropriate visual
terms specific metaphysical or religious concepts.
Thus his imagery, while substantive and not without
meaning, may initially have had no referent outside
itself. The Shang artist may not have been bound by
any prescribed iconography save that which his fore-
bears created. Any concept of the significance of this
imagery therefore becomes inseparable from our understanding of its evolution.

The imagery that we find fully developed on vessels
of the Anyang period had come into being slowly,
through the passage of centuries, as the product of artistic inventiveness. It started not from given motifs
but seemingly out of nothing, for we now know that
the earliest cast bronze vessels in China, unearthed at
Yen-shih Erh-li-t'ou, are nearly always plain.[3] The nascent decoration, in which pairs of eyes emerge from
a pattern of curling lines, may reflect a lingering of
the far older tradition of spiraling configurations on
Neolithic painted ware,[4] now in combination with a
desire to introduce, through zoomorphic images, the
expressiveness of animate life. Nonetheless, while endowed with recognizable attributes, these new images
of faces and animallike forms ordinarily stayed clear
of the world of objective reality. Such consummate
skill and control as are displayed by Shang sacrificial
vessels should be sufficient indication that had the
artist chosen to turn his abilities to the recreation of
natural phenomena, he would have proceeded without
difficulty. Upon the rare occasion when this was his
choice, as in the case of the marvelously realistic rhinoceros in the Brundage Collection, his immediate
success is fully evident.[5] But it was the nature of
Shang art that such was precisely what he avoided.

The important excavations of such pre-Anyang sites
as Yen-shih Erh-li-t'ou, Cheng-chou, and more re-

cently P'an-lung-ch'eng in Huang-p'i-hsien in the south have supplied a view of the developing bronze styles preceding relocation of the Shang capital to present-day Anyang—a move generally believed to have taken place during the reign of P'an Keng around 1300 B.C. These same discoveries altered our concept of the history of bronze art during the period of the Anyang capital as well, since on their account it has become clear that Style I through an early phase of Style III was the invention of pre-Anyang masters. It is generally believed that these newly discovered sites are roughly equivalent in time to the legendary early capitals of Po and Ao.[6] The intervening time between Ao and Yin (or Anyang) saw, however, the successive occupation of three other capital cities (Hsiang, Pi, and Yen)—dynastic centers of which we have no knowledge other than their presumed existence. Without archaeological information from this period we can only speculate what advances in bronze decoration may have taken place. Yet, surprising as it may seem, perhaps only the creation of Style V can now be credited to the Anyang artists. While Style III may not have reached its maturity until Early Anyang times, the preceding period almost certainly witnessed its initial emergence, as well as the nascent phase of Style IV. Our conception of the duration of Styles IV and V is thereby considerably lengthened to encompass the entire Anyang period. Until recently we were without securely datable material to guide us toward a more accurate understanding of the history of those styles.

Tomb No. 5 at Hsiao-t'un

It was long assumed that the more assertive Style V, or high-relief decor, was not achieved until the Middle Anyang period.[7] But with the momentous discovery of Tomb No. 5 in the Hsiao-t'un sector of Anyang in 1976 and the publication of the finds from this tomb the following year, this assumption has been opened to question.[8] Tomb 5, which was discovered in undisturbed condition, yielded some four hundred fifty objects of bronze, approximately half of them vessels; over seven hundred fifty items of jade; and other articles of shell, ivory, and turquoise. One of the most significant aspects of these finds, to historians and art historians alike, was that many of the sacrificial vessels carried inscriptions, providing the names of the persons for whom they were cast.

The most important of these names are those of Fu Hao, or Lady Hao, and the posthumous designation Mu Hsin "Mother Hsin." From the oracle bone texts it has been ascertained that a person by the name of Fu Hao lived during the reign of the fourth Anyang ruler Wu Ting, that she was probably his consort or queen, and further that over a considerable period of time she played a large role in the affairs of state. Since the oracle bones also record that one of the consorts of Wu Ting was referred to after her death as Mu Hsin or as Pi Hsin "Ancestress Hsin," it is now believed that Fu Hao and Mu Hsin refer to one and the same person, who lived during the Wu Ting period, and moreover that Tomb 5 is in fact the bur-

ial of Fu Hao. The oracle bone texts also indicate that Fu Hao predeceased Wu Ting, and thus we are provided with a *terminus ante quem* for the objects found within her tomb, which we may legitimately conclude can be no later than the end of Wu Ting's reign.

Because a substantial number of the bronze vessels and other objects of bronze recovered from this tomb must be classified as belonging to Style V (e.g., Figures 13 and 14), we are led to the realization that the consistent and customary use of high-relief decoration was well established before the end of the first century of the Anyang period. This new relief style did not supplant Style IV; instead the two continued to coexist as alternative decorative modes. In light of the new evidence provided by Tomb 5, the attempt to discern the various stages in the evolution of both Style IV and the relief style during the approximately three hundred years of Anyang bronze art is the challenge that lies ahead.

Because the finds from Tomb 5 are of such critical importance in the chronological reassessment of the history of Shang bronzes, it is first necessary to lay to rest any speculation that the Lady Hao in question may have lived at some later time. Although there is no doubt about there having been a Fu Hao of the Wu Ting period, mention is also made of a person by that name in divination texts ascribed by some scholars to Tung Tso-pin's Period IV, corresponding to the reigns of Wu I and Wen Wu Ting. Particularly among the Chinese historians and archaeologists this matter has been the subject of much recent debate.

The Question of Fu Hao's Identity

One aspect of the problem lies with our interpretation of the name Fu Hao. It has been generally believed for some time that the character *fu* as it occurs in the Shang divination texts designates a female whose position was that of wife or consort.[9] According to Li Hsüeh-ch'in, the term signifies a family relationship, not a rank;[10] but it is nevertheless clear that the Fu X ladies mentioned in those texts were high ranking members of the court.[11] Specifically, we must assume that Fu Hao, who was apparently later granted the title of *hou,* was the consort of a king.[12]

The question remains, however, whether the graph that follows the designation *fu* is to be understood as a clan or family name, or as a personal name. If it is a clan name, the probability is high that there may have been more than one consort known as Fu Hao, as several rulers might have taken as their consorts women from the same clan. If, instead, it is a personal name, as suggested by Li Hsüeh-ch'in, the likelihood of there being more than one consort of this name is reduced somewhat, but not eliminated.[13]

In either case, however, there is strong evidence that all references to Fu Hao in the oracle texts are to one person. In those of Period I, as previously described, a Fu Hao of considerable historical importance receives frequent mention. The name does not appear in divination texts of other periods with one significant exception: It is found several times in the

17

so-called Li-set, which has been assigned to Period IV, encompassing the reigns of Wu I and Wen Wu Ting. Among those scholars who persist in regarding the bronzes from Tomb 5 as too advanced in style to accord with their conception of the artistic achievements during Early Anyang, there is a preference to place Tomb 5 within the span of Period IV and to equate Fu Hao with the consort of K'ang Ting, whose posthumous name included the cyclical designation *hsin*.[14]

Li Hsüeh-ch'in, however, has presented a compelling argument that the Li-set itself should be reassigned to Period I. If he is correct, then we have to do with only one Fu Hao, who lived during Period I. Critical for resolving the date of Tomb 5, his argumentation concerning matters of script style, phraseology, and content merits serious attention. It is based upon five points.

(1) He observes, first, that in the Li-set the graph for *wang* "king" is in the particular form it takes during Period I; as early as the end of Tsu Chia's reign the same character had come to be written with the addition of a horizontal stroke at the top.[15]

(2) Further, the phraseology of the Li-set accords more closely with that of the oracle texts from the time of Wu Ting to Tsu Keng than with those of later periods. For instance, by the reign of K'ang Ting (Period III) conventional terms such as *erh-kao* "two pleas" and *hsiao-kao* "small plea," both of which appear in the Li-set, were replaced by others, like *chi* "auspicious" and *ta-chi* "greatly auspicious."[16]

Tung Tso-pin originally proposed that these two features were evidence of an archaistic revival during Period IV of the script style and phraseology of the earlier Wu Ting period.[17] But Tung's explanation, which has always seemed somewhat forced and unconvincing, cannot account for other distinctive traits of the Li-set that clearly point to its being earlier than Period IV.

(3) Li Hsüeh-ch'in provides an extensive list of the names of individuals drawn from the Li-set—including those of Tzu Yü, Fu Ching, and Wang Ch'eng—that are also mentioned in the texts of the Wu Ting period and in the Ch'u-set of Tsu Keng's time.[18]

(4) Moreover, there are cases in the Li-set oracle texts where the topic of divination exactly corresponds to that in either the Pin-set of the Wu Ting period or in the Ch'u-set. Instances include the king's order that X and Tzu Fang perform the *tsun* ceremony at the location called P'ing; the question whether Ch'üeh Chui Heng will receive a good harvest; and whether sacrifices should be offered to the ancestresses Pi Keng and Pi Ping to secure an efficacious childbirth.[19]

(5) As a final piece of evidence, Li notes that in two texts of the Li-set questions are put concerning sacrifice to X Chia Mu Keng (a consort of Yang Chia) and Hsiao Hsin Mu (associated with Hsiao Hsin), both of whom belong to Wu Ting's parental generation. Since in each case the women are referred to as *mu* "mother" rather than as *pi* "ancestress," there can be no question but that the two texts are of

the Wu Ting period.[20]

Li Hsüeh-ch'in's conclusion would seem unassailable: that the Li-set of oracle texts dates to Wu Ting's later years and to the time of his successor Tsu Keng, and consequently that the Fu Hao mentioned both in the Li-set and in the other Wu Ting and Tsu Keng texts is the same individual. The divination texts, then, provide compelling evidence that Tomb 5 at Hsiao-t'un is that of Wu Ting's consort Fu Hao.

Fu Hao as an Historical Figure

While the person of Fu Hao goes unmentioned in the traditional Chinese annals and has therefore remained unknown to historians generally, her name repeatedly occurs in the divination texts, in as many as 170–180 passages. From recent compilations of these short entries we receive a substantial idea of her elevated position and a record of her activities which, if incomplete, is amazingly precise for such an early period.[21] Nor is the impression we form of her without some sense of warmth and feeling, as provided by Wu Ting's many queries concerning her occasional ill-health, by the anticipation of her arrival at the capital from sojourns away, and not least by the frequency with which sacrifices to the various ancestors are offered for her protection and well-being.[22] Almost beyond doubt, Wu Ting's relationship to Fu Hao was deemed more important than that to most other women of the court.[23]

Naturally, among these passages there are also persistent questions concerning her ability to bear children,[24] and in certain texts the King specifically asks whether or not she will give birth to a son.[25] The actual outcome is not known.

Whatever her fate as the bearer of royal offspring, it is certain that she played a significant role in the important affairs of state, and it is in this regard that she emerges as a formidable historical figure. From the divination texts we learn that Fu Hao regularly received orders to direct the sacrificial ceremonies of the Yu, Pin, and Liao categories.[26] She not only participated in the rites of sacrifice, but in at least one instance carried the responsibility of *pu-kuan* or "prognostication officer."[27]

We are provided with considerable documentary evidence about the far-reaching military campaigns of Wu Ting. He is known for exterminating the Hu-fang in the south; vanquishing the T'u-fang in the north; subduing the Ch'iang in the west; driving back the I in the east; pacifying the Pa in the southwest. Partly because of these deeds, the Wu Ting period came to be known in much later times as the "Kao-tsung Restoration."[28] The extensive role that the Lady Hao played in these military exploits, however, is surprising. In the war against the Ch'iang, we are told, she was in command of some thirteen thousand men; against the Pa she seems to have held a position of authority equal to that of the famed general Chih Kuo; in an attack upon the I, the noted Hou Kao was under her banner; and she took part as well in the campaign against the T'u-fang.[29] Moreover she was ordered on several occasions to recruit the troops of the King's vanguard.[30]

In addition it has been suggested that Fu Hao may have been enfeoffed in an outlying territory or border state, although the evidence is not entirely convincing. This proposal, while quite plausible, is based upon Wu Ting's repeated concern about her returning to the Great City Shang, phrased in such questions as, "Will Fu Hao come next month, will Fu Hao not come?"–but it is not stated what sort of duties had actually taken her from the capital.[31]

What is established with certainty, however, is that Fu Hao died during Wu Ting's lifetime. It is recorded that Wu Ting performed various sacrifices for the departed Fu Hao in hopes that she, in another world, would fare well.[32] Moreover, the extensive account of her activities, provided by the oracle texts, would tend both to substantiate the long reign (fifty-nine years) traditionally ascribed to Wu Ting and to suggest that her own life was not short.

Nor can we fail to mention the important role Fu Hao continued to play after her death, when questions were raised as to which of the spirits of the departed royal ancestors she would become *ming-fu,* or "consort in the nether world." Ta I, Ta Chia, Tzu I and Wu Ting's father Fu I (Hsiao I) are mentioned as possibilities, but it was apparently also envisaged that she might become the betrothed of Shang Ti, the highest divinity of heaven.[33]

The oracle texts leave little doubt as to the status of Fu Hao during her lifetime or of the high esteem in which she was held after her death. This in turn leads us to a further conclusion bearing on archaeological matters. Despite its abundant contents, the tomb of Fu Hao is a relatively modest affair, small in size when compared to the cruciform tombs at Wu-kuan-ts'un and Hou-chia-chuang, and lacking even an entrance ramp. Since there is no evidence of any decline in her standing toward the end of her life, but much to the contrary, we are left to assume that a burial such as hers was deemed appropriate for even the highest ranking consorts. The discovery of her tomb, then, strongly suggests that the large cruciform tombs dating from the Early Anyang period and immediately thereafter—such as the Wu-kuan-ts'un *ta-mu,* Hsi-pei-kang M 1001 and 1004—were exclusively the graves of kings.

Style IV: Character of the *Lei-wen*

If, as now seems certain from the evidence provided by the Fu Hao tomb, Style V was already well established as the prevailing decorative mode as early as the end of the Wu Ting period, it is apparent that the maturity of Style IV must have been reached during the first century of the Anyang capital. At present we are in a position to describe the evolution of Style IV with a degree of precision that was not hitherto possible.

An important key to this development is afforded by the changing character of the *lei-wen* patterns that form the ground of the Style IV designs. This development may be documented most completely by a series of Early Anyang Style IV *hu,* following one another in

time (Figures 1A–1E). It is by now well established that the *lei-wen* patterns derive originally from the configurations of the quills and curls of Style III.[34] In its very early form—as seen, for instance, on the Sackler *hu* (Figure 1A)—the *lei-wen* are composed of two types of configurations. The first of these are the longish convolute shapes deviating from a purely rectilinear form by the slight curvature at the top, recalling the tip of the quill, and by a squarish protrusion at the base, probably corresponding to the crescentic element conventionally found at the base of the quill. For the rest, the *lei-wen* consist of squared spirals not unlike those seen on Style III designs at the root of the quills. At this particular stage of Style IV the quill-like configurations, by contrast to the squared spirals, are both the larger and more prominent feature of the *lei-wen* patterns.

On the Nanking *hu,* a vessel slightly later than the Sackler example, the same type of *lei-wen* is encountered again. In this case the quill-derived elements are reduced in number, while in its execution the *lei-wen* as a whole has acquired a greater fluency and ease, so that in relation to the main images, it contends for attention less than before (Figure 1B).

In the next phase of Style IV, represented by a *hu* in the Brundage Collection (Figure 1C), two alterations in the *lei-wen* pattern are immediately evident. The quill-like elements have vanished completely, having been transformed into, or reduced to, simple rectangles; and these rectangular elements, which in their original form served as the most conspicuous feature of the *lei-wen,* have become smaller in size, with the dominant role now assumed by the squared spirals.

In its fully evolved form, as visible on a *hu* in the Freer Gallery of Art (Figure 1D), the *lei-wen* is composed exclusively of squared spirals, differing from each other essentially only in their size. The rectangular shapes have all but vanished.[35] This stage in the development of the *lei-wen* was reached no later than the end of the Wu Ting period, as can be clearly seen from an examination, for example, of the *Fu Hao fang-ting* (Figure 1E). From this time onward, the *lei-wen,* whether rounded or squarish and whether applied to a Style IV or to a Style V surface, remain essentially uniform in shape; the only notable variation depends almost entirely upon the relative neatness, orderliness, and refinement in the manner of their execution.

Style IV: A Distinctive Early Group

There is, however, an important cluster of Style IV bronzes (Figures 2–6) displaying *lei-wen* patterns that do not fit into the evolution described above. The bronzes in question, ranging widely in type and size, are so closely related by their decoration as surely to be contemporary with one another. It would seem all but certain that these designs are more closely affiliated with Style III than with the mature Style IV patterns. In most cases the *t'ao-t'ieh* faces—much the same as in Style III—exhibit upswept scroll-like horns and usually a bracket-shaped mouth with pendant

1A

1B

1C

1D

1E

Figures

1A. *Hu* (detail). Arthur M. Sackler Collection, New York.

1B. *Hu* (detail). Academia Sinica, Nanking. After *Kunstaustellung der Volksrepublik China,* Staatiche Museum, Berlin, 1951, p. 85.

1C. *Hu* (detail). Avery Brundage Collection, Asian Art Museum, San Francisco.

1D. *Hu* (detail). Freer Gallery of Art, Washington, D.C.

1E. *Fu Hao fang-ting* (detail). After *The Great Bronze Age of China,* frontispiece.

2. *Chio.* Formerly in the Oskar Trautmann Collection. After Umehara, *Inkyo,* pl. 74.

2

hooks, presumably meant to suggest teeth. The triangular apron-like device visible in some instances beneath the mouth does not occur on Style III vessels; but it is seen, greatly reduced in size, on the early Style IV *hu* in the Sackler Collection and a companion piece formerly in the Kawai Collection, Kyoto (Figures 1A and 7), while it does not appear in later Style IV designs. Whereas the facial features of these *t'ao-t'ieh,* which occasionally even have ears, are fairly complete, their bodies remain often curiously undefined, as if their forms depended upon the shearing away of the quills and curls of the ground, without any preconceived notion of what shapes the creatures ultimately should take. Secondary motifs characteristic of Style IV in all but its earliest phase, such as birds and small dragons, are also generally absent from these bronzes.[36]

Because of these features this group of bronzes is set apart from others belonging to Style IV, while their relative earliness is further attested by two factors that link them, not to bronzes from Anyang, but to those from Cheng-chou. In two cases (Figures 3 and 4) the vessels are provided with openwork flanges formed as a series of "C"-shapes, diminishing in size as they descend the vessel surface. These flanges derive from a Cheng-chou prototype, although they are now smaller than those on the Style II *tsun* from Pai-chia-chaung.[37]

The other factor serving to connect these bronzes to a pre-Anyang tradition is far less obvious. There occurs repeatedly within the main images, and also amid the *lei-wen,* a curious configuration somewhat like a fork or tong, shaped as a thin stem with a small "C" attached to the end (Figure 4A). This particular device, absent from Style IV and apparently from all advanced Style III vessels as well, is a recurrent feature in pre-Anyang bronze designs, including those on the large advanced Style I *fang-ting* from Cheng-chou[38] (where it serves to divide horizontally the two halves of the *t'ao-t'ieh*'s "fish-tailed" bodies) and the *lei* in the Sackler Collections.[39] The device is also encountered on Style II vessels, for instance on a *kuei* and a *yu* from P'an-lung-ch'eng, and on early Style III vessels.[40]

By now, any doubts as to the earliness of these Style IV pieces should be dispelled. What, then, may be said of their *lei-wen* patterns. In one instance, that of the exquisite small *hu* in the Freer Gallery, the zoomorphic designs are set against a plain, slightly sunken ground; that is, there are no *lei-wen* (Figure 3). In the case of the *chio* formerly in the Trautmann Collection (Figure 2), the *lei-wen* consist of a maze of fine, wirelike lines raised from the sunken ground, some shaped as squared spirals, others reminiscent of the very fine quills that may be observed on some Style III vessels.[41] Similar but more widely spaced raised lines, shaped as quills, "tongs," and a complex of interlocked curls make up the *lei-wen* on both the large pear-shaped *ting*[42] and on the magnificent von Lochow axe in the Museum für Ostasiatische Kunst, Cologne (Figures 4 and 5). On the *ting* and the axe, whose designs are so closely alike (especially as re-

5

4

4A

Figures

3. *Hu.* Freer Gallery of Art, Washington, D.C.

4. *Ting.* Formerly in the Kawai Collection, Kyoto. After *Nihon seika,* 176.

4A. Detail of fig. 4.

5. Axe. Museum für Ostasiatische Kunst, Cologne. After *Sammlung Lochow,* vol. 2, no. 15.

gards the pair of dragons flanking the *t'ao-t'ieh*), it
may be noted that the shapes of the *lei-wen* are analogous to the linear embellishment on the surfaces of
the main images, save that they are formed of raised
rather than sunken lines.[43]

A *fang-hu* (Figure 6) formerly in the Werner
Jannings Collection and now in the Palace Museum,
Peking—a vessel of strikingly archaic shape—is unmistakably related to the foregoing series by its decoration.[44] The *lei-wen*, however, are quite different: They
are composed of quill-shapes and an array of curls so
dense and compact that the raised lines and the sunk-
en lines separating them have become precisely the
same width. As a consequence, the main images are
seen for the first time, not against a sunken field ornamented with raised lines, but—as in the case of all
subsequent Style IV patterns—against a *lei-wen* ground
that appears flush with the main images. This new
procedure would be recognized at once to provide a
stronger and less ambiguous contrast between the images and the ground, especially if the vessel was observed at a distance.[45]

It is clear that the aforementioned bronzes (Figures
2–6) can be accommodated nowhere into the later
history of Shang bronzes. The only fitting conclusion
is that they represent the very beginnings of Style IV.
Understood as such, they afford evidence of an important phase in the evolution of the *lei-wen* preceding those stages that we have traced (Figures 1A–
1E).[46] Quite possibly these bronzes, marking an initial
stage of Style IV, were pillaged from Anyang tombs;
but whether they were in fact cast at Anyang is a
matter that cannot now be determined. It is not, on
the other hand, entirely unlikely that they represent a
bronze style that flourished at one of the capitals immediately antecedent to Anyang. Whatever the particular case may be, this earliest manifestation of Style
IV had a distinctive character of its own, which did
not recur in bronze decor, although its influence
may have lingered on in other media such as ivory
carving.

Style IV of the Early Anyang Period

Only a small number of bronzes are available to
suggest one other important aspect of the earliest
phases of Style IV. These consist of the vessels excavated from the large cruciform tomb discovered at
Wu-kuan-ts'un in 1950[47] and others associated with
them stylistically—including the Kawai and Sackler
hu, and a *ku* in the Royal Ontario Museum (Figures
1A, 7 and 8). Together, they may provide us with a
hint of the changing stylistic tendencies around the
beginning of the Anyang period.

By contrast to the *t'ao-t'ieh* on the *fang-hu* of Figure 6, that on the Sackler and Kawai *hu* appears
compressed, and the design is rhythmically less intense. The fiery and agitated images of the *t'ao-t'ieh*
seem now muted. Around this outline the hooks and
flourishes are restrained, and a new and prevailing
stress on horizontality seems to affect not only the
shape of the creature's body but its facial features as
well, transforming the outline of the eyes and narrow-

6

7

ing the mouth.

Coincident with an emphasis on orderliness and horizontality is the incorporation into the decorative program of narrow bands ornamented with long barbed strings extending outward from the eye-like nuclei (visible on both the Sackler and Kawai *hu* [Figures 1A and 7]). One other new feature appearing fairly consistently on these pieces are the small *k'uei* dragons, seen on the Royal Ontario Museam *ku* and on the *ting* from Wu-kuan-ts'un E 14 (Figures 8 and 9).[48] The ancestry of these particular dragons may be traced back to Style III and ultimately to Style II patterns.[49] But it is only with this early phase of Style IV that these dragons—discrete, yet playfully undefined entities—acquire sufficient individuality to become the first of the secondary images to carry an expressiveness truly distinct from that of the primary image, or *t'ao-t'ieh*. They foretell the increasing diversification of imagery, inherent in Styles IV and V.

The cruciform tomb at Wu-kuan-ts'un, although emptied of its more important treasures on some occasion previous to the scientific excavation of 1950, nevertheless yielded a sufficient number of bronzes that its approximate date may be inferred. Apart from the Style IV vessels mentioned above, the only other mode of decoration represented is Style III. When compared to the inventory of bronzes from the Fu Hao tomb, those from Wu-kuan-ts'un appear to be earlier without exception. The very size of the Wu-kuan-ts'un tomb, not to mention the multitude of human sacrifices that accompanied the burial rites, strongly suggests that the tomb was that of a king. If this is so, and if the contents of the tomb are earlier than those from the Fu Hao burial, then logically the tomb principal should be one of the first generation Anyang rulers: P'an Keng, or his brothers Hsiao Hsin or Hsiao I. Thus a date toward the beginning of the Anyang period seems in order for the particular phase of Style IV that we have just touched upon.

Evidence for the continuing development of Style IV into the later part of the Early Anyang period is provided by several vessels comparable in decoration and associated by the inscription they share. This inscription consists of two human figures in profile, holding between them what appears to be a standard or banner, and a third figure standing opposite them. The vessels bearing this inscription include the Brundage *hu* previously mentioned (Figures 1C and 10); a *chia* (sold by Sotheby Parke Bernet, New York; present whereabouts unknown);[50] a *p'an,* also in the Brundage Collection;[51] and the magnificent Pillsbury *kuang* (Figure 11). With the exception of the *kuang,* the chief distinguishing feature of the decoration of these vessels is the strikingly mosaic-like quality of the images whose angular contours seem as if they were determined by the squared *lei-wen* forming the ground, rather than vice-versa. These fine *lei-wen* permit a far sharper contrast between design and ground than we have seen hitherto, while the images themselves—more discrete than before and of an unprecedented diversity—are exhibited with precision and clarity.

8

Figures

6. *Fang-hu.* Formerly in the Werner Jannings Collection, Palace Museum, Peking. After Consten, *Das alte China,* color pl. 1.

7. *Hu.* Formerly in the Kawai Collection, Kyoto. After *Nihon seika,* 31.

8. *Ku.* Royal Ontario Museum, Toronto.

9

10

11

Figures

9. *Ting* from Wu-kuan-ts'un *ta mu*. After *Chung-kuo K'ao-ku Hsüeh-pao,* vol. 5, 1951, pl. 18:1.

10. *Hu.* Avery Brundage Collection, Asian Art Museum of San Francisco.

11. *Kuang.* Alfred F. Pillsbury Collection, Minneapolis Institute of Arts.

At this stage in the history of Style IV there are also significant changes in the motifs themselves. The curious-looking *k'uei* dragon—known, for instance, from the *ting* from E 14 in the large tomb at Wu-kuants'un and the Royal Ontario Museum *ku* (Figures 8 and 9)—is transformed into the clearly defined image of a bird-headed dragon. This new bird-dragon, which appears indentically on the "standard-bearer" *hu* (Figure 10) and *chia*, persisted with very little further alteration as one of the most frequently used motifs even into Early Chou times. A second image, invented during this phase of Style IV, which was to endure for an equally long period of time, is that of a face from which to either side extend two long barbed strips—a version of what Karlgren has termed the "animal triple band."[52] It is visible in the narrow band separating the two main *t'ao-t'ieh* faces on the Brundage *hu* (Figure 10) and on the foot of the *p'an* in the same collection.[53]

The fourth vessel inscribed with the "standard-bearer" inscription, the Pillsbury *kuang*, which seems slightly more advanced than some specimens from the Fu Hao tomb,[54] is notable for the superlative dragon figures in the upper register and for those to either side of the lid. This vessel may indicate the state of Style IV near the end of the Wu Ting period or slightly later.[55]

Style V of the Early Anyang Period: The Fu Hao Vessels

Style IV is strikingly represented among bronzes from the Fu Hao tomb by the large, six-legged table which was designed to support three cauldrons (Figure 12). Around the sides of the table runs a wide frieze of expertly designed dragons separated by round, slightly raised bosses. These motifs and the *lei-wen* configurations appear more advanced than those belonging to the "standard-bearer" set just discussed, with the possible exception of the Pillsbury *kuang*. Apart from this table, however, the majority of the more important bronzes from this tomb employ Style V decoration.

Among the numerous and impressive bronzes from within the tomb is the *ou-fang-i*, or casket-like container (Figure 13), measuring almost a meter long and sixty centimeters high. In the treatment of its roof-shaped lid and in the large projections along the top, it resembles some massive architecture. At the center, the lid shows the deeply molded face of a horned owl with protruding round eyes, flanked to the sides by two large birds in profile, with their long tail feathers shown in stepped relief. A row of these same birds, all facing inward, occupies the frieze beneath the level of the beams. Lower down and in flattish relief we find a large *t'ao-t'ieh*, surrounded by a medley of dragons, birds, and creatures that combine the features of both. Large animal heads are placed at the center of all four sides; two apparently are elephants.

No less outstanding are the figures of a horned owl (Figure 14) with large hooked beak, big back-swept wings and colossal legs, supported at the rear by tail feathers arranged in a semicircle. The bird's ears, like

12

13

14

Figures

12. Six-legged table from the Fu Hao tomb. After *Kaogu Xuebao*, no. 2, 1977, pl. 5:4.

13. *Ou-fang-i* from the Fu Hao tomb. After *Jen-min Hua-pao*, no. 6, 1977, p. 23, upper right.

14. Pair of owl *tsun* from the Fu Hao tomb. After *Jen-min Hua-pao*, no. 1, 1978, p. 24, top.

small half-disks, protrude at an angle; the horns are fashioned as dragons, whose bodies rise like wings. The artist, unable to desist, adds still other creatures— the full-round figures of a bird and a dragon, who follow each other up the back of the owl's head. When viewed from the front, the bird seems to emerge at the top, small as if seen aproaching from a distance. Were it not for the handle at the back and the removable lid above—for which the small bird and dragon serve as a handle—we would have no sense that this object is a vessel, but might rather think it a piece of sculpture. The overwhelming concern for zoomorphic imagery at this particular time was such that it resulted in the transformation of entire vessels into sculptures of fantastic beasts. Even if in such objects, which are neither wholly vessel nor wholly sculpture, there results a certain awkwardness, both the exuberance of the form and the extraordinary quality of the designs are adequate compensation.

Although nearly all of the major vessels from the Fu Hao tomb are ornamented in relief, many are less unconventional in shape and more restrained in their decoration than those just described. The relief decoration on these vessels (Figures 15A–19A) reveals its relative immaturity when compared with later examples. The raised designs tend to be low and flattish, despite the fact that such features as the outline of the *t'ao-t'ieh*'s mouth and the tips of the horns may be given an emphatic touch in higher relief. Only in the case of the more realistically presented bovine heads, snake bodies, and birds (Figure 18A) is the relief treated more plastically. The relatively clumsy and unmodulated image of the *t'ao-t'ieh* stands out from the ground sometimes less precisely and definitely than do Style IV designs of the same period.[56]

The Vessels with the *Ya-i* Inscription

It is by means of the more conventional vessels from the Fu Hao tomb that we are led, I believe, to a discovery concerning a number of vessels that form a set of no small significance within the history of Chinese bronzes at large (Figures 15B–19B). The vessels that compose this set are dispersed throughout Japanese and Western collections; the majority of the most important pieces, however, are found in the Nezu Museum, Tokyo. These vessels are linked in part by the inscription which they all bear. This inscription (Figure 15C) consists of a human figure seen frontally, whose head is shaped like a horseshoe placed sideways. Beneath the figure's hand (usually the proper right) is often what appears to be a walking stick or baton. Joined to the head above is the cruciform insigne known as the *ya-hsing*. The pictogram (or the two pictograms in combination) is conventionally transcribed *ya-i*. Its meaning remains unclear.[57]

The vessels, however, are connected by factors other than their shared inscription. The six vessels that make up the core of this set are of outstanding quality with regard to their design and casting, and their unusually imposing appearance is due also to their exceptionally large size. They exhibit a high degree of

15A

15B

15C

Figures

15A. *Hou T'u Mu tsun* from the Fu Hao tomb. After *Yin-hsü Fu Hao mu,* pl. 21:1.

15B. *Ya-i tsun.* Nezu Museum, Tokyo. After *Nihon seika,* 9.

15C. *Ya-i* inscription from a *chia* in the Nezu Museum, Tokyo. After Umehara, *Kanan Anyō ihō,* pl. 48.

stylistic consistency with one another, which suggests that they are contemporary; and further they are to be associated closely with the Fu Hao bronzes.

The first of the *Ya-i* vessels to be mentioned is the magnificent shouldered *tsun* in the Nezu Collection (Figure 15B), which is in all regards closely analagous to the *Hou T'u Mu tsun* (Figure 15A) from the Fu Hao tomb. In fact these two vessels apparently can be told apart by only two features: The *Ya-i tsun* is somewhat more stoutly proportioned, and flanges have been added to its neck. Both these features would indicate that the *Ya-i* version is the slightly more advanced of the two.

The *Ya-i fang-lei* (Figure 16B), formerly in the possession of Yamanaka and Company, displays on its shoulder the same undulating snakelike bodies seen on both the Nezu and the *Fu Hao tsun.* The most telling features differentiating this vessel from the *Fu Hao fang-lei* (Figure 16A) are the following: The vessel is now raised by a very low foot; greater promi-

nence is given the handles on the shoulder, while yet another handle has been placed low on the body to facilitate lifting; and the overall form, including the lid, is accentuated by the addition of flanges. A final decorative element not to be overlooked are the elegant hanging blades, which now extend almost to the base.

A comparison of the *Hou T'u Mu chia* from Tomb 5 and the pair of *Ya-i chia*—one in the Nezu Museum, the other in the Brundage Collection—reveals many of the same distinctions (Figures 17A–B).[58] Contrasted with the *Hou T'u Mu chia,* the *Ya-i* examples are more gracefully shaped, the handles span a longer arc, and the full-relief heads adorning the upper part of the handles are at once more deftly sculpted and more ornate. Flanges slightly less heavy than those on the Fu Hao *chia* now extend to the neck and down the middle of the legs, while flanges in miniature are added to the finials.

An even more telling comparison is afforded by the

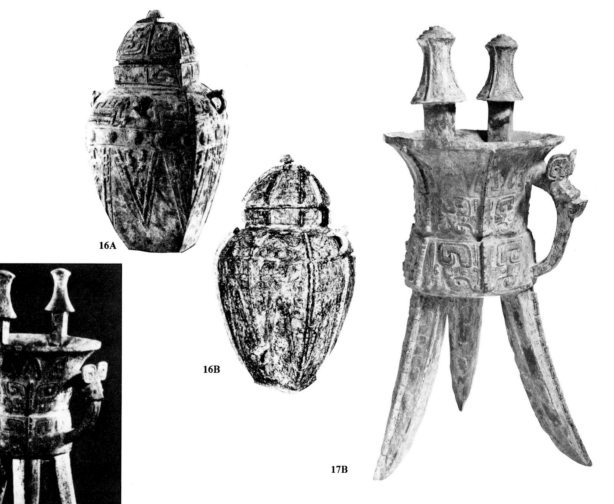

16A

16B

17B

17A

Figures

16A. *Fu Hao fang-lei.* After *Yin-hsü Fu Hao mu,* pl. 32:1.

16B. *Ya-i fang-lei.* Formerly Yamanaka and Company. After *Nihon seika,* 6.

17A. *Hou T'u Mu chia* from the Fu Hao tomb. After *Yin-hsü Fu Hao mu,* pl. 35:1.

17B. *Ya-i chia.* Avery Brundage Collection, Asian Art Museum of San Francisco.

29

Hou T'u Mu fang-hu (Figure 18A) and the splendid *Ya-i fang-yu* in the Hakutsuru Collection (Figure 18B). These two vessels with their squared shapes and elegantly sloping necks, joined to the body at a sharp angle, accord very well with one another; although it should be remembered that despite their shared features each vessel derives its shape from an already established prototype within its own typological category.[59] What chiefly accounts for the similarity of these two vessels, apart from their shapes, is the unusual treatment of the decoration on their bodies, consisting of large animal faces which are not placed at the centers of the friezes but span the corners. On both vessels these faces are closely analogous in all their features, displaying the same twisted horns, open and somewhat angular mouths, and leaf-shaped ears.[60] The principal difference between the decoration on these pieces resides not in the choice of motifs, which is remarkably alike, but in their treatment. A higher degree of artistic control is exhibited by the *fang-yu,* where an interplay between flat and relief decoration is permitted, and where those elements that appear in relief are rendered with far more subtlety and precision. In the case of the *yu,* an effect of clarity, restraint, and elegance everywhere replaces the more boisterous and uncouth character of the Fu Hao *fang-hu.*

The final major vessel of the *Ya-i* set to find its counterpart among the Fu Hao bronzes is the Nezu *p'ou,* a vessel whose rounded shape swells to truly gigantic proportions (Figure 19B). The Nezu *p'ou* corresponds exactly to the far smaller Fu Hao example in its shape, and similarly it is flanged and carries a domical lid, with a handle of comparable design (Figure 19A). The Nezu *p'ou,* with the exception of the narrow band of elevated rondels, is decorated, however, not in relief but in a Style IV mode that recalls the Hakutsuru *fang-yu* in its general refinement, and in such details as the long-tailed birds around the edge of the rim.

The proximity between the *Ya-i* vessels and those from the Fu Hao tomb would seem adequately revealed by the comparisons above. But the linkage between the two sets becomes still closer when we consider a pair of *ku,* decorated in openwork, that were acquired at Anyang in 1933 by Bishop White for the Royal Ontario Museum (Figure 20B).[61] These vessels, inscribed on the outer surfaces of their necks with the *Ya-i* pictogram, exactly match in size, shape, and decoration the five openwork *ku* recovered from the Fu Hao burial (Figure 20A), and also a sixth example bearing the inscription *Fu Hao,* which was at one time owned by C.T. Loo and Company.[62]

Other, but less conspicuous vessels related by inscription to the same set include a Style III *chüeh,*[63] several Style IV *chüeh* resembling the oval-bodied *chüeh* inscribed *Tung-ch'üan* "Eastern Spring" from the Fu Hao tomb,[64] as well as the *Ya-i p'an* and the small *Ya-i p'ou* in the Sackler Collection.[65] In addition, a clumsily shaped *ting,* bearing the *Ya-i* insigne followed by five boldly written characters, appears to be of the same period.[66]

18A

18B

19A

20A

20B

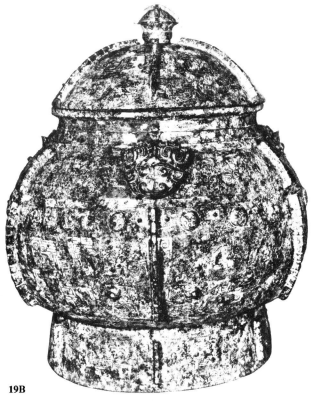

19B

Figures

18A. *Hou T'u Mu fang-hu* from the Fu Hao tomb. After *Yin-hsü Fu Hao mu*, pl. 23:2.

18B. *Ya-i fang-yu*. Hakutsuru Museum, Hyōgo. After *Chūgoku sansen bi-no-bi*, Tokyo, 1973, pl. 1.

19A. *Fu Hao p'ou*. After *Yin-hsü Fu Hao mu*, pl. 29:2.

19B. *Ya-i p'ou*. Nezu Museum, Tokyo. After *Nihon seika*, 5.

20A. Pair of *Fu Hao ku*. After *Kaogu Xuebao*, no. 2, 1977, pl. 11:1.

20B. Pair of *Ya-i ku*. Royal Ontario Museum, Toronto.

Finally, mention should be made of a sizable number of smaller bronze objects inscribed *Ya-i* that possibly derive from the same find as the six large vessels previously described. Among these may be listed two *yüeh* (axes), their socketed tangs inlaid with turquoise;[67] a *ko*;[68] a large hollow implement of unusual shape, pointed at the tip;[69] a chisel;[70] a knife blade;[71] several shield-shaped harness ornaments;[72] and a series of small bells of both the *nao* and *ling* varieties, very like those from the Fu Hao tomb.[73]

In summary, we note three matters of significance concerning the *Ya-i* bronzes: (1) These objects, linked by inscription and by style, originally must have belonged together as part of a group. (2) The larger of these vessels (Figures 15A–19B) are so monumental in size as to rule out the possibility that they were commissioned by, or cast for, anyone but the highest ranking members of the royal family. (3) The *Ya-i* bronzes are in all cases closely comparable to items from the Fu Hao tomb, but slightly more advanced or refined in style, suggesting a brief time lag between the two groups of objects. Taking into account that Fu Hao is known to have predeceased Wu Ting, we are justified in proposing that the *Ya-i* bronzes may well have come from the tomb of Wu Ting himself.[74]

The Nezu Museum Set of Three *Li-ho*

Nor is any consideration of the vessels attributable to the time of Wu Ting or immediately thereafter complete without mention of three of the most impressive bronze vessels ever cast in China: namely the three *li-ho* of the Nezu Museum (Figure 21). Designed as a matched set, these vessels are identical in shape and size. On their interiors they are inscribed, respectively, with the characters for "left," "middle," and "right," suggesting that they were intended to be displayed on the sacrificial altar in a specific order. The vessels are squared in shape and strongly architectonic in form. Their massive flanges, mounting the corners and the centers of each side and turning outward at the top, suggest architectural members supporting the square ledge of the domed cover. The legs, squared along the outside and subtly rounded on their inner sides, seem almost like great hewn timbers.

The disposition of the relief decor on each of these vessels is the same, but there is a considerable and lively variation to the motifs themselves. The *t'ao-t'ieh* faces spanning the corners of the legs are provided on each vessel with horns of different shapes; the same is true of the great monster faces with clawed feet on the dome, while the horns of these creatures in no case repeat those of the *t'ao-t'ieh* below. The birds of the frieze of the left-hand vessel are replaced on the central vessel by open-mouthed dragons, and on the vessel to the right by bird-headed fish. The creatures in the triangles above and those in the horizontal frieze below them are similarly varied. The heavy sculptures that form the handles are also treated individually: the one on the left as a bird with a bulbous down-turned beak; the one in the center as a tiger with a cavernous mouth, his hind legs tucked up to his stomach and his forelegs clasped to his chest; and

the one on the right-hand vessel as a tiger of strange anatomy with clenched teeth and pointed ears. Even the dragons on the spouts are distinguished from each other, principally by their horns, which are pointed, bottle-shaped, or like big saucers. Perhaps never again in the history of Chinese bronzes do we find such a diversity of motifs treated so masterfully or with such expressiveness. At the same time, these creatures, while ostensibly fearsome in character, cannot be regarded as entirely malevolent, for there is also about them a touch of playfulness. It is not unthinkable that these three large and magnificent vessels, stylistically not far removed from the Fu Hao and *Ya-i* pieces, may have been among the objects associated with the burial of Wu Ting or those of his successors Tsu Keng or Tsu Chia.

The *Hou Mu Mou fang-ting*

The information provided by the Fu Hao tomb further requires that we reconsider the dating of yet one other vessel, whose historical importance derives from its enormous size and from its highly important inscription (Figures 22 and 22A). The vessel in question, standing 133 centimeters high and weighing nearly two thousand pounds, is known as the *Hou Mu Mou fang-ting*. Unearthed in the vicinity of Wu-kuan-ts'un as early as 1939, it was re-buried in view of the impending Japanese invasion and was not recovered until the close of World War II. When it was published in 1954 it was acclaimed as the largest Chinese bronze ever cast—a distinction it retains to this day.[75]

Kane's thesis that the "unrivaled size of this vessel strongly suggests that the casting was commissioned . . . by a royal patron—presumably one of the An-yang kings"[76]—seems all the more probable today if, as now appears likely, the first character of its inscription is to be read not as *ssu* or *tz'u* (signifying either a clan name or the verb "to sacrifice"), but rather as *hou*, meaning "queen." The interpretation of the graph as *hou* has received the sanction of many Chinese scholars, including Li Hsüeh-ch'in and T'ang Lan, in reference to its occurrence in the Hou Mu Hsin and *Hou T'u Mu* inscriptions on vessels from Anyang Tomb 5.[77]

It remains, then, only to determine for which of the Anyang queens the *Hou Mu Mou fang-ting* was cast. Two Anyang rulers are recorded by the oracle bone texts as having had consorts whose posthumous names included the cyclical designation *mou*: Wu Ting and Tsu Chia, the second of Wu Ting's sons to attain kingship. But, as pointed out by Kane, the lengthy and important inscription on a Late Anyang *kuei* in the Sackler Collection reveals that the consort of yet a third Anyang king—Wu I—was also assigned the cyclical designation *mou*.[78] It has been argued that Hou Mu Mou was the consort of Wu I and that the *fang-ting* itself was commissioned during the reign of his successor Wen Wu Ting, who ruled at the end of the Middle Anyang period. This argument appears to be based primarily upon two observations: (1) that the character *mou* inscribed on the *fang-ting* corresponds to the form in which the graph occurs in oracle bone script during Tung Tso-pin's Periods I–IV, thereby indicating a date for the vessel previous to the reigns of Ti I and Ti Hsin; and (2) the paucity of inscribed ancestor dedications prior to the period of Ti I and Ti Hsin that include the cyclical character *mou*.[79] The first of these observations does not rule out the possibility that Hou Mu Mou might have been the consort of either Wu Ting or Tsu Chia, whereas the second observation, by which the vessel is assigned to the period of Wen Wu Ting, is too circumstantial to carry much weight.

Before the discovery of the Fu Hao tomb, the belief was tenable that ancestor dedications were unknown on bronze vessels earlier than the reign of Wen Wu Ting and that Style V relief decoration, such as we find it on the *fang-ting,* came as a late development in the history of Anyang bronzes. In addition, the presence of both ancestor dedications and Style V relief on vessels from the Fu Hao tomb does not contradict an attribution of the *fang-ting* to the time of Wen Wu Ting. However, we ought to take note that the inscription on the *Hou Mu Mou fang-ting* is written in a style analogous to, if perhaps slightly more advanced than, comparable inscriptions on vessels from Tomb 5. Although the decoration on the sides of the *fang-ting* finds no exact parallel on any of the vessels from Tomb 5, the rather coarse relief style seen on this vessel compares far better with the relief style of the Early Anyang and early Middle Anyang periods than with that of later times.[80] One other feature not to be overlooked is the motif seen on the handles of the *fang-ting* of two tigers whose gaping mouths enclose a human head; this striking motif also makes one of its very rare appearances on an axe from Tomb 5 (Figures 22B and 22C).

Taken collectively these features suggest that the *Hou Mu Mou fang-ting* cannot be widely separated in time from the Fu Hao tomb. More likely than not the *fang-ting* was commissioned, not for Wu I's consort, but for the consort of Wu Ting referred to in the oracle bones as Mu Mou or Pi Mou. Because Mu Mou is not mentioned in the oracle bones until the time of Tsu Chia,[81] it seems that she may have outlived Fu Hao, Wu Ting, and perhaps his immediate successor Tsu Keng. Consequently the vessel itself may not have been cast until the reign of Tsu Chia. The possibility that the woman in question was instead the wife of Tsu Chia cannot, of course, be dismissed offhand, although the relationship between the *fang-ting* and the Fu Hao bronzes is sufficiently close as to render this the less likely of the two alternatives. In any case the *Hou Mu Mou fang-ting* may now be counted among the growing number of vessels that may be convincingly attributed to the first half of the Middle Anyang period.

The Culmination of Shang Bronze Imagery

Surprisingly we discover, on the basis of the material that can now be assigned to the Early Anyang and to the beginning of Middle Anyang, that the development of Shang bronze imagery reached its culmination not toward the end of Anyang times, as would previously have been expected, but instead during the period corresponding to the reigns of Wu Ting and his immediate successors Tsu Keng and Tsu Chia. It was during this time—as revealed by many of the Fu Hao bronzes, by the Nezu *ho,* and by other vessels that may be tentatively attributed to this period[82]—that the repertory of images was most diversified and the images, shown in high relief and often bordering on the realm of sculpture, attained an intense and robust expressiveness.

Although by no means implying any decline in the artistic quality of the decoration—for what is perhaps the finest period in the history of Chinese bronzes lay in the future—the inventory of motifs ceases to grow beyond this time and thereafter becomes relatively conventional and standardized. Moreover, it is noteworthy that the decline in the Shang imagery, sometime after the beginning of Middle Anyang, seems to have coincided with a similar decline in Shang divination practice, which began after the reign of Wu Ting, in David Keightley's estimate.[83] Because this coincidence, if it is one day more fully established and understood, may cast light on the history both of Shang art and metaphysics, Keightley's observations are worth quoting in some detail. He remarks that between Period I (corresponding to Wu Ting's reign) and Period V (the reigns of Ti and Ti Hsin) a radical change in the procedure of divination and in the assumptions underlying them takes place:

> The whole process of divination has become more artificial, more routine, less spontaneous, less dramatic, less important. . . . The entire scope of Shang divination, in fact, had become constricted remarkably by Period V so that questions about many problematical matters of the Period I universe, such as the weather, sickness, dreams, ancestral curses, requests for harvest . . . were rarely divined about, if at all. The bulk of Period V divination was concerned with three topics: the routine execution of the rigid sacrificial schedule, the ten-day period, and the king's hunts. . . . The charges no longer involved specific forecasts about what the ultra-human powers might do to man. The inscriptions record, as it were, the whispering of charms and wishes, a constant bureaucratic murmur, forming a routine background of invocation to the daily life of the late Shang kings, now talking, perhaps, more to themselves than to the ultra-human powers. Optimistic ritual formula had replaced belief. . . . Man, rather than Ti and the ancestors, was thought to be increasingly capable of handling his own fate.[84]

Later Middle Anyang Styles

Though we lack scientifically excavated tombs or firmly datable landmarks to guide us in understanding the Shang imagery subsequent to the reign of Wu

21

22

22B

22A

Figures

21. *Li-ho.* Nezu Museum, Tokyo. Umehara Sueji, *Seizansō Seishō,* Tokyo, 1942, vol. 6, no. 2.

22. *Hou Mu Mou fang-ting.* After *Jen-min Hua-pao,* no. 6, 1977, p. 20, lower left.

22A. Inscription *(Hou Mu Mou fang-ting).*

22B. Detail: handle *(Hou Mu Mou fang-ting).* After Akiyama, *Arts of China: Neolithic Cultures to the T'ang Dynasty,* pl. 9.

22C. Axe from the Fu Hao tomb. After *Yin-hsü Fu Hao mu,* pl. 13:1.

Ting and his direct successors, its development may be tentatively sketched on the basis of stylistic analysis alone. It was especially the robustness and sculptural intensity of the earlier images that were lost to the succeeding generations of bronze artists. In general, the tendencies recognizable in the development that followed may be characterized as a seemingly deliberate reduction and regularization of the imagery from the preceding period, as well as a shift in emphasis from the imagery itself and its expressiveness toward refinement of execution. There was a shift from a primary interest in the imagery toward matters more purely and exclusively artistic. This new tendency took essentially two forms.

Lei-wen Relief Decor—Style V (a)

The first of these is embodied in the Style V (a) mode of decoration, where an imagery of a somewhat different sort is employed (Figure 23). The characteristic decoration of these pieces has been aptly termed *lei-wen* relief;[85] that is, the designs raised from the surface are covered by a pattern which often is very nearly indistinguishable from that of the ground. Necessarily, this mode of decoration de-emphasizes the images themselves. In addition, reference to the *t'ao-t'ieh,* which is not given as a complete unit, much less as a sculptural presence, is at best somewhat oblique. *The t'ao-t'ieh* is, as it were, without substance, shorn of its physical power and reduced to a kind of cryptogram. With this more moderate and less expressive image, the artist's concern now rests chiefly with aesthetic matters.

What is stressed is the elegant perfection of every detail of the design. We note, for instance, that the squared spirals forming the ground assume a more important role than before, and not infrequently their evenness and symmetry is such as to produce a kind of moiré effect. We also observe that the flanges on such pieces have been redesigned: Now small and finely scored they harmonize with the precision and refinement of the surface decoration. With these vessels, the resounding impact of the bronzes from around the time of Wu Ting, like some tumultuous

22C

storm, subsides into a style which may be characterized as one of peacefulness and repose.

The florescence of Style V (a), as evidenced by the Freer *tsun* and by other vessels closely related to it,[86] would seem to represent a distinctive stylistic trend following directly upon the Ya-i set. These vessels are perhaps attributable to the reigns of the fourth and fifth generations of the Anyang rulers.[87]

The Classic Style

The second stylistic trend of the late Middle Anyang period, which in certain regards is not dissimilar in spirit from the first, represents the continuation both of the more usual relief mode—Style V (b)—and of Style IV, featuring a *t'ao-t'ieh* of entirely recognizable type (Figure 24). But the designs are neither charged with the energy of the Wu Ting pieces nor can they be considered innovative, insofar as the repertory of designs has become quite restricted. Instead, through an increasing simplification and standardization of the imagery and by continued perfection of execution, this tradition produced the most classic of all Shang vessels.

These vessels have about them a definiteness and assurance unknown before and are perhaps best characterized by such terms as "strength," "balance," and "clarity." Seemingly unimprovable in form, they are articulated by strong flanges which not only are interrupted or broken to reflect the horizontal divisions, but which also assume an expressive function of their own that further enlivens the silhouette by being cusped or pointed at the tips.

When contrasted with comparable earlier patterns (Figures 13–19, 21 and 22), the advanced nature of their relief decoration is evident. Certain alterations to the features of the *t'ao-t'ieh*'s face—simplification of the horns to conventional "C-"shapes, the enlargement of the ear in proportion to the horns, the larger eyes and the addition of prominent eyebrows—effect both greater balance among the parts and a bolder image in general. Moreover, a reduction in the amount of linear embellishment on the raised surfaces separates the *t'ao-t'ieh* face more clearly from the surrounding *lei-wen* ground, and more importantly, permits further exploration of the relief mode itself. The creature's horns, previously rendered in flattish or rounded relief and often surrounded along their outer edge by a border in lower relief scored to resemble a flange, are now shown as smooth concave planes, while the ears of the *t'ao-t'ieh* and even those of the smaller dragons are similarly treated. The *t'ao-t'ieh*'s eyebrows, in the past usually indicated by incised lines, are shaped in slanting relief. So, too, the planes of the face are often subtly modeled. The classic phase may have reached its fruition somewhat later than did Style V (a).

The Late Anyang Styles

The continuation of this style into the Late Anyang period and its transformation into what may justifiably be called a "post-classical" phase can also be discerned. Serving as our first example of this phase is a

23

24

25

yü in the Minneapolis Institute of Arts (Figure 25), supported by a heavy molded base and provided with a thick everted rim and prominent flanges, with an emphasis on weightiness and blunt regularity.[88] Of an entirely conventional type, the *t'ao-t'ieh* on this *yü* nevertheless differs in character from that on the preceding specimen (Figure 24) by a straightforward plainness which replaces the subtle and lively refinements in relief modeling and linear embellishment of the earlier pieces. The dragons in the upper and lower zones, by contrast to those on the Freer *yu*, are weakly articulated and comparatively smooth in appearance, as if they had been executed in a relatively soft medium. This particular relief mode possibly counts as one of the symptomatic traits of this phase.

A *kuang* in the Brundage Collection (Figure 26) reveals similar post-classical tendencies: a relief style compatible with that on the Minneapolis *yü,* heavy flanges, and a high base of constricted diameter which contributes to a greater sense of the vessel's height and even to an effect of top-heaviness. Throughout this phase a slight mannerist touch is often present, whether regarding form or relief decoration.

Apart from vessels belonging to the "post-classical" phase and the continuing use of various decorative modes established earlier, two new and diametrically opposed decorative styles appear during the Late Anyang period. These two styles are most often associated with vessel shapes that evolved only toward the end of Shang and may be considered those especially characteristic of this period: the *chih* of oval section, the cylindrical *tsun,* the globular *yu,* and the cylindrical *yu.* On the one hand we find vessels decorated by narrow horizontal bands of purely geometric patterns, with the largest portion of the surface left plain (Figure 27); on the other, designs covering the entire surface in high relief, stark in effect, with minimal linear embellishment, and typically raised from a ground that is perfectly smooth (Figure 28). With their angular mouths and sharp fangs, huge eyes and cruel-looking horns that at the tips stand free of the vessel, these *t'ao-t'ieh* display a cold and forced expressiveness and a straining after dramatic effect, suggesting that the image had by then so declined in intrinsic meaning that it could be reclaimed only through exaggeration. These two opposing styles of decoration—the one in which zoomorphic imagery is virtually eliminated, and the other in which it is presented with such violence—are both symptomatic of the same situation: that the old images had by then lost much of their original significance and their inner life.

It was this time-worn tradition, and specifically the dichotomy between the "plain style" vessels and those of overly dramatic character, that were continued by the dynastic Chou, to be transformed subsequently into an aesthetic wholly their own. Given the particular phase in the development of the imagery toward the end of Shang, it is no cause for wonder that the Chou artists turned their concerted effort to the exploration of the formal properties of the designs, while adding essentially little by way of new motifs.

Figures

23. *Tsun.* Freer Gallery of Art, Washington, D.C.
24. *Yu.* Freer Gallery of Art, Washington, D.C.
25. *Yü.* Alfred F. Pillsbury Collection, Minneapolis Institute of Arts.

27

Figures

26. *Kuang.* Avery Brundage Collection, Asian Art Museum of San Francisco.
27. *Yu.* Royal Ontario Museum, Toronto.
28. *Yu.* Museum of Fine Arts, Boston.

Notes

1. An exception is the character *lung* "dragon" which may well be a pictogram for the image given on bronzes and in other visual media. Its specific meaning in divination texts remains unclear, although in some cases it seems to have functioned as a name. (See: Shima Kunio, *Inkyo bokuji sōrui,* Tokyo: Kyū-ko Shoin, rev. ed., 1971, p. 241 ff.)

2. Max Loehr, "The Bronze Styles of the Anyang Period," *Archives of the Chinese Art Society of America,* vol. 7, 1953, pp. 42–53.

3. One instance of early ornamentation on a cast bronze is the simple row of five raised nubs on the finely shaped *chüeh* excavated from Erh-li-t'ou in 1975, *Kaogu,* 1978, no. 4, p. 270, fig. 2, pl. 12:1; Wen Fong, ed., *The Great Bronze Age of China,* New York: Metropolitan Museum of Art, 1980, no. 1.

4. That spiral designs were retained into the Bronze Age is substantiated by the occurrence on two vessels—a lobed *ting* and a *ku* from Li Ml at P'an-lung-ch'eng (*Wenwu,* 1976, no. 2, p. 28, fig. 11; p. 29, fig. 15; p. 31, fig. 30:9, 12)—of spirals not dissimilar in appearance from those known from Miao-ti-kou and from Neolithic sites in northern Kiangsu (*Miao-ti-kou yü San-li-ch'iao,* Peking: Institute of Archaeology, Academia Sinica, 1959, pl. 27:1; *Kiangsu ts'ai-t'ao,* Peking: Wenwu Press, 1978, pls. 14 and 16–19).

5. René-Yvon Lefebvre d'Argencé, *Bronze Vessels of Ancient China in the Avery Brundage Collection,* San Francisco: Asian Art Museum, 1977, pl. 13.

6. Only the third and fourth strata at Erh-li-t'ou are now generally considered to be of Shang date, while the lower levels are assigned to the preceding Hsia period (see, for instance, *Kaogu,* 1976, no. 4, pp. 259–63; Yin Wei-ch'ang, *Kaogu,* 1978, no. 1, pp. 1–4; Tsou Heng, *Wenwu,* 1979, no. 3, pp. 64–69). Although Erh-li-t'ou may be representative of the earliest phase of Shang culture, the initial proposals to identify this site with the first Shang capital, known as Po, are perhaps now less tenable. Po is thought to have served as a capital during the reigns of approximately ten kings, while the remains from Erh-li-t'ou that are currently assigned to Shang do not seem to indicate that it functioned as a major seat for a correspondingly long period.

7. Alexander C. Soper ("Early, Middle and Late Shang: A Note," *Artibus Asiae,* vol. 28, [1966], p. 28) is of the opinion that the two *fang-ting* from Hsi-pei-kang M 1004 were "in the service" of Tsu Keng or his brother Prince Chi and that their "designs use the resources of the new style with a ponderous directness that suggests an early phase." While recognizing that Style v may have been introduced by the time of Tsu Keng, he nevertheless assigns the *Hou Mu Mou fang-ting* to the period of Wen Wu Ting (ibid.), thus implying that the maturity of Style v lay still later, presumably within the last fifty years of the Anyang period. Virginia Kane attributes the "onset of Style v to the reign of Tsu Chia" ("A Re-examination of An-yang Archaeology," *Ars Orientalis,* vol. 10, [1975], p. 101, n. 18), but shares Soper's opinion about the date of the *Hou Mu Mou fang-ting* ("The Chronological Significance of the Inscribed Ancestor Dedication in the Periodization of Shang Dynasty Bronze Vessels," *Artibus Asiae,* vol. 35, no. 4, 1973, pp. 340–41).

8. *Kaogu Xuebao,* 1977, no. 2, pp. 57–98, pls. 1–36; *Kaogu,* 1977, no. 3, pp. 151–53, pls. 5–9; *Yin hsü Fu Hao mu,* Peking: Wenwu Press, 1980. Color reproductions of some of the finds are also available in *Jen-min Hua-pao,* 1977, no. 6, p. 23; 1978, no. 1, pp. 24–27; and *The Great Bronze Age of China,* nos. 29–40.

9. Kuo Mo-jo, *Ku-tai ming-k'e hui-t'ao hsü-pien,* Tokyo: Bunkyōdō, 1934; Chou Hung-hsiang, "Fu-X Ladies of the Shang Dynasty," *Monumenta Serica,* vol. 29, 1970–71, pp. 348–55; Léon Vandermeersch, *Wangdao ou La Voie royale,* vol. 1, Paris, 1977, p. 262–77; vol. 2, 1980, pp. 29–32. For an opposing view, compare Shima Kunio, *Inkyo bokuji kenkyū,* Tokyo: Kyū-ko Sho-in, 1976, pp. 456–60.

10. Li Hsüeh-ch'in, *Wenwu,* 1977, no. 11, p. 34.

11. Chou Hung-hsiang attempts to develop a broader background of the *fu* ("Fu-X Ladies," pp. 356–61).

12. Ibid., pp. 34–35; T'ang Lan, *Kaogu,* 1977, no. 5, p. 346.

13. Vandermeersch argues for a variant of the former possibility, that the name denotes what he calls "corporations aristocratiques" (*Wangdao,* vol. 1, pp. 270–77). He is nonetheless convinced that Fu Hao (or Fu Tzu) refers to one individual (ibid., vol. 2, pp. 31–32).

    Ch'iu Hsi-kuei (*Kaogu,* 1977, no. 4, p. 343), basing his opinion upon that expressed by Li Hsüeh-ch'in in an article published in 1957, also advocates the first of these two alternatives. He too claims that Hao is composed of the term *tzu,* the designation of the Shang royal clan, with the addition of the "female" radical. As such, the name would indicate a female member of the Tzu clan. But Li Hsüeh-ch'in has of late reversed his own stand on the matter (see n. 10). His present argument that Hao should be regarded as a personal name arises from the following observations: (1) Clan names recorded in the divination texts are few in number; (2) In the Fu X instances in these texts, the X in no case corresponds to a known clan name. Li is convinced that "since Fu Hao involves a personal name introduced by an epithet, it can refer only to one person." This conclusion cannot be considered as final, since as previously noted, it seems unlikely that a personal name, any more than a clan name, would be reserved exclusively for one person or for one consort.

14. Only three of the nineteen members of the Symposium convened in Peking in 1977 to discuss the dating of the Fu Hao tomb incline to this view: Ch'iu Hsi-kuei, Tsou Heng, and Kao Ming. (See *Kaogu,* 1977, no. 5, pp. 343, 344, and 346.) Also see Li Po-chin, *Kaogu,* 1979, no. 2, pp. 165–70.

15. Li Hsüeh-ch'in (see n. 10, p. 36). According to Tung Tso-pin (*Fifty Years of Studies in Oracle Inscriptions,* Tokyo: Center for East Asian Cultural Studies, 1964, pp. 100–1), it was J.M. Menzies who first noted the difference between the two forms of the character *wang.* As regards the Li-set, Li claims that the forms of other characters in frequent use, such as the *kan-chih,* also are closest to those of the Wu Ting period (see n. 10).

16. See n. 10, p. 36.

17. Tung Tso-pin, "Chia-ku-wen tuan-tai yen-chiu-li," in *Ch'ing-chu Ts'ai Yüan-p'ei hsien-sheng liu-shih-wu sui lun-wen-chi,* Peking: Academia Sinica, pp. 412–13 and 421–23. Ch'iu Hsi-kuei's objection (see n. 13, p. 344) to placing Tomb 5 in the Wu Ting period—that the style of the inscription on the jade *ko* from this tomb (see *Kaogu Xuebao,* 1977, no. 2, p. 89, fig. 19:2) corresponds to that of Tung's Periods III–IV—is easily reversed: The inscription on the *ko* can alternately serve as evidence that this script style was practiced during Period I.

18. See n. 10, p. 36.

19. Ibid.

20. Ibid., p. 37; and *Wenwu,* 1981, no. 5, pp. 25–30 for new evidence for the date of the Li-set.

21. The most complete account of references to Fu Hao in the oracle bone texts may be found in Wang Yü-hsin, Chang Yang-shan, and Yang Sheng-nan, *Kaogu Xuebao,* 1977, no. 2, pp. 1–22. The present discussion depends upon the information presented in this article.

22. Among the illnesses from which Fu Hao suffered from time to time were colds (*Kaogu Xuebao,* 1977, no. 2, p. 15, item 85); bad teeth (ibid., p. 15, item 86, and p. 17, item 104); and abdominal troubles (ibid., item 87). Sacrifices to ensure her well-being were often made to Fu I (Wu Ting's father Hsiao I, ibid., p. 16, items 97–102) and to various ancestresses, usually Pi Keng (consort of Wu Ting's grandfather Tsu Ting, ibid., p. 17, items 105–6). Different ceremonial functions were performed, but those of the Yu category seem particularly common (ibid., p. 8, items 34–39; also see Vandermeersch, n. 9, vol. 1, pp. 140–41).

23. As noted in *Kaogu Xuebao,* 1977, no. 2, p. 1, "Oracles concerning Fu Hao, compared with those concerning other consorts such as Fu Ching, Fu Liang, Fu Shu, Fu Chu, Fu Lung and others, are not only more numerous but also wider in scope." Chou Hung-hsiang (see n. 9, p. 367) makes a similar remark, as does Vandermeersch (see n. 9, vol. 1, p. 277).

24. In one of the many instances, the King's question whether Fu Hao has the ability to give birth receives an affirmative answer, inscribed on the reverse side: "The King having seen the *pu-*

chao ('divining crack'), said, 'Fine, she has the ability to give birth.' " (Ibid., p. 10, item 52)

25. Ibid., p. 10, items 54–55; p. 11, items 56–58. Wu Ting expresses his anxiety as to whether the spirits of the ancestors will protect the child (ibid., p. 11, item 59; for the term rendered as "protect," see discussion following item 59), and clearly he also worries that Fu Hao's being with child may lead to her death (ibid., item 60). Some fifty days—and then eighteen days—before the expected birth, he inquires once more if there will be a male child (ibid., p. 11, item 61, and p. 12, item 63).

26. Those to whom sacrifices were made were the *hsien pi* (ancestresses), *fu* (father), *mu* (mother) and the sacred springs. The sacrifices included prisoners and other human victims, as well as oxen. Ibid., pp. 8–9, items 34–48.

27. Ibid., p. 9, item 49.

28. Ibid., p. 2.

29. Ibid., p. 2, item 9; p. 4, items 13–15; p. 5, item 18; and p. 4, items 11–12, respectively. Compare Chou Hung-hsiang, pp. 268–369.

30. Ibid., p. 2, items 3–6.

31. Ibid., p. 6, items 20–25.

32. Ibid., p. 18, items 111–23. For other evidence that some of the Fu-X laides may have been rulers of states or fiefs, see Chou Hung-hsiang (n. 9, pp. 357–58 and 361–65). Compare Vandermeersch's suggestion that the *fu*, apart from regional affiliations, could rather belong to so-called "aristocratic corporations"; Fu Hao would be the prime example (see n. 9, vol. 1, p. 274, and vol. 2, p. 31).

33. Ibid., p. 19, items 124–26.

34. Loehr, "Bronze Styles of the Anyang Period," pp. 47–48; figs. 9–12.

35. Rectangularized elements are nevertheless retained for some time longer in the case of certain specific designs, as for instance the "animal triple band." Similarly, quill-like *lei-wen* are occasionally found immediately adjacent to the remnant quills projecting from the main image in somewhat later Style IV designs.

36. The dragons seen in descending position on the Kawai *ting* and von Lochow axe (figs. 4 and 5) are related to the figures on Style III vessels, such as the Brundage *p'ou* (d'Argencé, *Bronze Vessels*, pl. 10, upper right).

37. *The Chinese Exhibition,* Kansas City: Nelson Gallery-Atkins Museum, 1975, no. 74.

38. *Wenwu*, 1975, no. 6, pp. 64–68; pl. 1; *The Great Bronze Age of China*, no. 11.

39. Max Loehr, *Ritual Vessels of Bronze Age China,* New York: The Asia Society, 1968, no. 3. The *lei* and the Cheng-chou *fang-ting,* both advanced Style I vessels, must be virtually contemporary with one another.

40. *Wenwu*, 1976, no. 2, p. 29, fig. 14; pl. 3:2; *The Great Bronze Age of China*, nos. 8 and 9; an early Style III example is the Sackler *p'ou* (Loehr, *Ritual Vessels*, no. 15).

41. An example of such a Style III design may be seen on a *ku* of quite primitive shape at one time in the Kawai Collection, Kyoto (Umehara Sueji, *Nihon shūcho Shina kodō seika,* Osaka, 1961, no. 174). The interstices between the raised lines on the Trautmann *chio* and the sunken lines of the main images are said by Ecke to be inlaid with a reddish substance (Gustav Ecke, *Frühe Chinesische Bronzen aus der Sammlung Oskar Trautmann,* Peking, 1939, no. 16).

42. *Ting* with pear-shaped bodies are uncommon; but a comparison of the form of that illustrated in fig. 4 and the Style IV example from Hsi-pei-kang 1435 (Umehara Sueji, *Inkyo,* Tokyo: Asahi Shimbunsha, 1964, p. 62:1) corroborates the relative earliness of the former.

43. The accomplished von Lochow *li-chia* (*Sammlung Lochow Chinesische Bronzen,* vol. 2, Peking, 1944, no. 9; *Meisterwerke aus China, Korea und Japan,* Cologne: Museum für Ostasiatische Kunst, 1977, no. 5), which also belongs to the earliest phase of Style IV, provides an example of a *"lei-wen"* ground formed almost entirely of sunken lines. An interesting comparison may be made between this vessel and a *chia* in the Shanghai Museum, embellished all over with Style III patterns of a

relatively early type (*Sekai kōkogaku taikei,* Tokyo: Heibonsha, 1958, vol. 6, no. 2: *Inshū jidai,* pl. 47). The decoration of the handles of these two pieces is strikingly similar. The von Lochow *li-chia* may be of non-Anyang, possibly southern, manufacture.

44. On the *hu,* as on the Trautmann *chio* (see n. 41), the sunken parts of the design in places apparently retain a substance of reddish color.

45. There also existed at least one variant of the style just described, as indicated by a *p'ou* in the Brundage Collection (d'Argencé, *Bronze Vessels*, p. 10, upper left). Judged by the *t'ao-t'ieh* face appearing on its swelling bowl, there can have been no appreciable lapse in time between this item and those illustrated in figs. 2–6; the earliness of the *p'ou* was first pointed out by Loehr, who felt it was "rather still closer to the Third Style" ("Bronze Styles of the Anyang Period," p. 48). The only new feature of its decoration is the treatment of the creature's body, and of the remainder of the design, in long ribbon-like bands or strips, which are bordered by *lei-wen* in orderly alignment. Much the same type of pattern is again seen on what may be an earlier rendition on a lobed *ting* in the Musée Cernuschi (Vadime Elisséef, *Bronze archaïques chinois au Musée Cernuschi,* Paris: L'Asiatheque, 1977, no. 1), whose design in many regards recalls that of the Trautmann *chio* (fig. 2). The Cernuschi *ting* has also been mentioned by Loehr as an early example of Style IV (see n. 39). A comparable, but possibly slightly later *ting* is in the Royal Ontario Museum (acquisition no. 960.234.13). The difference between the design on the Cernuschi *ting* and that on the *p'ou* resides primarily in the addition of *lei-wen* within the outlines of the *t'ao-t'ieh*'s body and tail; this simple and fanciful transformation may have led to the development of ribbon-like designs that occur, not only on the *p'ou,* but on other Early and Middle Anyang vessels, sometimes in openwork (e.g., figs. 20A and 20B).

46. Other vessels apparently belonging to the period of early Style IV include the *ting* with dragon legs and a lobed *ting* in the Museum of Far Eastern Antiquities, Bernhard Karlgren, "Some Characteristics of Yin Art," *Bulletin of the Museum of Far Eastern Antiquities,* no. 34, [1962], pls. 1b and 78b; William Watson, *Ancient Chinese Bronzes,* London: Faber and Faber, 2nd. ed., 1977, pl. 1b). The latter shows an early attempt at relief decoration; but note the similarity of the small bird-headed dragons on either side of the *t'ao-t'ieh* face to those on the upper register of the *hu,* fig. 6.

47. *Chung-kuo K'ao-ku Hsüeh-pao,* vol. 5, 1951, pp. 1–48; pls. 1–31 and 45. See also William Watson, *Archaeology in China,* London: Max Parrish, 1960, pp. 22–23; pls. 54–55.

48. A *ting* in the Neiraku Museum, Nara, decorated with a frieze of snakes also belongs to this group (*Neiraku-fu,* Nara: Nairaku Bijutsukan, 1969, no. 1). It carries the same *Pei-tan Ko* inscription as several vessels from Wu-kuan-ts'un E 9 (*Chung-kuo K'ao-ku Hsüeh-pao,* vol. 5, [1951], pl. 25), and in addition the decor of snakes is seen on a *ku* recovered from Wu-kuan-ts'un W 8 (ibid., pl. 20:2).

49. E.g., the Style II decoration on a *chia* in the Royal Ontario Museum, where curving lines surrounding the raised eyes take on the semblance of a bird's beak and down-swept crest (W.C. White, *Bronze Culture of Ancient China,* University of Toronto Press, 1956, pl. 78a).

50. Catalogue of Sotheby Parke Bernet auction, Nov. 4, 1978, lot 317.

51. d'Argencé, *Bronze Vessels*, pl. 18, front.

52. Bernhard Karlgren, "Notes on the Grammar of Early Bronze Decor," *Bulletin of the Museum of Far Eastern Antiquities,* no. 23, 1951, pp. 29–30.

53. Two other vessels deserving mention as examples of this phase of Style IV are the Buckingham *chia* (Charles Fabens Kelley and Ch'en Meng-chia, *Chinese Bronzes from the Buckingham Collection,* The Art Institute of Chicago, 1946, pls. 5–7), and a *tsun* formerly in the Kawai collection (*Nihon seika,* pl. 123).

54. *Yin-hsü Fu Hao mu,* pl. 27, 1–2.

55. The relative lateness of the *kuang* among those vessels carrying the "standard-bearer" inscription is also indicated by the palaeographic form of the inscription itself. Whereas the human

figures on either side of the standard on the *hu, chia,* and *p'an* inscriptions recall those which appear back to back in the *Pei-tan Ko* inscriptions associated with the finds from the large tomb at Wu-kuan-ts'un from the beginning of Early Anyang, they are shown here with smaller heads and less rigid in stance. The inscription as a whole seems carved in a more gentle and controlled manner (Karlgren, *Pillsbury Collection,* p. 93, fig. 39).

56. These are numerous instances of bronze objects carrying the same inscriptions as those from the Fu Hao tomb. One such piece was known to scholars as early as the Sung period (see Wang Hou-chih, *Chung-ting kuan-shih* in *Pai-i-lu chin-shih ts'ung-shu,* vol. 3, p. 20b. Another—a lid—was unearthed from Hsiao-t'un YM 066 (Li Chi, ed., *Studies of Fifty-three Ritual Bronzes,* Nanking: Academia Sinica, 1972, pl. 50). These items, stylistically consistent with the Fu Hao bronzes generally, are omitted from the present discussion.

57. Umehara long ago remarked upon the close connection between the *Ya-i* vessels (*Kodōki keitai no kōgogaku-teki kenkyū,* Kyoto: Tōhō Bunka Kenkyūsho, 1940, pp. 40–41; pl. 41:2–6; *Kanan* Anyo ihō, Kyoto: Kobayashi, 1940, pp. 42–47). Virginia Kane has suggested that these vessels "may have come from the same tomb" ("An-yang Archaeology," p. 101, n. 17). The inscription continues to occur on vessels of later date (see n. 65), indicating that the graph is probably to be interpreted as a name. Roswell Britton has discussed the *Ya-i* inscriptions at length (*Fifty Shang Inscriptions,* Princeton, 1940, pp. 41–51). He notes that a diviner by the name of I appears in oracle bone texts of the period of Tsu Keng and Tsu Chia (ibid., p. 74). On the diviner I, also see Jao Tsung-i, *Yin-tai chen-pu jen-wu t'ung-k'ao,* Hong Kong University Press, 1959, 2 vols., pp. 961–71.

58. The two *Ya-i chia* are so closely matched that they can be told apart only by the decor of their finials: Those on the Nezu piece show long-tailed birds around the lower edge (*Nihon seika,* pl. 7), whereas on the Brundage version (fig. 17B) there are dragons instead.

59. A precedent for the *Hou T'u Mu fang-hu* may be seen, for instance, in the early Style IV *fang-hu* of fig. 6, while forerunners of an almost equal antiquity exist for the Hakutsuru *fang-yu.* Precursors of the Hakutsuru vessel include a *fang-yu* in the Tokyo National Museum (*Nihon seika,* pl. 45), one in Minneapolis Institute of Arts (Karlgren, *Pillsbury Bronzes,* no. 22), and another recovered from M 331 at Hsiao-t'un (Li Chi, ed., *Fifty-three Bronzes,* pl. 44). Notwithstanding the introduction of relief ornament on the Minneapolis and M 331 specimens, these vessels and the Tokyo version are contemporary with a very early phase of Style IV. The M 331 *fang-yu* also provides a precedent for the bovine heads at the corners of the Fu Hao *fang-hu* and the *Ya-i fang-yu.*

60. It may also be noted that the full-relief heads—with their smooth apron-like snouts and bottle horns—serving as terminations of the swing handles on the *fang-yu* are duplicated in smaller size on the *hu* by the sculptural heads above the centers of the main frieze. The design on the foot of the *hu* is approximated by the Style IV mask on the neck of the *yu,* while Style IV variants of the long-tailed birds on the shoulder of the *hu* appear in the same position on the *yu.*

61. White, *Bronze Culture of Ancient China,* p. 15. There are many other openwork *ku* of this type (e.g., Huang Chun, *Yeh-chung p'ien-yü,* Peking, 1942, no. 3, vol. 1, pl. 40; Watson, *Ancient Chinese Bronzes,* pl. 22b). The piece illustrated in *Yeh-chung* is inscribed with a graph corresponding to the name of a Wu Ting period diviner (see Britton, *Fifty Shang Inscriptions,* p. 74).

62. *An Exhibition of Ancient Chinese Ritual Bronzes Loaned by C.T. Loo and Co.,* Detroit Institute of Arts, 1940, no. 16.

63. Umehara Sueji, *Kankarō kikkin-zu,* Kyoto, 1947, vol. 2, no. 29.

64. *Yeh-chung,* no. 2, vol. 1, pl. 26; Robert Poor, *Ancient Chinese Bronzes, Ceramics and Jade in the Collection of the Honolulu Academy of Arts,* Honolulu Academy of Arts, 1979, no. 22; Wang Ch'en, *Hsü Yin wen-tsun,* Peking, 1935, vol. 2, p. 3b, fig. 1; Lo Chen-yü, *Cheng-sung-t'ang chi-chin-t'u,* Peking, 1935, vol. 2, pp. 26–28; and a further example in Indianapolis Museum of

Art (Louisa Huber, "Ancient Chinese Bronzes," *Arts of Asia,* vol. 2, [Mar.–Apr. 1981], p. 76); *Yin-hsü Fu Hao mu,* pl. 18:1–2.

65. *Yeh-chung,* no. 2, vol. 1, figs. 34–36; Eleanor von Erdberg, *Chinese Bronzes from the Chester Dale and Dolly Carter Collection,* Ascona, Switzerland: Artibus Asiae supplementum, 35, 1978, no. 73; a note of caution should perhaps be introduced with regard to the inclusion of the *Ya-i p'an* and the small *Ya-i p'ou* within the larger group. On later vessels the graph occurs in a somewhat altered form, with the human figure either separate from the *ya-hsing* or enclosed within it (e.g., Ch'en Meng-chia, *A Corpus of Chinese Bronzes in American Collections,* Tokyo: Kyū-ko Shoin, 1977, vol. 2, R 141–144b; Wu Ta-ch'eng *K'o-chai chi-ku-lu,* Peking, 1896, vol. 2, p. 18; *Kaogu,* 1974, no. 5, p. 314, fig. 11:1. The changing form of the *ya-i* inscriptions is pointed out by Kane, "An-yang Archaeology," p. 101, n. 17. In its original form the graph is also known from at least one vessel—a Style V (a) *ku*—which appears to be later stylistically than any vessel in the group under discussion (Jung Keng, *Hai-wai chi-chin t'u-lu,* Peking, 1935, pl. 77). The graph may also be seen on the *fang-i* in Cincinnati Art Museum (Loehr, *Ritual Vessels,* no. 38, and Ch'en Meng-chia, *Corpus,* vol. 1, A 642, and vol. 2, R 140) but the authenticity of this inscription is not beyond question. More than one *ting* is recorded as carrying the same inscription (Yü Hsing-wu, *Shang Chou chin-wen lu-i,* Peking, Science Press, 1957, no. 40; Wang Ch'en, *Hsü Yin wen-ts'un,* vol. 1, p. 5b, figs. 3 and 4), but since the vessels are not available in reproduction, any assessment of their relationship to the *Ya-i* set remains impossible. On the other hand, the *p'an* and the *p'ou* do have the advantage of being roughly contemporary with the larger set.

66. Li T'ai-fen, *Ch'ih-an ts'ang-chin,* Peking, 1940, 2; Shirakawa Shizuka, *Kimbunshū,* Tokyo: Nigensha, 1965, nos. 67 and 68. If the inscription on this vessel is authentic, which offhand we have no reason to question, then it probably counts as the longest bronze inscription so far known from this period.

67. White, *Bronze Culture,* p. 58, fig. A; Bernhard Karlgren and Jan Wirgin, *Chinese Bronzes: The Natanael Wessén Collection,* Stockholm: Ostasiatiska Museet, 1969, no. 39, color pl. 8.

68. Yü Hsing-wu, *Shang Chou,* no. 545.

69. *Yeh-chung,* no. 1, vol. 2, pl. 5.

70. *Shodō Zenshū,* vol. 1: *Chūgoku,* Tokyo: Heibonsha, 1954, no. 24.

71. Wang Ch'en, *Hsü Yin wen-ts'un,* vol. 2, p. 90, fig. 2.

72. *Yeh-chung,* no. 2, vol. 2, pl. 7.

73. *Yeh-chung,* no. 2, vol. 1, pls. 1–2; White, *Bronze Culture,* p. 47, figs. A–B; *Yin-hsü Fu Hao mu,* pls. 62:1 and 79:1–2.

74. The supposition that the *Ya-i* bronzes originated from the same tomb raises several questions of an archaeological nature which remain unresolved. There are two possibilities: (1) either Wu Ting's tomb has yet to be discovered, or (2) it was one of the large cruciform tombs at Anyang pillaged of their more important contents by bands of grave robbers, some of them at work shortly before the scientific excavations of the 1930s. If the *Ya-i* bronzes do in fact originate from the burial of Wu Ting, we can dismiss the first possibility and make a case for the second.

The close relationship between the Fu Hao tomb and the cruciform tombs 1001 and 1004 at Hou-chia-chuang has been remarked upon in the current archaeological journals (*Kaogu,* 1977, no. 5, pp. 341 and 344–45; *Kaogu Xuebao,* 1977, no. 2, pp. 94–95; *Wenwu,* 1977, no. 11, p. 33). But both these large tombs, having been nearly emptied by plunderers, afford only paltry clues as to their precise relationship to Tomb 5 and no indication as to who in either case the tomb principal may have been. Because the south and east entrance passages of 1004 cut into 1001, it is certain that 1001 is the earlier of the two; and the contents excavated from these tombs suggest that neither is later than the beginning of Middle Anyang. Since the two tombs are so close in time, it has been tempting to regard 1001 as that of Wu Ting and 1004 as that of Tsu Keng or Tsu Chia, more probably the former, whose reign is believed to have been relatively short (Tsu Keng is generally believed to have reigned seven years; see, however, David Keightley, *Sources of Shang History,* Berkeley: University of California Press, 1978, p. 227,

n. g). Yet such a theory remains without means of proof. Li Hsüeh-ch'in's assumption that the three Nezu *ho* came from the "Eastern Ear" of M 1001 is without foundation. (Li Hsüeh-ch'in, *Wenwu*, 1977, no. 11, pp. 32–33. Also see Li Chi, *An-yang*, Seattle: University of Washington, 1977, p. 77, who presents an account of the appearance on the art market around 1933 of "huge bronzes," among which the most notorious were the three *ho*.)

In addition, a decided problem would seem to be posed by the two well-known *fang-ting*—the one decorated chiefly by bovine heads, the other with unusual looking deer heads—that were discovered *in situ* within Tomb 1004 (Kao Ch'ü-hsün, ed., *Hou-chia-chuang*, vol. 5; *Hsi-pei-kang M 1004*, Taipei: Academia Sinica, 1970, pls. 106–17). The pictograms for "ox" and "deer" inscribed on the respective vessels are consistent with the type of inscription found on the Nezu *ho*, insofar as they would seem to denote ritual functions rather than names. In regard to their decoration, the bird figures to either side of the ox and deer heads correspond to the many jade carvings of birds from the Fu Hao tomb (e.g., *Yin-hsü Fu Hao mu*, pl. 143:2) and in their relief modeling, the two *fang-ting* are, generally speaking, compatible with the Fu Hao bronzes and those of the following generation. But in actual design and execution their decoration may appear comparatively awkward and primitive and rather earlier than the *Ya-i* vessels or the Nezu *ho*. To some extent, of course, this awkwardness may be a result of the large size of the vessels; or possibly the vessels were not new when they were placed in the burial.

Soper thought to assign M 1001 to Wu Ting and the complex of other tombs around it—1004, 1002, and 1550—to his sons Tsu Keng, Tsu Chia, and the non-ruling Tsu Chia (Soper, see n. 7, p. 26). Virginia Kane also felt that 1001 might have been built for Wu Ting ("An-yang Archaeology," p. 109).

75. The excavation of the huge *fang-ting* and its history up to its final installation in Peking Historical Museum is recounted by Ch'en Meng-chia, *K'ao-ku Hsüeh-pao*, vol. 7, 1954, pp. 29–30, and is mentioned by Kane, "Ancestor Dedication," p. 340.

76. Kane, ibid.

77. Li Hsüeh-ch'in, *Wenwu*, 1977, no. 11, pp. 33–35. T'ang Lan (*Kaogu*, 1977, no. 5, p. 346) adopts the same usage based upon different evidence. Kane herself recognized some difficulty in interpreting the character as a verb. More recently David Keightley has also tentatively accepted the reading *hou* (*Sources*, p. XVI).

78. Kane, ibid., pp. 340–41.

79. Ibid., pp. 341–42. Soper, too, believed the *fang-ting* should be dated to the reign of Wen Wu Ting (see n. 7).

80. Li Hsüeh-ch'in has also remarked upon the close stylistic correspondence between the *Hou Mu Mou fang-ting* and the Fu Hao vessels (see n. 10, p. 33); and Tu Nai-sung has claimed that the vessel belongs to the early Yin-hsü period (*Kaogu*, 1977, no. 5, p. 347).

81. *Wenwu*, 1977, no. 11, p. 35.

82. The growing list of other vessels decorated in relief and likely to date from the end of Early Anyang or the beginning of Middle Anyang include:

1. Two *fang-chia*, one in Nelson-Atkins Gallery (Loehr, *Ritual Vessels*, no. 32), the other in the Brundage collection (B 60 B 1019).

2. A *ting* supported by legs shaped as birds (d'Argencé, *Brundage Bronzes*, pl. 5, right; the vessel carries the same inscription as a bronze helmet recovered from Hsi-pei-kang M 1004 (Kao Ch'ü-hsün, *Hou-chia-chuang*, vol. 5; *Hsi-pei-kang M 1004*, pl. 134).

3. The Hakutsuru *fang-i* (*Hakkaku kikkin-shū*, no. 20).

4. The *fang-lei* in Nelson-Atkins Gallery (*Handbook of the Collections in the William Rockhill Nelson Gallery of Art and Mary Atkins Museum of Fine Arts*, vol. 2, *Art of the Orient*, Kansas City, 1973, p. 10, lower left).

5. A lid published by Umehara, *Kanan Anyō ihō*, pl. 52.

83. David N. Keightley, "Legitimation in Shang China." Unpublished ms. of a paper presented at the Conference on Legitimation of Chinese Imperial Regimes, Asilomar, California, June 15–24, 1975, p. 49.

84. Ibid., pp. 49–51.

85. Virginia Kane, *Chinese Bronzes of the Shang and Western Chou Periods*, doctoral dissertation, Harvard University, 1970, p. 76 ff. Kane was the first to note that the florescence of Style V (a) represented for a "brief span of time" a "main area of stylistic . . . advance" (ibid., p. 78). The appropriateness of this decorative mode to vessels of squared shape is obvious.

86. Style V (a) vessels forming a closely related series insofar as each is typologically only slightly more advanced than its counterpart in the Fu Hao and Ya-i sets include the Hakutsuru *fang-lei* (*Hakutsuru Bijutsukan meihin senshū*, Kobe, n.d., no. 5) and the Idemitsu *p'ou* (Sugimura Yūzō, *Chūgoku kodōki*, Tokyo: Heibonsha, 1966, no. 18). Other instances of this phase in the development of Style V (a) to be mentioned are the Freer *fang-chia* (John Pope, et al., *The Freer Chinese Bronzes*, vol. 1, Washington, D.C., 1967, no. 22), a *kuang* and a *kuei* in the same collection (ibid., nos. 42 and 62), and not least, the Sackler *fang-i* (Loehr, *Ritual Vessels*, no. 37). In addition, a Style V (a) *ku* in the Freer (*Freer Chinese Bronzes*, no. 8) carries the same inscription as the Hakutsuru *fang-lei*.

Style V (a) was, however, by no means the invention of the Middle Anyang masters. It was a pre-existing, although infrequently used alternative mode available to them, which they evidently found especially suitable to their own needs. Previous manifestations of this variety of decoration, toward the end of Early Anyang, are documented by several vessels from the Fu Hao burial (e.g., *Yin-hsü Fu Hao mu*, pl. 20:1; pl. 28:1, 2; pl. 33:1, 2; pl. 35:2 and pl. 38:1; also see *The Great Bronze Age of China*, nos. 31 and 33). Still earlier stages in the development of this mode are evidenced by the Pillsbury *fang-yu*, corresponding in date to the very early period of Style IV, on which the face of the *t'ao-t'ieh* on its four sides is given solely by its separate parts that appear in relief, but largely unembellished, on a *lei-wen* ground (Karlgren, *Pillsbury Bronzes*, no. 22) and by a Style III *p'ou* excavated from T'ai-hsi-ts'un, Kao-ch'eng-hsien, Hopei in 1972 (*The Great Bronze Age of China*, no. 13).

A distinctive group of Shang jades embellished with fine raised lines of angular shapes in tidy parallel arrangements—best exemplified by the bird figure in the Museum of Fine Arts, Boston (see Diane Nelson, "The Stylistic Development of Decorated Jade from the Early and Middle Anyang Periods," *Oriental Art*, vol. 25, 1979, pp. 332–39)—may signify a stage in the decoration of jades coinciding with the *lei-wen* relief style in bronze. In their decoration the jades belonging to this group contrast with those from the Fu Hao tomb with their freer and more irregular configurations of quills and curls and their more jagged silhouettes (e.g., *Yin-hsü Fu Hao mu*, pl. 143:2). Raised lines in angular arrangements are also a feature of some stone carvings from Hsi-pei-kang M 1002, a burial established by stratigraphy as later than M 1004 (see Liang Ssu-yung, *Hou-chia-chuang*, vol. 3., *Hsi-pei-kang M 1002*, ed. Kao Ch'ü-hsün, Taipei: Academia Sinica, 1965, pls. 18:4 and 24:1–7).

87. The relative date here tentatively proposed for the florescence of Style V (a) is only slightly later than that first suggested by Kane (*Chinese Bronzes of the Shang and Western Chou Periods*, p. 76). A finely designed Style V (a) chariot fitting was unearthed from M 1003 at Hsi-pei-kang (Liang Ssu-yung, *Hou-chia-chuang*, vol. 4, *Hsi-pei-kang M 1003*, ed. Kao Ch'ü-hsün, Taipei: Academia Sinica, 1967, pls. 95:9 and 97:1). Other Style V (a) vessels excavated from tombs in the Anyang area (for instance, the *fang-i* from M 1022 and the *ku* and *chüeh* from Ta-ssu-k'ung-ts'un (*Fifty-Three Bronzes*, pl. 15; *K'ao-ku Hsüeh-pao*, 1955, no. 9, pl. 9; p. 49, fig. 19; pl. 8:4; p. 48, fig. 18) are of later date, as pointed out by Kane (*Chinese Bronzes of Shang and Western Chou*, p. 90), exhibiting a hardened and stereotyped treatment of this decorative mode. It is not unlikely that vessels in this mode continued to be produced until the end of the Anyang period, although there seems to be little evidence of its use among the Chou peoples either before or after the Conquest.

88. A Late Anyang date for the Minneapolis *yü* is secured by its inscription which includes the cyclical character *kuei* written in a form unknown in oracle bone script before the period of Ti I.

Western Chou History Reconstructed from Bronze Inscriptions

David S. Nivison
Professor of Philosophy and Asian Studies
Stanford University

THERE ARE VARIOUS WAYS ritual bronze vessels can be used to enrich our historical understanding of Shang and Western Chou. We can use them to try to reconstruct a history of the technology that produced them, or the development of the artistic taste they exhibit. If they are inscribed, they are likely to say or imply why they were made and what they were used for, and from this information we can learn something of the social and political relationships of the elite, and of their religious beliefs and practices. Sometimes an inscription gives more than this: It will mention or recount an event that is the occasion for making the vessel. Perhaps the maker served in a military campaign and was rewarded, and used part of his reward to finance the casting, and he tells us about it in the inscription. We don't know from this when the event took place; but by arranging all vessels in a plausible series of artistic-technological-morphological development, we can do some not completely uncontrolled guessing.

I try to do this too. But there are two other ways scholars have tried to use these things, that have engaged my attention particularly.

First, we have certain old books that describe events of the Western Chou period (and it is this period I shall be concerned with now, exclusively). This is the first part of the "dynasty" that includes in its second, longer part the great philosophers Confucius, Mencius, and Chuang Tzu. This earlier part of the dynasty came to an end in 771 B.C., when the western capital, the city Tsung Chou near modern Sian, was overrun and the last king, Yu Wang, was killed.

Naturally, scholars try to use accounts of the period in these books as a framework, and then to approximate the dates of events referred to in the bronzes in terms of that framework: This bronze refers to a campaign against such and such places and mentions this or that person; so it must have been made in the reign of Ch'eng Wang (the second king), and so on. The most important texts that are used in this way are these: (1) the *Shang Shu,* one of the "Classics," pretending to be a collection of historical documents, some of which were written in the Western Chou period; (2) the *Shih-chi,* a long history of 130 chapters written about 100 B.C. by Ssu-ma Ch'ien; it includes a chapter on the history of the Chou royal house, and chapters on the history of states that were vassals of the Chou; and (3) the *Chu-shu Chi-nien* or "Bamboo Annals," which is a court chronicle pretending to record events—very sketchily—from the mythical emperor Huang Ti in the third millennium B.C. down to the year 299 B.C..

This last book was put in the tomb of a local king, Ai-hsiang Wang (or Ai Wang, or Hsiang Wang), of the Wei state (capital near modern K'ai-feng) in 296 B.C. It was discovered when thieves broke into the tomb in 281 A.D. It is quoted in many early commentaries and encyclopedias, and all these quotations have been carefully collected. The original text of this chronicle has been lost. There is, however, a book called the *Chu-shu Chi-nien,* which must be shorter than the original. Almost everybody believes that this short, two-chapter book was forged after the original had been lost, because it differs, sometimes significantly, from the quoted fragments, and there is very little in it that cannot be found elsewhere (except that it does have a full set of dates, and gives an exact date to every event.)[1]

These various texts, and others I could list, often contradict one another. Evidently the ancient Chinese themselves were very uncertain of the historical details of the Western Chou, and there was much guesswork. In particular, they could agree on precise dating for almost none of this period. So scholars have tried to use bronze inscriptions to evaluate these texts and what they say, to see what can be trusted and what cannot be.

For the second approach, of the many hundreds of vessels with at least short inscriptions, there are fifty-four (known to me) that have what I will call "full internal dates." Many more have some kind of dating—perhaps it is just the mention, at the beginning, of an event everyone would have known about (though we, alas, do not). But a "full internal date" will give tantalizing information, usually at the very beginning of the inscription. A typical date will read as follows: "It was the fourth year, second month, second quarter, day *wu-hsü.*"

The "fourth year" in this example is presumably the fourth year of some king; we are almost never told which. (There are two exceptions: two of the fifty-four identify the king as Kung Wang, the sixth king of the dynasty.) The "second month" is not self-explanatory either, because sometimes the official year began with the lunar month containing the winter solstice, sometimes the month before, or the month after, or even the month after that. Or else we have to assume that sometimes an extra month was inserted in the calendar in the middle of the year. Furthermore, my translation "second quarter"—the term here is *chi sheng p'o,* literally "after the *p'o* stage of the moon had begun"—is controversial. Similar dates occur in the *Shang Shu,* and the meaning of the word *p'o* has been disputed for two thousand years. Some scholars think such terms in the bronzes are names of days, not lunar quarters; and if they are quarters (as I believe), we are not sure when they began or ended. The most solid information is "day *wu-hsü.*" *Wu-hsü* is "thirty-five" in the classical counting cycle of sixty, which has probably been in use continuously since antiquity for counting days.

The game, now, is to use this sixty-day cycle, together with astronomical tables that give the cycle designations for the first days of lunar months, year by year, projected back to the Western Chou period. Armed with such a research tool, we will then examine the vessel's form and decor, and the wording, graph style and content of the inscription, and try to guess the identity of the king in whose reign it was cast. We can then, we hope, calculate what years are mathematically possible as the first year of that king. One does this for all fifty-four of these inscriptions that have "full internal dates." Then one tries from these results to find a set of assignments of first-year dates of kings that is "compossible" for the whole set of inscriptions. Many scholars of recent years have worked at this game—notably Chou Fa-kao and the late Tung Tso-pin in Taiwan, Shirakawa Shizuka in Japan, and such scholars as Liu Ch'i-i, the late T'ang Lan and the late Ch'en Meng-chia in the People's Republic. And as they proceed, these scholars of course try to use accounts they find in the old books such as the *Shang Shu* and the *Shih-chi,* to guide them in their dating conjectures.

This is what I have been doing, too. But I have done one other thing no one else has dared to do. I have dared to imagine that the supposedly faked *Bamboo Annals* text is not a fake after all. The *Annals* is the one text that does have a complete set of dates. It is easy to show that they are wrong. But that's not enough. I made a simple experiment: I took a small group of inscriptions that seemed to belong together, that by their content could plausibly be assigned to the first part of the reign of Li Wang, the tenth king and the latest one whose dates are disputed. I found, mathematically, a first-year date that would satisfy these inscriptions: It was the year 857. (Traditionally, the date has been taken to be 878.) The *Annals* gives 853 as Li Wang's first year. There was one more inscription that seemed to belong with the others, but 857 wouldn't work for it. (It is the inscription from which I just took my sample date—the *Hsing Hsü,* discovered in 1976.)[2] So I went back to the *Annals* and found that its date for the preceding king, Yi Wang, is 861. I subtracted: 857 less 853 is 4; then added: 4 plus 861 is 865. When I used 865 as Yi Wang's first year, the *Hsing Hsü* date, "fourth year," had to be 862—and that worked. So I concluded that the *Annals* chronology must be a systematic distortion of the correct chronology.

From here on it was a new game. After much time and work I was able to use my fifty-four inscriptions, together with the *Annals* dates and certain astronomical data, to deduce the precise nature of the distortion—and to find the explanation for it—and so to recover the correct chronology for the whole of Western Chou. Then I could go to the *Annals* and use this text, with appropriate critical caution, to obtain the outline of a genuine history of the dynasty from its beginning, filling in the outline with material from the inscriptions, with some assurance that those inscriptions belong exactly where I put them.

Using this approach as a basis—a new reading of old historical texts, particularly the *Annals* and the *Shih-chi*: a reading guided by and at the same time guiding a reading of inscriptions—I will try to do two things at once. First, I will sketch the history of the dynasty as it appears to me under this new perspective. Second, as I do this, I will point to problems and surprises that have continued to force me to recheck my inferences and interpretations. This part of historical research historians are supposed to do quietly by themselves, presenting their results to the public only when such problems are solved—or when the historian is willing to pretend they are solved. But the history of Western Chou has been problematic too long for this to be honest, and even the criteria for resolving problems are still controversial.

The present *Annals* book shows the hand of an editor or rewriter who is convinced that number is the key to great historical events. For him the Western Chou began in 1071 B.C., exactly 300 years before its collapse in 771 B.C. For 1071 B.C. he records a conjunction of the five planets (the ones visible to the naked eye, for he knew of no others). He has moved the date and made it be what he knew it had to be. There was a very spectacular conjunction at about this time, not in 1071 but in 1059 B.C., peaking on May 28. As the *Annals* text suggests, this was taken by the Chou as a sign that Heaven had given Chou its favor. King Wen probably declared the next year the beginning of his dynasty's rule of the world, when the "year star" Jupiter was located in the zodiac station "Quail Fire," thought to be especially auspicious for the Chou state. Two years later, in 1056 B.C., he apparently formally claimed the title *wang* ("king") and began a new royal calendar.

As we will see, there is evidence in the inscriptions that normally a king took this step in the third year of his reign, after completion of mourning for his predecessor. Wen's "predecessor" in this case would be himself, unmourned. But it would be natural for him to follow the third-year tradition and reassert his claim more strongly at this time. He was a rebel, who had to keep up a certain momentum. Moreover, there was another spectacular celestial event the year before, in 1057 B.C. This was a year of return for Halley's Comet (which we will see again in 1986, for the first time since 1910).[3] For the Chinese, of course, Halley's return was an astonishing surprise, for they had no conception of it as a recurring phenomenon. Comets were portents of ill for reigning rulers, and so, of success for rebels. This spectacle in the sky by itself could have prompted Wen to announce a new "royal" calendar to begin with the next new year.

There followed a program of military campaigns, still unfinished when Wen Wang died in 1050 B.C. His son Wu Wang launched the final campaign late in 1046. (Wu Wang himself took the field on December 15.) This too was a year when Jupiter was in "Quail Fire," for its cycle is about twelve years. Early the next year Ti Hsin, the last Shang king, killed himself in his own capital after the Chou victory of Mu-yeh—on the day *chia-tzu,* January 15, 1045 B.C.

It is a reading of the *Annals* together with the *Shih-chi* that leads to ascertaining this date; and obviously it was therefore crucially important to have seen that the *Annals* must be taken seriously. The *Annals* text tells us about the conjunction of the planets, and records that Wen Wang died nine years later. The *Shih-chi* chapter on the history of Chou says Wen's death was in his fiftieth year as lord of Chou and in his seventh year as king. It then gives data we can interpret as implying that the victorious campaign was launched at the end of the fourth year of his successor Wu Wang. This is then confirmed by astronomy, four times over: (1) Another old text, the *Yi Chou Shu,* tells of an eclipse of the moon on the night of the day *ping-tzu* of the first month (of spring) of Wen Wang's thirty-fifth year.[4] This would have to be the night of March 12, 1065 B.C.; there was indeed a long and dramatic lunar eclipse that night in north China. (2) The date of the attack has to be—and is—a year when Jupiter was in the right place.[5] (3) The year 1045 must be—and is—one with lunar months beginning with the right days in the sixty-day cycle, so that lunar phase dates given in several chapters of the *Shang Shu* are satisfied.[6] (4) One

would have to look forward or backward five hundred years to find another conjunction of even four of the five planets.

More than this: As my story shows, 1056 should be regarded as the formal (as distinct from the celestial) beginning of the dynasty's "Mandate"; and the original *Annals* said that the reign of the fifth king, Mu Wang, began just one hundred years after the "receiving of the Mandate." On my analysis of the *Annals* and of inscriptions, this turns out to be exactly right: Mu succeeded to the throne in 956. Further, in 256 B.C. the king of Ch'in removed the last Chou king Nan Wang from his throne and forced him to surrender his few remaining lands. The year 256 was the exact eighth centennial of the founding of the dynasty; this can hardly be an accident. Yet another numerical correspondence, of a different kind, is this: For many years, most scholars have taken the Conquest date to be 1027 B.C. In this they follow a fifth-century commentator on the *Shih-chi,* who quotes from the lost original text of the *Annals* a statement that the length of the dynasty, from the Conquest to the death of the last Western Chou king Yu Wang in 771 B.C., was 257 years. If "257" was a change from a still earlier original figure "275," the Conquest date must have been 1045.[7]

Satisfying the *Shang Shu* lunar phase dates is a particularly important aspect of the Conquest date problem. As I explained, the meaning of the dating terms is disputed. It turns out that only one of the competing theories works at this point—the lunar quarter interpretation, under one precise definition, which we can then apply to the entire corpus of dated inscriptions. When we do so apply it, the inscriptions reveal their true dates and lead us to an explanation of the distortions in the *Annals* chronology, once we allow for the demands of numerology and for the post-mourning calendar institution. (This must have been dead and forgotten when the *Annals* took shape.)

The accompanying chart summarizes all of this, and compares several chronologies with the true one. (Columns II and IV are my own reconstructions; it is beyond the scope of this study to show in detail how these reconstructions are obtained and how the several chronologies are related.)

I stress the strength of the case for the Conquest date not just because it is a famous problem. Paradoxically, it is the least of the problems that I have encountered in the revisionist reading of history to which the *Annals* and the inscriptions direct me. In some matters, the conclusions I am forced to are so surprising that I would have scoffed at them, were it not for the fact that the cost of doing so would be to reject my findings about the beginnings of the dynasty and the entire line of reasoning on which it is based. Here is the whole picture as I see it.

I. The Conquest Period

This begins under Wen Wang in 1056, culminates in the decisive victory under Wu Wang in 1045, and is consolidated with more campaigns and organization

Western Chou: Chronologies

Reigns (or events)	I: "Traditional" Dates (of Shao Yung)	II: "Original" Annals (DSN)	III: "Current" Annals	IV: "Actual" Dates (DSN)
Conjunction		1039	1071	1059
Wen (claims kingship)		1038	1070	1058/6 (2+7)
Wu		1031	1062/1 (a)	1049 (7)
Conquest	1122 (7)	1027 (6)	1051/0 (a)	1045
Ch'eng	1115 (37)	1021 (35)	1044 (37)	1042/0 (2+35)
K'ang	1078 (26)	984 (26)	1007 (26)	1005/3 (2+26)
Chao	1052 (51)	958 (19)	981 (19)	977/5 (2+19)
Mu	1001 (55)	939 (34)	962 (55)	956/4 (2+34)
Kung	946 (12)	907 (12)	907 (12)	922/0 (2+17)
Yih	934 (25)	895 (25)	895 (25)	903/1 (2+25)
Hsiao (regency)				882 (15)
Hsiao (as king)	909 (15)	870 (9)	870 (9)	876 (9)
Yi	894 (16)	861 (8)	861 (8)	867/5 (2+6)
Li	878 (51)	853 (30)	853 (26)	859/7 (2+30)
Li, majority				844
Li, exiled	842	838	842	842
"Kung Ho" period	841	837	841	841
Hsüan	827 (46)	823 (44)	827 (46)	827/5 (2+44)
Yu	781 (11)	779 (9)	781 (11)	781/79 (2+9)
Yu killed (end of Western Chou)	771	771	771	771
	(1122 through 842: 281 years)	(1027 through 771: 257 years) (b)	(1051 through 771: 281 years)	(1045 through 771: 275 years)
		(1039 to 939: 100 years) (c)	(1071 to 771: 300 years)	(1056 to 956: 100 years) (c)
			(1062 to 962: 100 years) (d)	(1056 to 256: 800 years)

(a) The "current" Bamboo Annals gives both dates.

(b) P'ei Yin, fifth century, quotes the (original) Annals as saying that from the destruction of Yin to Yu Wang was 257 years.

(c) Shu Shih is quoted in the Tsin Shu as saying that from the "receiving (of the Mandate)" to Mu Wang was one hundred years, according to the (original) Annals.

(d) The "current" Annals, comment under Mu's first year, says that from Wu Wang to Mu Wang was one hundred years.

under Ch'eng Wang. (The inscribed li kuei, in The Great Bronze Age of China exhibition, was discovered in 1976; it belongs to the Conquest year.)[8] We can accept the tradition that Ch'eng came to the throne as a minor, with his uncle Tan, Duke of Chou, at first as regent (perhaps through 1041) and then as dominant court official (until 1036; he retired in 1033 and died in 1032). Very serious revolts broke out almost immediately after Ch'eng's succession. These were brought under control by 1038. By 1036, the administrative components of a new capital, Ch'eng Chou (Lo-yang), in the middle of the new empire, had been completed. Two chapters of the Shang Shu deal with this year, and it is probably the date of the Ho tsun, which was discovered in 1965 and displayed in the 1981 exhibit.[9] Conquered territories were being passed out to princes and allies as fiefs. Occasional warfare continued for another fifteen years. By 1020 all was in order, and a grand assembly of regional lords and delegations of border peoples was convened in Ch'eng Chou—in Ch'eng Wang's twenty-third year, and the twenty-fifth anniversary of the Conquest.

II. Peaceful Development: Ch'eng, K'ang, (perhaps) Early Chao

I have to say "perhaps Chao" because I know nothing about Chao's reign except for the one event that would count as ending this stage if it didn't end sooner. He is the one king to whose reign I cannot, using my methods, assign a single inscription. I am sure there are some Chao inscriptions, but there are no exactly datable ones.

As for Ch'eng Wang and K'ang Wang: Ssu-ma Ch'ien in the Shih-chi says that in the reigns of Ch'eng and K'ang there was peace, with no need for punishments, for forty years. One must suppose the forty-year period to be inaugurated by the celebration of 1020. My analysis of the Annals dates for K'ang,

1007–982, shifts the succession date to 1005, and requires that he be given two more than the traditional twenty-six years allotted him. Inscriptions show that each Western Chou king had a formal installation, when a new calendar must have been started, in his third year; normally, this would be just after the completion of mourning for his predecessor. Mourning required twenty-seven months. Since the predecessor necessarily predeceased sometime in the year preceding the succession year, mourning would be completed sometime in the second year. We find quite clear cases in the reigns of Kung Wang, Yi Wang, and Hsüan Wang, where inscriptions unmistakably belonging to these reigns require two calendars beginning two years apart. (The two inscriptions naming Kung Wang are in different calendars, one for his succession year and one for his coronation year.)[10] K'ang thus had two plus twenty-six years, and died in 978—just forty-two years after 1020.

So Ssu-ma Ch'ien was two years off? Well, not quite. One of the longest inscriptions known is one that was on a cauldron discovered in the 1840s (and lost in the T'ai P'ing Rebellion). This is the Hsiao Yü *ting*.[11] The text (in all available copies) is badly damaged, but we can make out enough: It describes a victory celebration, with the interrogation and execution of captives of a rebellious people probably of the northwest frontier. The date on it is the "twenty-fifth year." The events include a burning sacrifice (*liao*), and there is reason to believe that such a sacrifice—indeed, such a celebration—ought to occur at the full moon.[12] Further, sacrifices are mentioned to kings Wen, Wu, and Ch'eng, who therefore must be dead. The date in the text is the third quarter of the eighth month, day *chia-shen* (twenty-one). The inscription, therefore, must describe a celebration, following a suppressed rebellion, which must turn out to be on the sixteenth of the eighth month of K'ang Wang's twenty-fifth year. If we count from K'ang's coronation date 1003, the year is 979, and the sixteenth of the eighth month was indeed *chia-shen*.[13]

So, Ssu-ma Ch'ien was right after all. His "forty years" of quiet was probably not intended as a precise figure, but it will do: The period he refers to is the forty years beginning with 1020 and ending just before 980, which would be the year of the rebellion whose suppression was celebrated in 979. Besides vindicating Ssu-ma Ch'ien, this inscription on the Hsiao Yü *ting* is rich in information on court procedures and rituals, and tells us much about the relationship between the king and his generals and regional princes.

Ssu-ma Ch'ien's statement means that this time was otherwise happily uneventful, so I must leave the rest of it to the art historians and the kinds of inferences they can make better than I. The *Annals* chronicle says almost nothing.

III. Middle Western Chou: End of Chao, Mu, Kung, Beginning of Yih

The chronicle says that in Chao's fourteenth year the duke of Lu was murdered and displaced by his younger brother. The date must be corrected: It was Chao's third year, 975.[14] This was an act that a strong king would have punished. In Chao's sixteenth year, the chronicle says—the date must have been 960—a campaign was put in motion against Ch'u, the Yangtse valley state that had never been conquered and had only occasionally acknowledged Chou hegemony. The campaign ended in disaster three years later, in 957 by my dating. The home army of the west was destroyed and Chao was killed. (Here, and also in many inscriptions, we read of a standing Chou military organization consisting of a six-division army in the western capital area and an eight-division army in the Ch'eng Chou area. I suspect these were standing cadres that could be filled out by levies and reserves with fixed service obligations.)

The dynasty could have ended then and there. The chief thing at present that inscriptions do for my understanding of the history that follows is to license confidence in the *Bamboo Annals* account, bare though it still is. (One *Annals* entry, the building of the Spring Palace in 954, is precisely verified, I believe, by the Shih Chü *kuei* inscription.)[15] The chronicle gives this picture—with obviously legendary matter left out, and with some interpretation on my part:

957: Chao Wang killed. Mu invites Yen, the ruler of Hsü, to his capital and appoints him chief of the eastern regional lords. (Hsü was a non-Chinese state in the southeast. This was obviously an alliance to counterbalance, temporarily, the defeat by Ch'u.)

955–950: Mu occupies himself with fence-mending on his northern and western borders, with a combination of diplomacy—involving some of the traveling for which Mu has become legendary—and military campaigns, including one in 951, under Mao Pan and others. (Mao Pan was probably the maker of the famous Pan *kuei*.)[16]

950: Yen of Hsü, betraying his alliance (as no doubt Mu expected), attacks the Lo-yang area. Mu is ready. He has now repaired his relations with Ch'u.

949: Mu "leads the lord of Ch'u in an attack on the hordes of Hsü and defeats them." (But Mu must have known that he was bound to have more trouble with Ch'u, with Hsü no longer a check on that power.)

945: The regional lords come to court to pay homage to the king. (This year was actually the centennial of the Conquest.)

928: Ch'u makes its move, attacking Hsü again. Mu is again ready: A royal army under Mao Ch'ien defeats the Ch'u army.

926: This victory is followed up by a royal campaign penetrating far into the southeast, with a nine-division force. The result: Ch'u sends a delegation to the Chou court with tribute.

924: Mu Wang confirms his triumph, assembling the regional lords again, at T'u Shan in modern Anhwei.

Mu Wang died the following year, on my analysis, in the thirty-fourth year of his reign. But in the thirty-four years of activity I have reviewed, he had completely reversed the situation he had inherited. Mu has been treated shabbily by historians. He is said to have been a king overly fond of his women, given to frivolous travels and much palace-building. (Witness the archaic novelette *Mu T'ien-tzu Chuan.*) There were surely elements of display in his reign. (Even inscriptions, we see, speak of the palace-building.) But there was also brilliance of another kind. Display itself, for Mu, was an instrument of policy, used with effect, and far less expensive in the long run than failure would have been. One recently discovered vessel, undatable but mentioning Mu Wang by name, finds the King at a wine party; Mu then calls for an archery contest, and rewards one of his officers who assists in the rite.[17] This picture of easy but dignified accessibility suggests that he may have been a popular king.

The security Mu restored to his dynasty makes the next thirty years uneventful reading. At least, I do not find major events in the reign of Kung Wang or the first dozen years of Yih Wang. One long inscription, on the Shih Chiang p'an (discovered in 1976—the longest inscription discovered since World War II), by a court recorder descended from a Shang subject who had entered the service of the Chou at the beginning of the dynasty, sketches the history of the Chou kings and of the inscriber's ancestors. He says of Mu Wang that he "followed the great policies" of the founders, and "passed on renewed security to the (present) Son of Heaven," i.e., to Kung Wang.[18]

Late Mu Wang and Kung Wang inscriptions do reveal two interesting institutional developments. One inscription, the Ch'iu Wei *kuei,* discovered in 1975 and datable to the year 930 B.C., is the earliest example known to me of an inscription form that becomes very common.[19] It is a ritualistic move-by-move description of the author's reception at court: who escorted him into the king's presence, where each person stood, the king's order to the recorder to record certain gifts, etc. Perhaps the function of such an inscription is to realize the full prestige value, for the maker's family, of even a trivial demonstration of royal favor. Most late Western Chou inscriptions are of this kind.

Another in the same find, the fifth-year Ch'iu Wei *ting,* datable 918, records and authenticates a real estate transaction.[20] Again we have a full ritualistic description: the words and terms of the two contracting parties quoted; record of an oath exacted of the other party by officers, named, who validate the action, and names of witnesses on both sides. The inscription closes with the usual dedication, in this case to the maker's deceased father. Apparently one possible function of an inscribed bronze is to serve as a property deed. There are more of these in the next century, sometimes very difficult to read.

IV. Late Western Chou (1): Yih and Hsiao

We enter a period when the royal institution is ceasing to work, and one different attempt after another is made by home area lords (who are close to the throne and so are dependent on it) to keep it go-

ing. Each of these attempts is ultimately unsuccessful.

The contribution of the inscriptions to the sketch I have given of Mu Wang's reign was mainly indirect. Inscriptions datable to Mu Wang on the basis of script and vessel style could supply a rich background. They show that there was, indeed, much military activity on the frontiers during this time, sometimes quite far removed from the Chou capitals.[21] But I have not yet been able to give dates to these military events recorded in the inscriptions. My sketch of Mu Wang therefore was developed from the *Annals* account; inscriptions merely show me how far I can reasonably trust that account. In contrast, the histories, even the *Bamboo Annals*, say almost nothing about the reigns of Yih Wang, Hsiao Wang, and Yi Wang. But here, the many inscriptions imply, as I am forced to read them, a very surprising story. (There are more datable inscriptions for this period than for any other.) The histories do say that Yih was incompetent. He failed to keep the regional lords in order, failed even to keep the calendar of court events in order. He was ridiculed in popular satires. A long inscription discovered in 1942, the Yü *ting,* has no date but probably should be dated 891.[22] It records a revolt of one Yü-fang, Marquis of E, leading the southern and eastern non-Chinese peoples—mounting just the kind of threat that Ch'u and Hsü had posed earlier. (Other inscriptions show that this Yü-fang had previously been the main ally of the throne in the south. "Yü-fang" may be a title, "Defender of the borders.") The royal western and eastern armies proved helpless. The revolt was finally put down by the author of the inscription, commanding the chariots and foot soldiers of his own lord, who came to the aid of the king.

We come now to a major problem of interpretation. I think I have it right, but I would find a different solution if I could, and I do not expect others to agree with me quickly. The difficulty is that there are four inscriptions with full internal dates, that I think (for various reasons) must be dated in the first half of the ninth century; but their internal dates place them late in a very long reign: twenty-seventh year, twenty-eighth year, thirty-first year, thirty-third year. The mathematics of lunar phases allows me to date them between 876 and 869, using one of Yih Wang's two calendars, the one beginning in his succession year (903) or the one beginning in his coronation year (901). But the *Annals* chronology, as revised under my analysis, implies that Yih Wang's reign ended in 877, and was two plus twenty-five years in length—if it stopped with the beginning of Hsiao Wang's reign. All four of these inscriptions must be dated after the year 877.[23]

What shall I do? Conclude that my analysis is wrong, or that the *Annals* chronology that it takes as premise has no evidential value? But this analysis has repeatedly given me verifiable results. (One need look no further than the Conquest date.) It is logically possible that I have repeatedly been led, as it happens, to true conclusions by a bad argument or useless premises, but this is so unlikely that I discard the possibility. I see only one way out, and that is to conclude that for some reason Yih Wang's calendars continued to be used by some (not all) persons throughout Hsiao Wang's following reign.

If this is what we have, what could be the explanation? Before I sketch a possible sequence of events, note one more item: The *Annals* gives Hsiao Wang nine years; but the "traditional" chronologies (that date the Conquest 1122) give him fifteen years. I had two inscriptions (of the ritual court reception sort) mentioning persons figuring in other inscriptions datable in the 860s, but I couldn't find dates for these two.[24] So I took 868 (see my chronological chart) as Hsiao's last year and counted back fifteen, to 882. With 882 as his first year, these two inscriptions could be dated easily, in 871 and 870. And note also this: Hsiao was not the son of Yih Wang, the king he follows, but was the king's junior uncle. This is the only such irregular succession in all of Western Chou.

Here, then, is what I think may have happened:

891: The E Hou revolt; the throne barely escapes disaster. It becomes increasingly evident that Yih Wang is not a competent king.

882: The king's junior uncle, P'i-fang, later Hsiao Wang, becomes acting regent. After Hsiao becomes king, this date is sometimes used as a "first year" for him. Yih is (perhaps for some time has been) gradually eased out of royal functions.

881: In this year, the chronicle says, Yih moved his court to a village named Huai Li, outside the western capital city; perhaps this was actually a forced or induced retirement.

878: Ssu-ma Ch'ien, in his narrative of the Chou court, says as of the year 845 that "for thirty-four years the regional lords had not come to court in homage"—i.e., since 878. Perhaps, then, in this year Hsiao took the first ritual steps to make himself king—finding that status as regent just wasn't enough to enable him to function effectively. With the real king on the sidelines and an illegitimate "king" moving toward the throne, the lords would stay away.

876: Hsiao formally crowns himself. This date is used as a "first year" in some inscriptions, apparently, and is the date that gives Hsiao nine years.

868: Yih Wang dies. Ssu-ma Chi'ien writes that on Hsiao Wang's death the regional lords "restored" Yih's crown prince Hsieh to the throne, as Yi Wang. Perhaps, then, Hsiao too died at this time or soon after. Or, perhaps the "restoration" did not wait for his passing: Hsiao may have lived on, to be forcibly removed sometime before Yi's coronation date, which was 865.

865: Yi Wang is crowned, retroactively claiming 867 as his actual succession year. The "Ssu-ma Kung" inscriptions of Yi Wang's reign—see below—require both 867 and 865 as "first year" dates.[25] Probably the party of lords that supported the restoration was led by Marquis Ch'ing of Wei, who came to his rule in 866; for Ssu-ma Ch'ien says that this lord "bribed" Yi Wang to raise his status from *po* to *hou*.[26] Possibly another party of lords supported Hsiao, and lost: The *Annals* says that Yi in his third

year (i.e., 865 by my dating) had Duke Ai of Ch'i "boiled in a cauldron"—so, he may have been on the losing side.

I ask you to study this conjecture, as to the dates and the sequence of events of the Yih-Hsiao-Yi period, as I address, again, two questions:

(1) *Must* we assume that Yih's and Hsiao's calendars ran concurrently from 876 through 868?

(2) *Why* should they have done so?

We must make that assumption. For, (a) there is no reasonable way to date the beginning of Yi Wang's reign *later* than 867. The next mathematical possibility would be 862/860. This would require Li Wang's reign to begin, not 859/857 but 854/852; this in turn would push the Shih Li *kuei* (see below) to 842, and the related Fu Shih Li *kuei,* describing a royal audience, would then have to be 840, after the beginning of Li's exile in 841.[27] And there is Ssu-ma Ch'ien's testimony: He says Li reigned thirty years, and this has to mean 857–828.

Further, (b) the beginning of Yih Wang's reign cannot be moved *back.* His succession year was 903. The *Annals* record for Yih's first year says that in this year "the sky twice dawned in Cheng"—"Cheng" being West Cheng, near Tsung Chou, and the royal residence since Mu Wang's reign. The phrase, "the sky twice dawned," is technical language referring to an eclipse of the sun. There was in fact a fairly dramatic partial eclipse, in mid-forenoon (at about 10:20) in the Tsung Chou area, on July 3, 903 B.C. Such a celestial event is rare enough to rule out mere coincidence.

Furthermore, eclipses were ominous. The very fact that this eclipse is recorded indicates that some misfortune befell Yih Wang. We can now see what this must have been.

But *why* the use of Yih Wang's calendars under Hsiao Wang? We can imagine that there might have been partisans of the two kings, using different calendars; or even two rival courts in different places. But the inscriptions belie this. There is no hint in them of such a situation.

A likely explanation, it seems to me, is this: Hsiao Wang, I am arguing, was a *substitute* king. This would mean that what thin claim he had to legitimate royal status depended on his filling the role, not just of a "king," but of a *particular* king, Yih Wang. This would mean that once Yih Wang's reign—and calendar—were formally terminated, Hsiao's role as king must cease. (It is quite possible that during this time Yih Wang may not have been still living. Wu Wang, from 1049 through 1044 or later, continued Wen Wang's calendar (for different reasons), even though Wen died in 1050.) So, probably Hsiao himself directed that Yih's calendars continue to be observed after 876.

V. Late Western Chou (2): The Career of Kung Ho, 865–828

The first inscriptions mentioning Kung Ho ("Ssu-ma Kung," "Shih Ho Fu," or "Po Ho Fu") must be dated 865. There is disagreement about identifying

Kung Ho as the man named by these names. The reason for this is that the inscriptions containing these names must be dated in the earlier part of Li Wang's reign, or still earlier, and for two thousand years Ssu-ma Ch'ien's account in the *Shih-chi* has been misread as saying that Li had already ruled for thirty years before the events of Li's reign that Ch'ien narrates. This would make Li's first year 878—totally irreconcilable with my own analysis of the chronology. (Actually, Ch'ien says that Li's entire reign, including his exile, was thirty years.)[28] So, it was thought, any person in these inscriptions could not be the Kung Ho that the *Annals* gives us as regent during Li's exile, 841–828. If we read the *Shih-chi* correctly, there is no problem about taking "Ssu-ma Kung," etc., in the inscriptions as Kung Ho. We must then, however, infer from the inscriptions that Kung Ho comes on the scene, suddenly one of the highest officials in the court, in 865. But why?

Ssu-ma Ch'ien was confused about Kung Ho. The so-called "Kung Ho" period (of Li's exile) was for him a year-period such as he knew in the Han dynasty, meaning "common harmony," i.e., a period of collegial government by Duke Mu of Shao and Duke Ting of Chou. He does mention Kung Ho, the man. For him, Kung Ho is the prince of Wei who intimidated his elder brother Kung Yü, the heir, and drove him to suicide in 813, becoming Duke Wu of Wei, with a long reign thereafter.[29] We must assume, I think, that Ch'ien here follows a bad source. The "Lesser Preface" to the Mao text of the *Shih Ching* points to the solution of the puzzle. It says of Ode 256 ("Yi") that the ode was written by Duke Wu of Wei as an admonition to himself *and* to Li Wang. Duke Wu was therefore much earlier than Ssu-ma Ch'ien makes him, and was indeed an elder contemporary of Li Wang, in a position to counsel the king before the king's exile in 841. Probably the whole story of the succession struggle of 813 is a piece of popular fiction of a later time. When we read the ode, furthermore, we find that it is addressed by a mature, even old man to a young and foolish king. Kung Ho, therefore, was a prince of the Wei state. (When he succeeded as duke we cannot tell.) "Kung," his surname, was also the name of a sub-domain of Wei northeast of Lo-yang, probably the personal domain of the Wei ruling family. We may then infer that Kung Ho enters the court scene in 865 as part of the settlement that put Yi Wang on his throne—i.e., that a high post for Kung Ho was part of the reward to Wei for its support of the king. Ho's sudden prominence in the inscriptions is thus not surprising.

The traditional date 878 as first year for Li Wang is made quite implausible by Ssu-ma Ch'ien's account of the disturbances that drove him into exile in 842. His eldest son and heir—probably his only son at that time—was only a small child, who was rescued by the Duke of Shao and brought up in the Duke's household, later to be crowned as Hsuan Wang. Evidently Li Wang was still a young man at the time; in fact in the *Annals* a note gives his birthdate as 864. That date is verified by a hitherto problematic inscription,

the third-year Shih Tui *kuei,* which by content must be later than but in the same reign with the first-year Shih Tui *kuei.* The two cannot be dated in the same calendar, however, and this is a problem that has vexed all students of the matter.[30] If Li had a new calendar when he attained manhood in 844, there is no problem, for then the third-year Shih Tui *kuei* easily takes the date 842. Both inscriptions refer to "Shih Ho Fu" as having duties of a *ssu-ma* with Shih Tui becoming his substitute (proof again that "Ho," i.e., "Shih Ho Fu," is the same as "Ssu-ma Kung").

Kung Ho's role at this time becomes clearer from another inscription, the Shih Li *kuei,* eleventh year, datable 847—when young King Li had not quite attained manhood.[31] Li Wang presides over a court reception and confers appointments and gifts, but what he is to say is apparently brought in to him as a "report" from "Shih Ho Fu." (The inscription's opening has caused much debate. It should go, "Shih Ho Fu had me, Li, make a formal report to the King . . . .") Kung Ho, then, was regent not only during Li's exile, 841–828, but also earlier, during his minority, 859–845.

The entire thirty-eight years from 865 through 828, then, can be called a "Kung Ho" era. Furthermore, Li Wang, it seems to me, has obviously been treated rather unfairly by the historians. They rate him proverbially as one of the worst kings in Chinese history. But Li Wang was not on stage long enough to justify any such judgment. He was a functioning king for only three or four years. He was probably a spoiled child, and may have been overreacting to feelings of insecurity. But it is not impossible that his ouster was the consequence of the Wei faction seeing power slipping from its hands: The confirmation of Shih Tui's position in the third-year Shih Tui *kuei*—it was previously only an acting one—may have been a thrust at Kung Ho.

That Li Wang still was king after 841, though he had withdrawn from the capital for his own safety, is shown by two more difficult inscriptions, the fifth- and sixth-year Tiao Sheng *kuei* (837–836).[32] One of these shows that the Duke of Shao was representing "the King's" financial interests while the latter was staying in a place called "P'ang Ching," perhaps "detached capital," evidently a royal retreat (sometimes mentioned as a royal residence in Mu Wang inscriptions).[33] But what was this political situation like? The *Shih-chi* and the *Annals* say that there were satires against Li Wang too (like Yih Wang), and that he tried to track down the satirists and have them executed—over the remonstrances of advisors. So repression produced a popular explosion. But if this is true (it need not be), what sort of society was it that could function in this way? Who were the "people" so expressing themselves? We are not going to get answers to these questions from inscriptions.

We cannot leave Li Wang without looking at two more vessels, the Tsung Chou *chung* (a bell, sometimes claimed to be fake), and the Hu *kuei* (discovered in 1978; the largest *kuei* ever found).[34] Both have inscriptions, in exquisite script, by a certain "Hu," who describes himself as a "young man" (hsiao tzu), and refers to himself as "king." "Hu" (another graph, but the two can be identified) was Li Wang's personal name; and the late T'ang Lan has concluded that these must be vessels authored by King Li himself. There are other scholars who laugh at this idea. I am with T'ang Lan. The date of the kuei, "twelfth year," must be 846, and of the bell, 845 or 844. The texts say just the sorts of things one would expect the young king to be saying. (The bell reports, and inflates, a trivial military adventure that its casting celebrates: The king was evidently inaugurating his majority reign with a regional "tour of inspection.") I myself do not think these two pieces are problematic, but it is extraordinary to have vessels and inscriptions actually authored by an identifiable king, and one would like to have agreement about it.

VI. Late Western Chou (3): Hsüan (827–782) and Yu (781–771)

The literary record for Hsüan's and Yu's reigns is much richer, and the inscriptions fewer. I myself have not yet found much instruction in them, but there is much disagreement here. Some experts would assign many more inscriptions to these reigns than I would, and would see Hsüan's reign, therefore, the way tradition represents it, as a truly glorious revival of the Chou royal house.

I believe this picture has to be looked at doubtfully. Hsüan was put on the throne by his protectors when barely of age (if that). While he was under their guidance the court's projects—at least the military ones—were successful. But then as he outgrew them this changed. The picture I form of the whole of the ninth century is that the Chou Chinese world—one cannot call it a "state," or an "empire," or even really a "kingdom"—had become something no king could rule, or be of very much relevance to, for very long.

The Chou power structure looked something like this: There was the Chou home area in the west, a cluster of small domains headed by lordlings who held offices in the court, and there was a similar power arrangement around Lo-yang, where the king had another court and spent part of his time. Then there were the larger territories of the distant vassals in the east and north and south, and the non-Chinese entities on all sides, including Ch'u, Hsü, the northwestern tribes, etc. The king himself did not need to be more powerful than these more distant states, so long as he could overbalance their power—singly or in any reasonably expected combination—when he mobilized his own home forces, the petty domains (Shao, Mao, Kuo, Yü, etc.) close to his capitals. He was dependent

on them. By the same token, they were completely dependent on him—that is, on there being a king. Without a king able enough to draw them together and lead them, they would be lost, in the long run. So we see repeated efforts of the lords around the throne to get a stronger man in the king's role when the incumbent was found wanting. From Yih Wang on, it never worked very well, and eventually it stopped working at all. Obviously there were limits to the king's economic resources, on which his gift-giving depended—always prominent in the royal receptions described in the inscriptions. One long inscription of the Yih Wang period—the Ta K'e ting—records dangerously lavish gifts of lands to a royal cousin.[35] Probably the outer states were living, more and more, quite independent histories, and could simply forget about the throne. When one did take note of it, it would be because the power problems of the inner court involved one of them directly as a participant, which could be very dangerous. Wei, one of the inner states relatively speaking, was not so small.

The danger became disaster when what should have been a petty succession squabble developed in Yu Wang's court, and certain regional lords intervened in favor of one of Yu's sons. In the end, one is tempted to say, Western Chou was not overthrown; it just petered out.

This picture of a gradual drift into irrelevance may describe the late Western Chou throne as a power, but it cannot describe the late Western Chou era as a way of life. The serenely beautiful Po Chü Sheng hu in the Brundage Collection in San Francisco probably was cast in 800, rather late in Hsüan's reign.[36] The maker tells us it is a wedding gift for one of his children. We are glimpsing in these objects a dignified, ordered, and cherished way of life for many scores or hundreds of thousands of persons. Of course this way of life meant that a few were high and many were low, but it was order. This way of life must have gone on, with only imperceptible changes for those who lived it, until a quick turn of the savage wheel of history brought on a brief season of sudden terror. Then, in panic, families gathered their treasured bronzes and buried them in pits—where we find them today—lest they be taken by strangers, and melted down and made into other vessels for other ancestors (just as the Chou conquerors had done with Shang booty in 1045). And then the people fled, if they could. This probably happened for many in 842. It happened again with greater violence in 771, when the lord of Shen and his "dog" barbarian allies took Tsung Chou, killed the king and his officers, and ended the Chou way of life in the Western Lands forever.

Notes

1. Unless otherwise noted, narrative details come from the (*Chinpen*) *Chu-shu Chi-nien,* and when the *Shih-chi* is cited, from the "Chou Pen-chi" chapter. For fuller argument supporting my conclusions, see my article "The Dates of Western Chou," to appear in the *Harvard Journal of Asiatic Studies.* I am indebted to Mr. David W. Pankenier for two important points: the significance and precise date of the conjunction of 1059 B.C.; and the statements from the *Kung-yang Chuan* supporting my hypothesis about the connection between royal mourning periods and the Chou calendar system.

   Translations cited are: (1) *(Chin-pen) Chu-shu chi-nien* ["Current" Bamboo Annals], in James Legge, trans., *The Chinese Classics,* vol. 3, *The Shoo King,* London, 1865, pt. 1, "Prolegomena," pp. 105–83, "The Annals of the Bamboo Books" (with Chinese text); (2) *Shih-chi* [Scribe's record, by Ssu-ma Ch'ien, c. 100 B.C.], "Chou Pen-chi" [Basic annals for the Chou], in Edouard Chavannes, trans., *Les Mémoires Historiques de Se-ma Ts'ien,* Paris, 1895–1905; reprinted, Leiden: E.J. Brill, 1967; vol. 1, chap. 4, "Les Tcheou," pp. 209–319.

2. Hsinq Hsü: See the Fu-feng excavation report in *Wenwu,* no. 3, 1978, p. 5.

3. The appearances of Halley's Comet from 1057 B.C. to 1986 A.D. are worked out in Chang Yü-che, "Ha-lei Sao-hsing ti Kuei-tao Yen-pien ti Ch'u-shih ho T'a ti Ku-tai Li-shih" [The tendency in orbital evolution of Halley's Comet and its ancient history], *T'ien-wen Hsüeh-pao* (Acta Astronomica Sinica), vol. 19, no. 1, June 1978, pp. 109–18. (All positions of the sun, moon, and planets important to my argument can be obtained from standard sources. See Bibliography, "Astronomical references.")

4. For the lunar eclipse of Mar. 13, 1065 B.C., see *Yi Chou Shu* (any edition), chap. 23, "Hsiao K'ai." The day given, *ping-tzu* [13], corresponds to Mar. 12. This shows us that the Chinese day began and ended at dawn. The eclipse was after midnight in North China.

5. Positions of the sun, the moon, and the planet Jupiter at the time of the launching of the Conquest campaign are given in *Kuo Yü* (discourses of the states, fourth century B.C.), "Chou Yü" no. 7. Philological and astronomical evaluation of this text is a very complex problem, which I cannot pursue here in detail. I have a proof that this text was forged, probably about 51 B.C. (the date of the Shih-ch'ü conference on the Classics); but the first sentence, locating Jupiter, is approximately correct, and is probably a Han calculation that attempts to make an earlier tradition more precise, from a Han scientific viewpoint (the calculator had the wrong date, of course). See my article, "*Kuo Yü* 'Wu Wang Fa Yin' T'ien-hsiang Pien-wei" [The forgery of the text in the *Kuo Yü* describing the celestial phenomena "when Wu Wang attacked Yin"], to appear in *Ku-wen-tzu Yen-chiu.*

6. The most important *Shang Shu* chapter for this purpose is the "Wu Ch'eng," no. 23. The present version of this chapter is a fake (of the third century A.D.), although it does appear to contain some old material. The original was quoted by the middle-Han scholar Liu Hsin, in a treatise incorporated into Pan Ku's *Han Shu,* chap. 21B. Dates in two other *Shang Shu* chapters, the "Shao Kao" (no. 32) and the "Lo Kao" (no. 33), concerning the last year of Chou Kung's regency, are also satisfied. These must be in the year 1036 B.C.; for according to the *Shih-chi,* "Feng Shan Shu," Wu Wang died two years after the Conquest; and Chou Kung's regency lasted seven years.

7. The likelihood that "257" is a garble for "275" has been noticed also by Zhong Mengyuan (Jung Meng-yüan), "Shitan Xi Zhou Jinian" [Remarks on Western Zhou chronology], *Zhonghua Wenshi Luncong,* 1980, no. 1, p. 19. Jung, however, adds "275" (inclusively) to 781 B.C. (first year of Yu Wang), arguing that the Conquest year was 1055 B.C.

8. The Li *kuei* commemorates a reward given its maker by the king eight days (inclusive) after the conquest victory at Mu-yeh (i.e., Jan. 22, 1045 B.C.). For the inscription and discussion of it see the excavation report in *Wenwu,* 1977, no. 8, pp. 1–2; also Wen Fong, ed., *The Great Bronze Age of China: An Exhibi-*tion from the People's Republic of China, New York: Metropolitan Museum of Art and Alfred A. Knopf, 1980, p. 203 and p. 215, pl. 41.

9. For brief articles on the Ho *tsun* by T'ang Lan, Ma Ch'eng-yuan and Chang Cheng-lang, see *Wenwu,* 1976, no. 1, pp. 60–66. For reproductions and English translation (which I would not accept), see *Bronze Age of China,* p. 203, and p. 216, pl. 42.

10. See *Kung-yang Chuan,* Wen Kung, ninth year: "The Son of Heaven styles himself 'king' only in his third year," after mourning is completed. The two Kung Wang inscriptions are (1) the fifth year Ch'iu Wei *ting* (Dec. 25, 919 B.C., which was the second day of the *tzu* (winter solstice) month of 918 B.C.; *yüan* year, 922 B.C.); and (2) the fifteenth year Ch'üeh Ts'ao *ting* (906 B.C.; *yüan* year 920 B.C.).

11. Hsiao Yü *ting:* For a translation of the inscription (with transcription of the text), see W.A.C.H. Dobson, *Early Archaic Chinese,* Toronto: University of Toronto Press, 1962, pp. 226–33. For a more accurate transcription and Japanese translation, see Shirakawa Shizuka, *Kimbun Tsūshaku,* Kobe: *Hakutsuru Bijutsukan Shi,* in series from 1962, no. 12, sec. 62, p. 682 ff. [NOTE: Hereafter Shirakawa is cited in this form: KB 12 (62) 682.]

12. A victory *liao* sacrifice in the fourth month of 1045, mentioned in the "Wu Ch'eng," turns out to be on Apr. 30 in my chronological reconstructions. This was the day following the night of the full moon. (This sacrifice is referred to explicitly in the spurious "Wu Ch'eng" as a *chai wang,* "burnt offering at the full moon.")

13. Here we must take the year as beginning—as it commonly does—with the second astronomical month, i.e., the month after the winter solstice month, and rearrange a few long and short months in a quite simple way. The first days of the months are not, as Tung Tso-pin's table gives them, "fifth month, *hsin-wei* (8); sixth month, *hsin-ch'ou* (38); seventh month, *hsin-wei* (8); eighth month, *keng-tzu* (37); ninth month, *keng-wu* (7), etc.— but "fifth month, *hsin-wei* (8); sixth month, *hsin-ch'ou* (38); seventh month, *keng-wu* (7); eighth month, *keng-tzu* (37); ninth month, *chi-ssu* (6); tenth month, *chi-hai* (36); eleventh month, *chi-ssu* (6)," etc. The two consecutive long (thirty-day) months, that the calendar must have at intervals, are simply located in a different place, so that the ninth astronomical month, which in the inscription will count as the eighth month, begins with *chi-ssu* (6) rather than with *keng-wu* (7). No matter when we suppose the "eighth month" in the Hsiao Yü *ting* to have been, day *chia-shen* (21) was Aug. 16, in the ninth astronomical month of 979 B.C. The actual moment of maximum fullness of the moon was 5:08 Greenwich time, or approximately 12:20 Tsung Chou time on that day. The inscription puts the *liao* at about 8:00 in the morning. The moon could easily have been seen as full when it set at dawn shortly before this time.

14. The correction follows Ssu-ma Ch'ien's reign-lengths for dukes of Lu in *Shih-chi,* chap. 33, "Lu Shih-chia."

15. Shih Chü *kuei:* KB 19 (100) 304.

16. Pan *kuei:* Dobson, *Early Archaic Chinese,* pp. 179–84; KB 15 (79) 34.

17. Ch'ang Fu *ho;* KB 19 (103) 339. The vessel was discovered in 1956. The year 935 B.C. would satisfy the partial date in the inscription. The description of the event suggests that it was a time of peace, and relatively late in Mu's reign.

18. Shih Ch'iang *p'an:* KB 50 (supp. 15) 335.

19. Ch'iu Wei *kuei: Wenwu,* 1976, no. 5, p. 27; KB 49 (supp. 11) 273.

20. Fifth year Ch'iu Wei *ting: Wenwu,* 1976, no. 5, p. 27; KB 49 (supp. 11) 262. Shirakawa thinks the "transaction" is a lawsuit, and he has a different interpretation of the date.

21. Virginia C. Kane has a careful analysis of these matters in an unpublished paper, "The Reign of the Fifth Western Chou King Mu-Wang As Seen in Bronze Inscriptions," presented at the annual meeting of the American Oriental Society in San Francisco, Apr. 1980.

22. Yü *ting:* KB 27 (162) 442. See also H.G. Creel, *The Origins of Statecraft in China,* vol. 1; *The Western Chou Empire,* Chicago

and London: University of Chicago Press, 1970, pp. 430–31. The date is controversial. I assume that the campaign recorded in the inscription is the one referred to in the Wu-chi *kuei* [KB 22 (128) 62], which has a full internal date requiring 891 B.C. in my chronological reconstruction. Other features of both vessels and their texts support this date.

23. The four inscriptions that must be dated after 877 are these:
    876: Yüan *pan*, twenty-eighth year (*yüan* 903), KB 29 (177) 590.
    875: Yi *kuei*, twenty-seventh year (*yüan* 901), KB 28, (169) 520.
    873: Ke Yu Ts'ung *ting*, thirty-first year (*yüan* 903), KB 29 (180) 627.
    869: Po *k'uei* (?) *Fu Hsü*, thirty-third year (*yüan* 901), *Wenwu*, 1979, no. 11, pp. 16–20.

24. The inscriptions are (1) Ta Shi Ts'o *kuei* [KB 22 (126) 38] and (2) Wang *kuei* [KB 22 (129) 67].

25. The inscriptions referring to "Ssu-ma Kung"—all in Yi Wang's reign in my reconstruction—are these:
    865: Shih Ch'en *ting*, third year (*yüan* 867), KB 22 (125) 18.
    865: Shih Yü *kuei*, third year (*yüan* 867), KB 22 (124) 9.
    863: Chien *kuei*, fifth year (*yüan* 867), KB 22 (127) 55.
    862: *Hsing Hsü*, fourth year (*yüan* 865) (see n. 2).

26. *Shih-chi*, chap. 37, "Wei K'ang-shu Shih-chia." Creel, *Statecraft*, p. 429, suggest that some kind of intrigue must be involved in the Hsiao Wang era and Yi Wang's "restoration."

27. Shih Li *kuei*: KB 31 (189) 767. See below, sec. V. The exact date should be Sept. 15, 847 B.C. Fu Shih Li *kuei*: KB 26 (151) 334. (Shirakawa does not relate these two inscriptions as I do, and would not require that the latter be later than the former.)

28. Zhong Mengyuan (Jung Meng-yüan), "Shitan Xi Zhou Jinian," has also noticed that Ssu-ma Ch'ien must have meant that Li Wang's entire reign, to his death, was thirty years (pp. 7–8).

29. *Shih-chi*, chap. 37, "Wei K'ang-shu Shih-chia."

30. First year Shih Tui *kuei*, 857, KB 31 (187) 751; third year Shih Tui *kuei* (*yüan* 844), 842, KB 31 (188) 758. (All dates are mine, not Shirakawa's.)

31. See n. 27.

32. Fifth year Tiao Sheng *kuei* (also called Shao Po Hu *kuei*), KB 33 (194) 841; sixth year Tiao Sheng *kuei*, KB 33 (195) 860.

33. The term *p'ang ching*, which I translate "detached capital," perhaps literally means "side citadel." It may be a general term used at different times to name different places. In the sixth-year Tiao Sheng *kuei* (836 B.C.) the term is abbreviated to *p'ang*. There it probably actually refers to Chih, the town on the Fen River where Li Wang spent his exile. The text appears to show "Shao Po Hu" communicating with the king, who replies that he authorizes a third person—who must be Tiao Sheng, identified in the Shih Li *kuei* (847 B.C.) as a royal steward *(tsai)* and now revealed to be a nephew or cousin of Shao Po—to expend money under his control to settle a litigation for Shao Po involving title to a town. There are many different interpretations of the inscription. Most interpretations date it not in the Kung Ho period but in Hsüan Wang's reign. (The Hsüan Wang assignment related to misunderstanding and misdating of the Shih Li *kuei*—see n. 27—which mentions Tiao Sheng as *tsai*.)

34. Tsung Chou *chung*: KB 18 (98) 260. (Some think this a Chao Wang period bell, because the inscription has the words "... *chao wang*" but the meaning is "... extended an invitation to the King.") Hu *kuei*: *Wenwu*, 1979, no. 4, pp. 89–91.

35. Ta K'e *ting*: KB 28 (167) 490. The K'e Hsü, by the same author (Shan-fu K'e), has a full date, requiring Dec. 1, 884 B.C. (eighteenth year, *yüan* 901) in my chronology; KB 28 (166) 485.

36. Po Chü Sheng *hu* (or Fan Chü Sheng *hu*): KB 27 (159) 417. The vessel shape and wave-band decor are found in early-middle ninth century, but the script shows this vessel to be later (note, especially, the graph for *yüeh*, "month"). In interpreting the date (twenty-sixth year) one must use Hsüan Wang's coronation *yüan* 825. See illustration and translation in René-Yvon Lefebvre d'Argencé, *Bronze Vessels of Ancient China in the Avery Brundage Collection* (produced by Kodansha International and printed in Japan by Dai Nippon Printing Co. for the Asian Art Museum of San Francisco), 1977, pp. 98–99, pl. XLI.

Bibliography

Astronomical References
    (1) Ahnert, Paul, *Astronomisch-chronologische Tafeln für Sonne, Mond und Planeten*, Leipzig: Johann Ambrosius Barth, Verlag, 1960.
    (2) Goldstine, Herman, H., *New and Full Moons, 1000 B.C. to 1651 A.D.*, Memoirs of the American Philosophical Society, vol. 94, Philadelphia American Philosophical Society, 1973.
    (3) Oppolzer, Th. Ritter v., *Canon der Finsternisse*, Denkschriffen der Kailerlichen Akademie der Wissenschaften, Mathematisch-Naturwissenschaftliche Classe, vol. 52, Vienna, 1887.
    (4) Stahlman, William D., and Owen Gingerich, *Solar and Planetary Longitudes, for Years -2500 to +2000 by 10-Day Intervals*, Madison: University of Wisconsin Press, 1963.

Chang Cheng-lang, "Ho Tsun Ming-wen Chieh-shih Pu-i" [Addenda to "An explanation of the Ho tsun inscription"], *Wenwu* [Cultural relics], 1976, no. 1, p. 66.

張政烺,"何尊銘文解釋補遺"(文物)

Chang Yü-che, "Ha-lei Sao-hsing ti Kuei-tao Yen-pien ti Ch'u-shih ho T'a ti Ku-tai Li-shih" [The tendency in orbital evolution of Halley's Comet and its ancient history], T'ien-wen Hsüeh-pao [Acta Astronomica Sinica], vol. 19, no. 1, June 1978, pp. 109–18.

張鈺哲,"哈雷彗星的軌道演變的趨勢和它的
古代歷史"(天文學報)

Chavannes, Édouard, *Les Mémoires Historiques de Se-ma Ts'ien*, 5

vols., 1895–1905, reprint, Leiden: E.J. Brill, 1967.

Creel, Herrlee G., *The Origins of Statecraft in China*, vol. 1: *The Western Chou Empire*, Chicago and London: University of Chicago Press, 1970.

d'Argencé René-Yvon Lefebvre, *Bronze Vessels of Ancient China in the Avery Brundage Collection*, San Francisco: Asian Art Museum (produced by Kodansha International and printed in Japan by Dai Nippon Printing Co.), 1977.

Dobson, W.A.C.H., *Early Archaic Chinese: A. Descriptive Grammar*, Toronto: University of Toronto Press, 1962.

Fong, Wen, ed., *The Great Bronze Age of China: An Exhibition from the People's Republic of China*, New York: Metropolitan Museum of Art and Alfred A. Knopf, 1980.

Jung Meng-yüan, "Shih-t'an Hsi Chou Chi-nien" [Remarks on Western Chou chronology], *Chung-hua Wen-shih Lun-ts'ung*, 1980, no. 1, pp. 1–21.

榮孟源,"試談西周紀年"(中華文史論叢)

Kane, Virginia C., "The Reign of the Fifth Western Chou King Mu-Wang As Seen in Bronze Inscriptions," unpublished paper presented at the thirtieth annual meeting of the American Oriental Society, San Francisco, Apr. 1980.

Legge, James, *The Chinese Classics*, 5 vols., Hong Kong and London, 1861–72, vol. 3, *The Shoo King*, London, 1865.

Ma Ch'eng-yüan, "Ho Tsun Ming-wen Ch'u Shih" [An initial interpretation of the Ho *tsun* inscription], *Wenwu*, 1976, no. 1, pp. 64–65 and 93.

馬承源,"何尊銘文初釋"(文物)

Shirakawa Shizuka, *Kimbun Tsūshaku* [Comprehensive interpretations of bronze texts], Kobe, *Hakutsuru Bijutsukan Shi,* in series from 1962.

白川 靜, 金文通釋 (白鶴美術館誌)

T'ang Lan, "Ho Tsun Ming-wen Chieh-shih [An explanation of the Ho *tsun* inscription], *Wenwu,* 1976, no. 1, p. 60.

唐蘭, "矞尊銘文解釋" (文物)

Wenwu Reports:

(1) 1976, no. 5, pp. 26–44: "Shan-hsi Sheng Ch'i-shan Hsien Tung-chia-ts'un Hsi Chou T'ung-ch'i Chiao-hsüeh Fa-chüeh Chien-pao" [Summary excavation report on the Western Chou bronze vessel pit at Tung-chia-ts'un, Ch'i-shan District, Shen-shi Province].

陝西省 岐山縣 董家村 西周銅器窖穴 發掘簡報

(2) 1977, no. 8, pp. 1–5: "Shan-hsi Chien-t'ung Fa-hsien Wu Wang Cheng Shang Kuei" [A *kuei* from Wu Wang's attack on Shang, discovered in Chien-t'ung, Shensi].

陝西臨潼發現武王征商盨

(3) 1978, no. 3, pp. 1–18: "Shen-hsi fu-fung Chuang-pai i-hao Hsi Chou Ch'ing-t'ung-ch'i Chiao-tsang Fa-chueh Chien-pao" [Summary excavation report on Chuang-pai no. 1 Western Chou bronze vessel hoard, Fu-feng, Shensi].

陝西扶風莊白一號西周青銅器窖藏發掘簡報

(4) 1979, no. 4, pp. 89–91: "Shan-hsi Fu-feng Fa-hsien Hsi Chou Li Wang Hu Kuei" [The *Hu Kuei,* by the Western Chou king Li Wang, discovered in Fu-feng, Shensi].

陝西扶風發現西周屬王𣆀𣪘

(5) 1979, no. 11, pp. 12–15: "Shan-hsi Ch'i-shan Feng-ch'u ts'un Hsi Chou Ch'ing-t'ung-ch'i Chiao-tsang Chien-pao" [Summary report on the Western Chou bronze vessel hoard at Feng-ch'u-ts'un, Ch'i-shan, Shensi].

陝西岐山鳳雛村西周青銅器窖藏簡報

Western Chou History: Names and Terms

chai wang 柴望
Ch'ang Fu *ho* 長白盉
chi sheng p'o 既生霸 (既生魄)
Chien *kuei* 諫𣪘
Chih 𣪘
Ch'iu Wei *kuei* 裘衛𣪘
Ch'üeh Ts'ao *ting* 遹書鼎
E Hou Yü-fang 噩侯馭方
Fan Chü Sheng *hu,*
see Po Chü Sheng *hu*
Fu Shih Li *kuei*
(or Fu Shih Fan *kuei*) 輔師嫠𣪘
Ho *tsun* 矞尊 (何尊)
Hsiao Yü *ting* 小盂鼎
Hsing Hsü 癲盨
Hu 胡, 𣆀
Hu *kuei* 𣆀𣪘
Ke Yu Ts'ung *ting* 鬲攸从鼎
K'e Hsü 克盨
Kung Ho 共和
Kung Yü 共餘
Li *kuei* 利𣪘
liao 燎
Pan kuei 班𣪘
P'ang Ching 蒡京
P'ei Yin 裴駰

Po Chü Sheng *hu* 番匊生壺
Po Ho Fu 伯龢父
Po K'uei Fu *hsü* 伯寬父盨
Shan-fu K'e 善夫克
Shao Po Hu *kuei* 召伯虎𣪘
Shih Ch'en *ting* 師晨鼎
Shih Ch'iang *p'an* 史牆盤
Shih Chü *kuei* 師遽𣪘
Shih Ho Fu 師龢父
Shih Li *kuei*
(or Shih Fan *kuei*) 師嫠𣪘
Shih Tui *kuei* 師兌𣪘
Shih Yü *kuei* 師艅𣪘
Shu Shih 束晳
Ssu-ma Kung 嗣馬共
Ta K'e *ting* 大克鼎
Ta Shih Ts'o *kuei* 大師虘𣪘
Tiao Sheng *kuei* 琱生𣪘
Tsung Chou *chung* 宗周鐘
Wang *kuei* 望𣪘
Wei 衛
Wu-chi *kuei* 無旲𣪘
Yen 匽, of Hsü 徐
Yi *kuei* 伊𣪘
Yü *ting* 禹鼎
Yüan *p'an* 袁盤

The Cultural Renaissance of Late Zhou

George Kuwayama
Senior Curator of Far Eastern Art
Los Angeles County Museum of Art

THE CENTURIES OF LATE Western Zhou (1027–771 B.C.) and early Spring and Autumn (770–481 B.C.) were a transitional period in the development of ritual bronze vessels. This paralleled the declining fortunes of the Royal House of Zhou, which was plagued with political fragmentation, the increasing independence of vassal states, and barbarian incursions. Inevitably the Zhou Empire collapsed and in 770 B.C. the capital was moved eastward to Luoyang. Nonetheless new forces soon evolved to revitalize the arts in the form of secularized usage of bronzes, expanded patronage, and technological innovations.

During the Shang (c. 1523–1028 B.C.) and Western Zhou periods ritual bronze vessels functioned in sacrificial rites to ancestral spirits, as part of important state functions. The bronzes symbolized aristocratic authority and the legitimacy of the ruling house, and adhered to a decorative schema sanctified by precedent. But gradually during the Zhou period their usage in sacrificial ceremonies no longer retained its original significance and was replaced by more secular purposes. By the middle of the Eastern Zhou period ritual bronze vessels became increasingly associated with their owners rather than as offerings to ancestral spirits, and they were not buried in tombs to ensure a proper afterlife for the deceased. The presence of bronze vessels in the graves of those of lesser status reflects the rise of private wealth during late Zhou.

By the middle of the Spring and Autumn period, feeble central authority and the existence of strong regional states radically affected the nature of patronage for ritual bronze vessels. The power rivalries among the emerging states and the shifting balances of power required treaties of alliance and royal marriages of convenience; these were formally sanctioned with ex-

changes of inscribed ritual vessels and the presentation of sumptuous bronzes as dowries. Local rulers, in seeking to legitimize their assumption of kingship, symbolically acquired sacrificial bronze vessels and observed the proper ceremonies. Edicts were announced and victories celebrated by the commissioning of bronze vessels.

Regional centers for bronze casting and the crafts arose under local sponsorship in many states. During Shang and Western Zhou the king's ministers controlled the activities of craftsmen and all commerce. However, during the Spring and Autumn period this control ended, and social barriers were broken with the increasing independence of merchants and artists. The new social position of the bronze caster is reflected in inscriptions of the Warring States period identifying the supervisor of a bronze atelier, according to unpublished reports by Chinese scholars. The private ownership of land, the creation of individual fortunes through tenant farming, and flourishing trade resulted in additional sources of patronage that encouraged artistic innovation and the proliferation of the arts.

Important ministers and high officials, rich landowners and merchants acquired bronze vessels as objects of beauty and as personal manifestations of wealth and prestige. Stunningly decorated bronzes were appreciated as an aesthetic pleasure and technical achievements marveled at for their virtuosity. With increased secularization of the arts, the bronze caster was free to seek new sources of inspiration unfettered by ceremonial canons. Spurred by the desire to produce something beautiful, diverse sources—including other artistic media—became a positive stimulus for creativity. The arts of the weaver, the potter,

56

and the lacquerer, whose designs were purely decorative and usually consisted of rhythmic, all-over patterns, may have been an important source of artistic inspiration for bronze vessels.

The introduction of iron during the Spring and Autumn period, about the sixth century,[1] revolutionized agriculture and gave the jade carver the tools with which he created objects of jade that have been unsurpassed for their beauty before or since. Improvements in the composition of bronze alloys to facilitate the accuracy of casting, the invention of new complex casting techniques, the introduction of lost-wax casting, and the methods of riveting, welding, and annealing all combined to maximize the creative possibilities for the artist. Indeed the *Kaogongji* compiled around the end of the Spring and Autumn period described the high degree of labor specialization in metalworking and the manufacture of six different bronze-copper alloys with specific properties for different usages.[2] A changed patronage, technological advances, and the advent of many independent artistic centers created a renaissance for the arts during the sixth and fifth centuries. This cultural reawakening is reflected not only in the metallurgical arts but in political philosophy and ethics, literature and poetry, and in the nascent art of painting as revealed in pictorial bronzes and lacquerwork.

Bronze Vessels

As hitherto noted, the interval between early Western Zhou and a renaissance of the arts in the sixth and fifth centuries was marked by artistic decline. Although pieces of considerable merit were occasionally produced, there is a general deterioration of technique, a reduced vocabulary of motifs, and a stylistic mode that was essentially transitional with incipient experiment. A Western Zhou style was gradually created that negated the monumentality, ordered structure, and balanced symmetry of Shang, and replaced organic zoomorphic forms with increasingly abstract patterns. The harmonious, unified, and static composition of Shang gave way to restless movement with a rhythmic scheme of repeated patterns and curvilinear motion. Designs were confined to bands that girded the vessel in dynamic progression.

Bird-like forms rendered in profile were popular motifs during the tenth century. By the reign of Mu Wang (965–928 B.C.) the long, curled bird tails often crossed to create a continuous sequence of rolling movement; this usually occurred on rearward looking birds as in a *yu* from Tunxi, Anhui.[3] Subsequently fanciful crests and flourishing tails underwent simplification and were decoratively abstracted into flat bands with hooks and curls, as exemplified by the base decoration of the Li *fang zun* and the Li *fang yi* from Licun, Mei Xian, Shaanxi, dating to the end of the tenth or the beginning of the ninth century.[4] They were composed into addorsed symmetrical arrangements or into horizontal bands retaining only a central eye to indicate their derivation from zoomorphic motifs such as birds and dissolved *taotie*.

Similarly, the large "S"-shaped dragons in profile

evolved through a series of stylistic stages beginning with early Western Zhou. The long hooked snout is shortened and ends in a roll, and the dragon forms are gradually simplified and reduced in size, forming bands of repeated "C"- and "S"-shapes comprised of the disintegrated parts of zoomorphic motifs.[5] Thus by late Western Zhou the vocabulary of ritual bronze designs narrowed into simple ribbons of abstract "S" patterns: repeated "C" and "S" shapes, scales, horizontal grooves and waves. For example, the all-over fish scale pattern often seen as a background pattern on late Shang bronzes as on a *zun* from NingXiang Xian, Hunan, became a horizontal band of scales by the ninth century as exemplified by the Zhong Yi Fu *ling* from Qishan Xian, Shaanxi.[6] The wave pattern, with its rhythmic movement that arose in late Western Zhou, epitomizes the ultimate end of Shang stylistic influences.

The artistic legacy at the beginning of Eastern Zhou was one of impoverishment when the innovative prospects of Western Zhou styles were exhausted. By the middle of the Spring and Autumn period, which spanned the seventh and early sixth centuries, new developments led to a creative revival in bronze making. A style of two-dimensional surface pattern had limited possibilities except for interlacing designs which were to become the prime vehicle for artistic development during the Eastern Zhou period. The traditional motifs of dragon and bird-like forms found infinite expressive possibilities in the interlace. The linear ribbons of decoration, confined to a band, turned back on themselves and interwove. Magnificent designs of overlapping, intertwining forms in infinite variation were to become the ultimate achievement of this period.

An early form of interlace was found at Xinzheng, from where the style derives its name. Patternized dragons and "C"- and "S"-shaped bands, seen on a Xinzheng *Fu,* were miniaturized into rectangular units that formed a decorative mosaic by the seventh century B.C.[7] It has been suggested that textured pottery from Southeast China was the source of inspiration for this waffle-like pattern.[8] It is also possible that the repetitive patternization and interwoven character of these designs may also have been inspired by textile designs.

Paralleling this miniaturization into rectangular, waffle-like units was the development of an all-over interlacing tapestry of serpentine forms. This interlacing pattern was alternatively rendered as interwoven feline-bird zoomorphs rendered in modeled relief. This latter form is exemplified by the spectacular pair of huge *fang hu* from Xinzheng attributable to the late seventh-sixth century.[9]

The sixth and early fifth centuries were a period when bronzes reached their highest development, and the stylistic richness of this era is best exemplified by the Liyu hoard found in 1923 in northern Shanxi.[10] Bronze vessels were discovered with flat interlacing zoomorphs rendered in two layers and arranged in horizontal friezes that are defined as the Liyu pattern. There were in addition bronze pieces that continued

1

the "waffle" patterns of the Xinzheng style into the late Spring and Autumn period.

Molds for Liyu style bronzes were discovered at Houma in southwestern Shanxi where the remains of a bronze foundry were excavated between 1956 and 1961.[11] Houma has subsequently been identified as the capital of the state of Jin from 584 to 453 B.C. where an elegant style of ritual vessels were produced with wide distribution throughout China. Houma further revealed the high degree of specialization and the use of mass production methods to meet both the demand for ritual and secular use. The objects from Liyu display artistic sophistication in the harmonious relationship of form and decor that rivals the best Shang ritual vessels. The finest Liyu bronzes are technically unsurpassed for their meticulous detail and precision of casting.

The recent excavations of the tomb of the marquis Yi of Zeng at Sui Xian, Hubei, dating to the fifth century B.C.,[12] yielded a large number of elaborately decorated bronze vessels. Characteristic is a baroque exuberance in their deeply undercut ornate designs teeming with writhing serpentine forms.

The intense energy of the Xinzheng and the Sui Xian bronzes indicate both the development and enormous creative vitality of provincial centers while their shape and style continue to reflect metropolitan traditions. This suggests the rapid communication and ease of contact between various regions of China. There is the coexistence of many styles during Eastern Zhou in a tolerant eclecticism that nurtured continuities and archaisms in style while simultaneously encouraging innovation. This is especially evident in the enormous variety of styles and motifs found among the mold fragments at Houma. There are of course regionally idiosyncratic styles: the central plains, the north, the northeast, the west, and the south. Most of the archaeological attention has so far been focused on the Central Plains, and the state of Chu in the south, with relatively little known about these other areas.

The three-dimensional elaboration of the hooks and spiraling flourishes on the interlacing band led to comma-shaped feather curls. This resulted from the studding and textural effects on the interlace. In its final form the interlace disappeared in a teeming frothy surface of curls. This tendency toward surface projection seems to have begun at least by the late sixth century in a love for lavish embellishment. A style of baroque exuberance found expression not only in the rococo swirls of the comma pattern but also in a brilliantly decorative style utilizing the technique of colorful inlays which became the prime decorative mode of the Warring States period. These features are illustrated by a silver inlaid mythological monster from the royal Zhongshan tomb of King Cuo at Ding Xian, Hebei,[13] and a *hu* from Baoji, Shaanxi.[14] It was a sumptuous style utilizing gold, silver, or turquoise inlays which appealed to a changed patronage that included the newly wealthy who acquired luxurious objects for personal prestige and enjoyment. The art of inlaid bronzes flourished with fluid lines swirling in curvilinear movement, enhanced by the influence of lacquer painting.[15]

During the Warring States period in some of the older metropolitan centers, the innovative brilliance of the previous two centuries had passed and earlier styles continued with conventionalized treatment.

2

3

Figures

1. *Fang hu* from Xinzheng, Henan (Metropolitan Museum of Art, *Treasures from the Great Bronze Age of China*, 1980, no. 67, pp. 128–29 and 187).

2. Silver inlaid mythological monster from the tomb of King Cuo, Zhongshan, Ding Xian, Hebei (Tokyo National Museum, *Treasures from the Tombs of Zhong Shan Guo Kings*, 1981, pl. 43).

3. Inlaid *hu* from Baoji, Shaanxi (Foreign Languages Press, *Hsin Chung-kuo Ch'u-t'u Wen-wu*, 1972, no. 73).

However, other centers arose to create some of the most spectacular, elaborate, and complex bronzes of China's Bronze Age as reflected in the aforementioned excavated materials from Sui Xian, Ding Xian, and other sites.

Pictorial Bronzes

One of the novel developments of Eastern Zhou are the pictorial bronzes. Their production has been attributed by Charles Weber to a period from about the third quarter of the sixth century through the mid-fifth century.[16] A sequential development from simple stylized renderings to a representational art illustrating real events is projected. Animal and human figures are arranged schematically on bronze vessels, as well as scenes of hunts, festivals, battles, or ceremonial events. The artistic conventions employed are conceptual rather than optical and restrict the composition to the frontal plane. Narrative themes are presented rationally, although sequential events are usually presented simultaneously in the same scene.

Weber has placed the center of production for pictorial bronzes in southern Shaanxi and northern Henan under the patronage of the Zhi clan. This was confirmed by the excavation of ceramic molds at Houma illustrating the mulberry festival and other scenes.[17] In addition, pictorial bronzes may have been produced in the south where a different regional style preferred animal illustrations in contrast to a northern one of figures with animals.

The sudden appearance of pictorial scenes depicting human figures interacting with animals in integral composition begs explanation. Diffusionists point to the Eurasian Steppe and ancient Greece as stylistic sources, but a coherent sequence of influence cannot be reconstructed from nomadic art of this period. Isolated motifs on Chinese pictorial bronzes owe their origin to the Steppe, such as the granulated line, the flying gallop, the reclining deer, and sausage and pear shapes decorating the body of animals, seen on the Freer hu.[18] The evidence for Chinese origin, on the other hand, is far greater. Almost all the motifs have earlier Chinese prototypes, and the scenes depicted conform to accounts given in ancient literary sources. For example, the bull sacrifices—a fertility rite—seen on the lower level of the Freer hu, illustrates a domesticated bull about to be sacrificially slain by a man with a sword. Other bronzes show characteristically Chinese themes like archery contests and the ritual selecting of mulberry branches for bows, which can be seen on the top register of a hu excavated at Chengdu, Sichuan.[19] On the second register of this vessel are scenes of bird hunting with corded arrows, dancers with spears, and musicians. The third register shows naval engagements and warriors scaling a fortification. The human figure being devoured by a tiger on a Liyu hu[20] is an evil spirit being exorcised by a protective tiger. It is a symbolic theme with antecedents in Shang bronzes exemplified by the Sumuwu ding excavated at Wuguancun, Anyang.[21]

Nomadic influences from the Eurasian Steppe on Chinese bronze designs were probably indirect and accidental. Bronze objects from the Steppe served as a creative stimulus, showing Chinese artists the possibilities of other artistic solutions. Nomadic and other foreign influences are undeniable in Chinese art and they increase during the Warring States period. However, these foreign elements are casual and interact with established native traditions.

There must have been a rich graphic tradition of study sketches for bronze designs during Shang and Zhou which found full expression in the pictorial bronze. Perhaps a naturalistic, utilitarian art always existed in China which utilized the less exalted media of textiles, pottery, wood, and metallic objects of daily use. However, it is the creative vitality of the sixth and fifth centuries B.C. fostered by benign patronage that led to the florescence of the pictorial bronze.

Naturalism

Throughout the Chinese Bronze Age there seems to have been the parallel coexistence of a hieratic ritual art and a more naturalistic art on objects that were used functionally and were secularly inspired. One may cite examples from the late neolithic period such as the extraordinary pottery bird from Huaying, Shaanxi.[22] The essential aspects of the bird powerfully express a rudimentary naturalism by means of simply modeled compact masses.

A Shang zun in the form of a rhinoceros from the Asian Art Museum, San Francisco, admirably captures the rotund proportions, menacing mien, and ponderous energy of a rhinoceros.[23]

By the sixth-fifth century the techniques for modeling naturalistic sculpture are amazingly sophisticated. The tiny relief sculptures of water buffalo, ducks, and rams embellishing the covers of Liyu bronzes are marvels of realistic rendering.[24] Close observation and study of animals are reflected in a practical understanding of anatomy, an awareness of proper proportions, the successful integration of anatomical parts to the whole, and the harmonious relationship of surface to structure. By the Warring States period the Chinese artist had conquered the technical means to create naturalistic sculpture. This is vividly illustrated by a late Warring States rhinoceros from Xingping Xian, Shaanxi.[25] It is curiously overlaid with an ornamental surface pattern of scalloped cloud scrolls.

The sophistication with which subjects from Nature were treated evolved gradually during China's Bronze Age. It was a native development with its own inner dynamics essentially independent of the animal style of the Eurasian Steppe.

Inlaid Bronzes

The art of inlay was revived during the sixth century, and in succeeding centuries it became the favorite mode for embellished bronzes. Silver inlay appears to be a technique unique to China and was found as early as Shang on chariot fittings. At Erlitou vessels were found with turquoise inlaid onto depressions cast into bronzes, and at Anyang innumerable cases of malachite and turquoise inlay may be cited.

During the sixth-fifth centuries the art of metallic

inlay was enriched with the use of copper, tin, and gold, and new methods of inlay were invented. The earliest datable Zhou example of metallic inlay fixed into case depressions is on a *pou* with an inscription mentioning Luan Shu, a state minister of Jin active between 597 and 573 B.C.[26] Forty gold characters seen in this rubbing were inlaid on the bronze body of this heirloom piece. During the late Spring and Autumn period copper sheets were attached to a mold and cast into position. This is exemplified by specimens from the tomb of the Marquis of Cai, 518–491, at

Shou Xian. With the development of iron tools, bronzes were engraved, and gold threads were hammered into position at least by the Warring States period. During the fifth century the metal inlays were often supplemented by colored glass, malachite, and turquoise, providing a dazzling effect with sumptuous materials and intricate designs.

The art of inlay spread rapidly with many regional ateliers adopting this technique. Inlaid bronzes of the sixth-fifth centuries may be tentatively categorized into a northern, central plains style from the states of

4

5

6

Figures

4. *Fang hu* (John A. Pope, *The Freer Chinese Bronzes*, 1967, pl. 92, pp. 502–7).

5. Schematic diagram of pictorial scenes on a *hu* from Chengdu, Sichuan Province (Metropolitan Museum of Art, *The Great Bronze Age of China*, 1980, no. 91, fig. 107, p. 317).

6. Bronze Rhinoceros *zun* from Xingping Xian, Shaanxi (Metropolitan Museum of Art, *The Great Bronze Age of China*, 1980, no. 93, p. 294 and fig. 109, p. 320).

Jin and its successors Zhao, Han, and Wei, and a southern style in Chu.[27] The northern mode is typified by the Jincun bronzes from Luoyang, Henan, and those from Jiagezhuang, Tangshan, and Beixinbo, Huailai, both in Hebei. Geometric patterns with rectilinear and diagonal lines ending in spirals are characteristic of northern inlaid designs. The southern style, initially reflecting the influence of the central plains, evolved into a distinctive regional mode which is exemplified by bronzes excavated from the Leigudun tomb, Sui Xian, and Wangshan, Jiangling, Hubei.[28] Here the inlaid compositions are more curvilinear and often incorporate dragons and other zoomorphic elements. The artistic traditions of the southern state of Chu were to become the dominant creative force during the Warring States period, and the foundation for much of the artistic production of the Han Dynasty.

Jade

The period from the late seventh century to the end of Eastern Zhou was an extraordinary one for jade carving. At its height during the sixth and fifth centuries supreme examples of jade work were produced that have never been surpassed. The introduction of fine abrasives, tough bronze alloys, and iron tools enabled the jade carver to produce elaborate designs with intricate details, while secularization of the arts liberated him from traditional conventions and stimulated creativity.

Eastern Zhou tombs of the late sixth and early fifth centuries reveal the magnificent quality of late Zhou jades. The tomb of the Marquis of Cai, datable to 518–491 B.C.,[29] Tombs 1 and 60 at Liulige,[30] and Tomb 1 at Guweicun, Hui Xian, Henan,[31] have yielded superb examples. However, the group of jades believed to be from Jincun are the apogee of jade carving. A number of examples are preserved in American museums, such as those from the Freer[32] and the Fogg.[33] They are unsurpassed for the artistic elegance of their conception and for the meticulous perfection of their execution.

The vocabulary of motifs that adorn ceremonial jades are similar to those of ritual bronzes. For example, the comma-spirals on Warring States jades correspond to bronzes with feather curls.[34] The elegant

shapes of late Zhou jades are often inspired by bronze prototypes.

Lacquers

The widespread use of lacquerwares has been verified by archaeological excavations of Eastern Zhou sites. During the Warring States period the art of lacquer blossoms forth with new styles, artistic techniques, and new methods of applying lacquer as well as preparing the base.

The styles of decoration on lacquerwares were strongly influenced by contemporary designs on bronzes with interlacery and scroll designs predominant.[35] In turn, inlaid bronze designs of many Warring States vessels were influenced by painted lacquers with their fluid flourishes and sweeping curvilinear lines. A remarkable lacquer fragment with pictorial scenes of fluidly drawn figures was recently excavated from Tomb 1, Changtaiguang, Xinyang Xian, Henan.[36] Paintings similar to these may have been the prototypes for pictorial bronzes.

A unique example of zoomorphic interlacery on lacquer is a sword fitting in the British Museum.[37] Its modeled design is an openwork relief of serpents and dragons, identified by their long noses and upturned snouts. The fitting has been attributed by various scholars to every century of the Eastern Zhou and Han periods, but its style relates closely to the zoomorphic modeled interlacery of the sixth-fifth century and may be a retarditaire rendering from the end of Zhou.

The medium of lacquer was especially favored by the artists and patrons of the Southern state of Chu. Other centers of lacquer production soon appeared in Sichuan, Henan, Shanxi, and Hunan, indicating the widespread popularity of this medium during the Warring States period. Indeed, during this period the most creative artistic innovations occurred in the medium of lacquer rather than in bronze.

The sixth-fifth century in China was a magnificent period of cultural brilliance in the arts, philosophy, and thought. Many of the artistic inventions and creative ideas were only to be fully exploited centuries later. One is reminded of a similar period in history— Italy during the Quattrocento.

7

Figures

7. Drawing of inlaid design on both sides of iron belt hook from Tomb 1, Wangshan, Jiangling, Hubei (Metropolitan Museum of Art, *The Great Bronze Age of China*, 1980, fig. 104, p. 314).

8. Jade pendant *huang* from Guweicun, Hui Xian, Henan (Metropolitan Museum of Art, *The Great Bronze Age of China*, 1980, no. 72, pp. 138 and 188).

8

Notes

1. The usage of iron in ancient China begins around 700 B.C., and by 500 B.C. it is widespread and highly developed. *Wenwu Gaoku Gongcuo Sanshi Nian 1949–1972,* Beijing: Wenwu Press, 1979, p. 312; see also Kwang-chih Chang, "The Bronze Age: A Modern Synthesis," Metropolitan Museum of Art, *The Great Bronze Age of China,* ed. Wen Fong, New York: Metropolitan Museum of Art, 1980, p. 40.

2. "K'ao Kung Chi" chap. in Chou Li, chüan 41, 17 pp. in *Ssupu-pei-yao,* Shanghai, 1930; or Edouard Biot, *Le Tcheou-Li ou Rites des Tcheou,* vol. 2, Paris, 1851, chap. 41, pp. 490–514; and for discussion of "K'ao Kung Chi" see Noel Barnard, *Monumenta Serica Monograph,* XIV, Canberra: Australian National University, 1981, pp. 7, 9, 178, 183 and 184.

3. Li Xueqin, *The Wonder of Chinese Bronzes,* Beijing: Foreign Languages Press, 1980, pl. 12.

4. Metropolitan Museum of Art, *Treasures from the Bronze Age of China,* New York: Metropolitan Museum of Art, 1980, no. 60, pp. 121 and 185, and no. 59, pp. 120 and 185.

5. George Kuwayama, *Ancient Ritual Bronzes of China,* Los Angeles: Far Eastern Art Council, 1976, no. 32, pp. 54–55, and no. 37, pp. 60–61.

6. Metropolitan Museum of Art, *Treasures from Bronze Age,* no. 20, pp. 74–75 and 179–80, and no. 61, pp. 122–23 and 186.

7. Ludwig Bachofer, *A Short History of Chinese Art,* London: B.T. Batsford, 1947, p. 41, fig. 10.

8. See: Pottery shards from Lamma Island, Hong Kong, Eastern Zhou period and from Starling Inlet, Hong Kong, c. 1000 B.C. in Jessica Rawson, *Ancient China,* New York: Harper and Row, 1980, p. 175, figs. 154–55; see also a *tan,* Spring and Autumn period, Zhenze, Jiangsu in Akiyama Terukazu, et al., *Arts of China,* Tokyo: Kodansha, Int., 1968, p. 45, fig. 64.

9. Metropolitan Museum of Art, *Treasures from Bronze Age,* no. 67, pp. 128–29 and 187.

10. Umehara Sueji, *Sengoku-shiki Dōki no Kenkyū* (Etude des bronzes des royaumes combattants), Kyoto, 1936, pls. I–XXVIII.

11. "Pottery Moulds Discovered Among the Eastern Chou Remains at Hou-ma, Shansi," *Wenwu,* 1960, no. 8, pp. 7–10; Chang Ling, "Eastern Chou Remains at Hou-ma of Ceramic Bronze Moulds with Patterns," *Wenwu,* 1961, no. 10, pp. 31–34; Chang Wan-chung, "The Techniques for Making the Eastern Chou Ceramic Moulds at Hou-ma," *Wenwu,* 1962, no. 4, pp. 37–42; and Hou-ma Municipal Archaeological Research Society, "Brief Report on the Excavated Chou Remains Southeast of the Old City Niu-ts'un, Hou-ma," *Kaogu,* 1962, no. 2, pp. 55–62.

12. Hubei Provincial Museum, *Sui Xian Zeng Hou Yi Mu,* Beijing, 1980, p. 1 passim.

13. Tokyo National Museum, *Treasures from the Tombs of Zhong Shan Guo Kings,* Tokyo: Tokyo National Museum, 1981, pl. 43.

14. Foreign Languages Press, *Hsin Chung-kuo Ch'u-t'u Wen-wu* [Historical relics unearthed in China], Peking: Foreign Languages Press, 1972, no. 73.

15. See: *Zun,* Jiangling, Hubei, in Wenwu Press, *Chung-hua Jenmin Kung-ho Kuo Ch'u-tu Wen-wu Jan Lan* [Exhibition of objects excavated in the People's Republic of China], Peking: Wenwu Press, 1973, pl. 63.

16. Charles Weber, "Chinese Pictorial Bronze Vessels of the Late Chou Period," *Artibus Asiae,* pt. 4, vol. 30, nos. 2 and 3, 1968, pp. 197–98.

17. Verbal communication with Chinese scholars.

18. John A. Pope, et al., *The Freer Chinese Bronzes,* Smithsonian Institution, Freer Gallery of Art, Oriental Studies, vol. 1, no. 7, Washington, D.C., 1967, pp. 502–7, pl. 92.

19. Fong, *Great Bronze Age,* no. 91, p. 317, fig. 107.

20. Ibid., no. 69, pp. 277–79.

21. Akiyama, *Arts of China,* vol. 3, pp. 24–25, figs. 9 and 10.

22. Private photograph courtesy of Jeffrey Riegal.

23. René-Yvon Lefebvre d'Argencé, *Ancient Chinese Bronzes in the Avery Brundage Collection,* Berkeley: deYoung Memorial Society and Diablo Press, 1966, pp. 48–49, pl. XIX.

24. Umehara Sueji, *Ōbei Shūcho Shina Kodō Seika,* Osaka, 1933, pls. 165–66.

25. Fong, *Great Bronze Age,* p. 294, pl. 93, and p. 320, fig. 109.

26. Li, *Wonder of Chinese Bronzes,* p. 38, fig. 25.

27. Ibid., p. 40.

28. Fong, *Great Bronze Age,* no. 76, pp. 286 and 314, fig. 104.

29. Yü Shi-chi, et al., *Shou-hsien Ts'ai-hou Mu Ch'u-t'u I-wu* [Archaeological finds at the tomb of the Marquis of Ts'ai in Shouhsien], Peking: Anhui Provincial Museum and Institute of Archaeology, Academia Sinica, 1956, pls. 28, 29, 105 and 106.

30. Hsia Nai, et al., *Hui-hsien Fa-chüeh Pao-kao* [Field report No. 1 on excavations at Hui-hsien], Peking: Institute of Archaeology, Academia Sinica, 1956, pl. 23; and Kuo Pao-chün, *Shan-piao-chen yü Liu-li-ko* [Shan-piao-chen and Liu-li-ko], Peking: Institute of Archaeology, Academia Sinica, 1959, pls. CX–CXIII.

31. Hsia Nai, *Hui-hsien,* pl. 53–55; and Metropolitan Museum of Art, *Treasures from Bronze Age,* no. 72, pp. 138 and 188.

32. *Masterpiece of Chinese and Japanese Art: Freer Gallery of Art Handbook,* Washington, D.C.: Smithsonian Institution, 1976, p. 32.

33. Max Loehr, *Ancient Chinese Jades from the Grenville L. Winthrop Collection,* Cambridge: Fogg Museum, Harvard University, 1975.

34. See: Jade *bi,* George Kuwayama, *Chinese Jade from Southern California Collections,* Los Angeles: Los Angeles County Museum of Art, 1977, no. 10, p. 29; see also a bronze *bian hu* with feather curl, Kuwayama, 1976, no. 46, pp. 74–75.

35. See: Lacquered leather shield from Wulibai. Chung-kuo K'o Hsüeh Yüan, K'ao-ku Yen Chiu So, *Chang-sha Fa-chüeh Pao-kao* [Report on the archaeological excavation at Chang-sha], Peking: Chung-kuo K'o Hsüeh Yüan, K'ao-ku Yen Chiu So, 1957, pl. 1; see also a silver and gold inlaid *zun* from Jiangling, Hubei, Foreign Languages Press, no. 77.

36. Akiyama, *Arts of China,* p. 109, fig. 185.

37. Harry Garner, *Chinese Lacquer,* London: Faber and Faber, 1979, p. 33.

Hu Vessels from Xinzheng:
Toward a Definition of Chu Style

Jenny F. So
Harvard University

THE TWO MONUMENTAL *fang hu* unearthed in 1923 at Xinzheng, Henan, and now in the collection of the Palace Museum, Beijing, are certainly among the most outstanding bronzes of the Eastern Zhou period (Figure 1). Their decoration is also unusually perplexing.[1] While such features as the rounded square shape, the petaled crown on the lid, and the interlacing surface patterns have late Western Zhou antecedents in vessels like the Song *hu*[2] and the Liang Qi *hu,*[3] others— the bird atop the cover, the feline supports, and the generous array of zoomorphic appendages—are new and striking. The only really close parallel is a pair of slightly smaller *hu* vessels from the same find that display similar dragon handles and feline supports (Figure 3).[4]

The unusual stylistic features of these four vessels have made them difficult to date with any precision. Past estimates have been closely tied to the date of the Xinzheng find as a whole, and this has in turn been deduced from the seven-character inscription of a brazier belonging to the find. This inscription has, however, been interpreted by different scholars to imply a variety of dates, ranging from the beginning of the seventh century to the Warring States period;[5] and even if agreement were reached on the date of the brazier, this information would be of limited use in dating the other bronzes from the hoard, since they show a number of disparate styles.[6]

Leaving out of account, therefore, this inconclusive epigraphic evidence, it can be asserted on the safer grounds of style that the four monumental *fang hu* from Xinzheng are among the latest bronzes from the find and are likely to date from the late seventh century or the beginning of the sixth.[7] This estimate is based partly on the comparatively minor role played by mature "Xinzheng-style" interlocking dragon pat-

terns in their decoration. The Xinzheng-style motifs were formulated by the end of the seventh century and were in common use by the beginning of the sixth; the four *hu* vessels must antedate the real vogue of these motifs.[8] On the smaller Xinzheng *hu* (Figure 3) most of the patterns represent early stages of Xinzheng-style designs; only a single band around the cover comes very close to the tightly interlocked rectangular configurations typical of fully developed Xinzheng-style patterns.[9] On the larger Xinzheng *hu* (Figure 1), carefully and crisply executed Xinzheng-style interlocking dragon units do occur, but still only as a single band around the foot and again on the flat cover in the center of the lid.[10] The two pairs of *fang hu* seem to be close contemporaries, but the smaller pair is perhaps slightly earlier.

A date for these vessels in the late seventh or early sixth century, most assuredly for the smaller pair (Figure 3), becomes plausible if they are seen in the context provided by a series of *hu* vessels related in style. The earliest vessel in the series belongs to the beginning of Eastern Zhou and was recently unearthed near Yicheng, Hubei at a site that was the Chu capital from the late fifth to the early third century and that was probably a Chu settlement well before that time.[11] In shape and decor the Yicheng *hu* (Figure 2) recalls late Western Zhou models from Shaanxi such as the Liang Qi *hu,* but it is much larger. The neck of the vessel is moreover unusually long and narrow in comparison with the Western Zhou prototype, giving it an eccentrically curved silhouette.

The smaller Xinzheng *fang hu* (Figure 3) is in every way a more developed and bolder descendant of the Yicheng *hu.* It retains the same basic decor scheme, which divides the body into panels, but the upper panels are densely filled with small dragons and

Figures

1. *Fang hu* from Xinzheng, Henan. One of a pair. Height, 118 cm. After *Chung-Kuo Ku Ch'ing-t'ung-ch'i Hsüan,* Beijing: Wenwu Press, 1976, pl. 56.

2. *Fang hu* from Yicheng, Hubei. Height, 53 cm. After *Kaogu*, 1980, no. 2, pl. 3:2.

65

3

dragon-like motifs.[12] An even more pronounced curvature appears in the slender, elongated neck joined to a full round belly. Large and sinuous dragon handles projecting from the sides, feline supports, and a flaring openwork crown further break up the outline of the shape.

A pair of *hu* vessels about 74 centimeters tall, crowned by openwork lids and supported by animals, is said to form part of the contents of the mid sixth-century tomb of a Chu minister excavated in Xichuan Xian, Henan.[13] The Xichuan vessels, which at the latest must belong to the first half of the sixth century, offer some corroboration of the date proposed on stylistic grounds for the four vessels from Xinzheng, which they evidently resemble.

From the late sixth century come two more *fang hu*, this time from the burial of a marquis of Cai at Shou Xian, Anhui (Figure 4).[14] The shape, decor scheme, and even ornamental details of the Xinzheng *hu* are duplicated on the Cai vessels, but the alternating curves of the silhouette have become more rigid and the dragon handles lifeless, while the slinking feline supports of the Xinzheng vessels have dwindled to busts.

Finally, among the bronzes from the late fifth-century tomb of the Zeng Hou Yi at Sui Xian, Hubei is a pair of *hu* vessels similar in decoration to the Shou Xian *hu* but round in shape (Figure 5).[15] The Sui Xian *hu* are fitted to a rectangular platform supported by four small "S"-shaped felines. These two vessels are the largest in the present series, standing 111 centimeters high and weighing 240 kilograms.

Ranging from the eighth to the fifth century, the vessels of the foregoing series have certain features in common. First and most striking is their significantly larger size measured against their late Western Zhou models.[16] Secondly, they display a marked disdain for the sober and prosaic late Western Zhou shape, exaggerating its curves and complicating its silhouette with flamboyant appendages. Clearly the dignity of simple forms could not satisfy the unconventional taste of the owners of these vessels.

The same exuberance is expressed vividly and at times with utter abandon in other bronzes from Zeng Hou Yi's tomb (Figures 6–7).[17] The complicated shape of the *zun-pan* (Figure 6), its handles and appendages in the form of dragons with lolling tongues, and its elaborate openwork parts amount to daring exaggerations of features noted on the *hu* vessels already discussed. The writhing serpentine energy of the bronze drum stand (Figure 7) carries this decorative flamboyance to an extreme that elsewhere is matched not in bronze but only in carved and lacquered wooden objects, long recognized as the representative Chu art form.[18] Two outstanding examples of Chu lacquerware might be cited as counterparts of the Zeng bronzes. One is a modest egg-shaped box from a Chu burial at Jiangling Yutaishan, Hubei (Figure 8),[19] the other a miniature openwork screen from a large Chu tomb at Jiangling Wangshan, Hubei.[20] Tightly intertwined serpents form the shape and sole decoration of the Yutaishan box; on the Wangshan screen they

4

5

Figures

3. *Fang hu* from Xinzheng, Henan. One of a pair. Height, 90 cm. Photograph courtesy of the Gugong Bowuyuan, Beijing.

4. *Fang hu* from Shou Xian, Anhui. One of a pair. Inscribed. Height, 80 cm. After *Wu Sheng Ch'u-t'u Chung-yao Wenwu Chan-lan T'u-lu*, Peking: Wenwu Press, 1958, pl. 46.

5. Paired *hu* on fitted platform from Sui Xian, Hubei. Height, 111 cm. After *China Pictorial*, 1980, no. 4, p. 38.

67

serve as the base for the openwork upper structure. While such complicated networks may be relatively easily carved from wood, their fabrication in bronze exhibits a technical bravura far beyond what has heretofore been credited to ChunQiu bronze casting.[21]

The burials at Yicheng and Xichuan can probably be taken as Chu; the Cai Hou and Zeng Hou tombs at Shou Xian and Sui Xian were not those of Chu personages but nevertheless were undoubtedly within the reach of Chu influence. Throughout the history of Cai its rulers had close though not always friendly political relations with Chu, and the Cai marquis buried at Shou Xian was no exception.[22] The connections between Chu and Zeng were at least equally close, for the latter small principality managed to survive only by becoming a vassal to Chu.[23] The tomb of the Zeng Hou Yi provides explicit confirmation of the close relations of Zeng and Chu in the form of a large bell cast by Chu Hui Wang in the fifty-sixth year of his reign, on the occasion of Zeng Hou Yi's death.[24] Incorporated into Zeng Hou Yi's set of sixty-five bells, the monumental Chu Hui Wang bell provides an approximate date of 433 B.C. for the tomb.[25]

In view of the links of all these finds with the Chu state, it is possible that the eccentric features of the bronzes surveyed above represent a hitherto unrecognized Chu decorative style. This suggestion becomes especially attractive when the parallels to the Zeng

6

8

7

Figures

6. *Zun-pan* from Sui Xian, Hubei. Height, 40.4 cm. After Li Xueqin, *The Wonder of Chinese Bronzes*, Beijing: Foreign Languages Press, 1980, pl. 23.

7. Drum base from Sui Xian, Hubei. Diameter, 80 cm. After *Zhongguo Wenwu*, 1980, no. 2, p. 21.

8. Lacquered box from Jiangling Yutaishan, Hubei. After *Kaogu*, 1980, no. 5, pl. 4:5.

bronzes in Chu lacquered objects are taken into account, and there are moreover a few Chu bronzes to give further support. A companion burial roughly contemporary with the mid sixth-century Chu tomb at Xichuan, Henan already mentioned—the only undoubtedly Chu find among those so far listed—is reported to contain a bronze altar table whose top and sides are executed in multi-layered openwork.[26] The legs of the table take the form of ten felines moving forward with their heads raised. These recall the felines supporting the four *hu* vessels from Xinzheng (Figures 1 and 3). This second burial at Xichuan also yielded monumental bronzes such as a set of *ding*—ranging from 60 to 67 centimeters high and 58 to 66 centimeters in diameter—which are decorated with elaborately intertwined dragon-like appendages.[27] The bells from this tomb are comparable to the Zeng Hou bells in size and weight although the set is smaller.[28] Both in size and style, the Xichuan bronzes seem to confirm that the characteristics remarked in the series of *hu* vessels should be identified with the Chu state.[29]

The larger pair of *hu* from Xinzheng shows one feature that does not recur on any of the other *hu* considered here, namely the bird with spread wings standing within the crown at the top of the vessel (Figure 1). Perhaps this too can be associated with Chu. The bird surmounting the lid of a vessel appears again, albeit far taller and less realistic, among the Zeng Hou bronzes (Figure 9). Here a pair of antlers is added arbitrarily to the bird's head, perhaps in imitation of other antlered creatures, frequently made from lacquered wood, found regularly in Chu tombs.[30] At least one such creature is a bird.[31]

The unique character of Chu taste illustrated in the series of *hu* vessels reviewed here evidently did not go unnoticed in regions outside the range of Chu's political influence. A pair of large *fang hu* from Houma Shangmacun, Shanxi, site of the Jin capital, is a close contemporary of the Xinzheng vessels.[32] The decor of the Shangmacun *hu* not only evokes late Western Zhou vessels such as the Song *hu* in the sweeping interlaced dragon bands on the body and the wave pattern at the neck but also reflects influences from the Xinzheng *hu*, notably the intertwined dragons attached to the corners of the vessel and the flaring openwork crown of the lid. The liveliness of the Xinzheng dragons is, however, replaced by a rigid formality on the Shangmacun vessels.

Much later than both the Xinzheng and Shangmacun bronzes but clearly inspired by them is another large *fang hu*, dating from around 310 B.C., that was excavated recently from the tomb of the Zhongshan king Cuo at Pingshan, Hebei (Figure 10).[33] The simple geometric shape and undecorated surface of this vessel provide a neat foil to the four large, floridly curved, winged dragons that hold deftly to its corners. These dragons are theatrical descendants of the winged creatures on the larger Xinzheng *hu* (Figure 3); unlike the dry creatures at the corners of the Shangmacun *hu*, they have a spirited lightness in which the grace and rhythm of their Chu ancestors live once more.

9

10

Figures

9. Bird from Sui Xian, Hubei. Height, 109 cm. After *China Pictorial*, 1980, no. 4, p. 39.

10. *Fang hu* from Pingshan, Hebei. Inscribed. Height, 61.5 cm. After *China Pictorial*, 1979, no. 3, p. 23.

Notes

1. See William Watson, *Ancient Chinese Bronzes,* London: Faber and Faber, 1962, pp. 57–58, and *The Great Bronze Age of China: An Exhibition from the People's Republic of China,* ed. Wen Fong, New York: Metropolitan Museum of Art, 1980, chap. 7 and entry no. 67.

2. *Ku-kung T'ung-ch'i Hsüan-ts'ui* [Masterworks of Chinese bronzes in the National Palace Museum], Taipei, 1969, no. 35.

3. The vessel and its mate are reported to be from Shaanxi Qishan. One of them is now in the Brundage Collection (René-Yvon d'Argencé, *Bronze Vessels of Ancient China in the Avery Brundage Collection,* San Francisco, 1977, pl. 43, top left); the other has remained in the collection of the Shaanxi Provincial Museum (*Ch'ing-t'ung-ch'i T'u-shih,* Peking: Wenwu Press, 1960, pl. 70).

4. This pair of *hu* is now divided between the collections of the Palace Museum in Beijing and the National Historical Museum in Taipei (T'an Tan-chiung, *Hsin-cheng T'ung-ch'i,* Taipei: National Historical Museum Collected Papers on History and Art of China, Third Collection, 1977, pls. 20–21).

5. T'an Tan-chiung, *Hsin-cheng T'ung-ch'i,* pp. 63–70; Sun Hai-po, *Hsin-cheng Yi-ch'i,* 2 vols., Peking, 1937, pp. 129–32. For an excellent summary of the differing views and assessment of their relative merits, see Max Loehr, *Chinese Bronze Age Weapons: The Werner Jannings Collection in the Chinese National Palace Museum, Peking,* Ann Arbor: University of Michigan Press, 1956, pp. 62–63, nn. 45–46. Extracts from Chinese discussions and further references can be found in T'an Tan-chiung, *Hsin-cheng T'ung-ch'i,* pp. 3–4, 63–70. A less detailed summary, also in Chinese, is given in *Shang Zhou Kaogu,* Beijing: Wenwu Press, 1979, pp. 257–58. A discussion of the provincial features of the brazier is given in Jenny F. So, *Bronze Styles of the Eastern Zhou Period,* Ph.D. dissertation, Harvard University, 1982, app.

6. The stylistic diversity of the bronzes from the Xinsheng hoard has long been recognized (see Loehr, *Weapons,* p. 63, n. 46; Watson, *Chinese Bronzes,* pp. 56–57), but Chen Meng-chia was the first to present a chronological grouping of the bronzes according to style (*Kaogu Xuebao,* 1956, no. 2, pp. 95–123, especially pp. 118–19). A similar analysis is offered in So, *Bronze Styles,* app.

7. Ch'en Meng-chia agrees that they are among the latest bronzes from the find, but dates them in relation to the Cai Hou vessels to the late sixth or early fifth century (ibid.). Charles Weber follows Ch'en's dating, but assigns them a much broader "sixth century" date (Charles D. Weber, *Chinese Pictorial Bronze Vessels of the Late Chou Period,* Ascona, Switzerland: Artibus Asiae Publishers, 1968, pp. 3–7). The authors of the exhibition catalogue (*Chung-kuo Ku Ch'ing-t'ung-chi Hsüan,* Peking: Wenwu Press, 1976, no. 56) did not offer a more specific date than middle or late Chunqiu period for the larger pair of *hu* from Xinzheng.

8. See So, *Bronze Styles,* chap. 3.

9. Sun Haipo, *Hsin-cheng Yi-ch'i,* p. 95.

10. This contrasts with the latest vessels from the find, on which Xinzheng-style patterns predominate (see Sun Haipo, *Hsin-cheng Yi-ch'i,* pp. 28–39, 47–54, 82–87).

11. *Kaogu,* 1980, no. 2, pp. 108–13 and 134.

12. Sun Haipo, *Hsin-cheng Yi-ch'i,* p. 96.

13. *Wenwu,* 1980, no. 10, pp. 13–20, 27–30; *Kaogu,* 1981, no. 2, pp. 119–27. No illustration of the pair has been published. The line drawing of the vessels *in situ* suggests that they carry a decor scheme similar to that of the Xinzheng and Yicheng vessels (*Kaogu,* 1980, no. 2, p. 120, fig. 1, item nos. 49–50). Jessica Rawson, Deputy Keeper at the Department of Oriental Antiquities in the British Museum, who saw some of the Xichuan bronzes at the Henan Provincial Museum during a recent trip to China confirms my suspicion, observing that the two Xichuan *fang hu* are so similar to the Xinzheng vessels (fig. 3) that they may be easily mistaken for each other. She does note, however, that there are minor differences in the motifs that fill the upper panels and neck of the Xichuan vessels. I am deeply grateful to Mrs. Rawson for her information.

14. A late fourth-century example inscribed to a Zeng consort who was herself from the Chu royal house is a virtual duplicate of the Cai *hu,* except that the feline supports are absent and the vessel is far cruder (*Jung Keng, Shan Chai Yi-chi T'u-lu,* Peking, 1936, pl. 105; now in the National Palace Museum, Taipei).

15. Excavation report in *Wenwu,* 1979, no. 7, pp. 1–50; an illustrated catalogue of the find is available as *Sui Xian Zeng Hou Yi Mu,* Beijing: Wenwu Press, 1980.

16. Exceptional size is a significant factor as it entails not only the expense of large quantities of metal but also considerable technical expertise. Apparently, the local patrons were ready to meet all costs in search of an ever greater monumentality to outstrip Zhou's traditional grandeur.

17. See *Sui Xian,* pls. 11, 50–51, and 88 for other examples. Note that the two *fang jian* are also supported by felines (ibid., pls. 50–51).

18. Chiang Yüan-yi, *Chang-shu: Ch'u Min-tsu Ch'i Yi-shu,* 2 vols., Shanghai, 1949; Shang Ch'eng-tso, *Ch'ang-sha Ch'u-t'u Chu Ch'i-ch'i T'u-lu,* Shanghai, 1955; Chang Kwang-chih, "Major Aspects of Ch'u Archaeology," in Noel Barnard and Douglas Frazer, eds., *Early Chinese Art and Its Possible Influence in the Pacific Basin,* New York: Intercultural Arts Press, 1972, pp. 26–40; William Watson, "Traditions of Material Cultures in the Territory of Ch'u," ibid., pp. 69–72.

19. Excavation report in *Kaogu,* 1980, no. 5, pp. 391–402.

20. *Wenwu,* 1966, no. 5., pls. 2–3; an English summary of the find is given by Annette L. Juliano, "Three Large Ch'u Graves Recently Excavated in the Chiangling District of Hupei Province," *Artibus Asiae,* vol. 34, no. 1, 1972, pp. 5–17; a replica of the screen is illustrated in *Chūka Jimmin Kyōwakoku Shutsudo Bunbutsu Ten* [Archaeological treasures excavated in the People's Republic of China], Tokyo: Asahi Shimbunsha, 1973, no. 21. The fifth-century date originally advanced for the burial has been revised down to the fourth century, as bamboo strips from the tomb mention the names of Chu kings who ruled as late as 381 B.C. (*Wenwu,* 1976, no. 8, pp. 66–67), while the presence of a Yue Wang sword among the finds suggests that the tomb may even date from the destruction of Yue in 311 B.C. (see *Jiang Han Kaogu,* no. 1, 1980, pp. 59–60).

21. Parts of the *zun-pan* are reported to have been cast using the lost-wax method, a technique hitherto believed by some scholars to have been unknown in China until the Han period (*Wenwu,* 1979, no. 7, pp. 47–48, 45). Surprisingly, however, the lost-wax method was apparently not used in the fabrication of the drum base, whose complex decor is described as made by soldering thirty-six separately cast parts together (ibid., pp. 47–48).

22. Alexander C. Soper, "The Tomb of the Marquis of Ts'ai," *Oriental Art,* no. 10, 1964, pp. 153–57; *The Great Bronze Age of China,* chap. 7; Ch'en Meng-chia, *Kaogu Xuebao,* 1956, no. 2, pp. 95–123; *Shou-hsien Ts'ai Hou Mu Ch'u-t'u Yi-wu,* Peking: Science Press, 1956, pp. 17–21.

23. *Wenwu,* 1980, no. 1, pp. 54–58; *Kaogu,* 1980, no. 5, pp. 436–43.

24. *Wenwu,* 1979, no. 7, pl. 4:2, discussion of the inscription on p. 25; *Sui Xian,* pl. 22.

25. Other objects from the burial reveal further connections between Zeng and Chu. Bamboo strips record numerous gifts from various Chu nobles and show that Zeng's bureaucratic system and writing system were modeled after Chu's (see Qiu Xigui in *Wenwu,* 1979, no. 7, pp. 26–27, 31–32). The iconography of Zeng Hou Yi's lacquered coffin also testifies to strong Chu influence in the realm of religion and superstition (*Sui Xian,* pl. 4).

26. As the table is badly damaged and undergoing repair, no illustration of it has been published with the report, and only a description is provided (*Wenwu,* 1980, no. 10, p. 16). The lost-wax method was apparently also used in the making of the table (ibid., p. 16; see also *Kaogu,* 1981, no. 2, pp. 174–76). Technological similarities between the Xichuan table and the

Sui Xian *zun-pan* form a further link between the two finds, while the history of lost-wax casting in China is pushed even further back into the sixth century by the Xichuan find. It seems possible that the invention or choice of lost-wax casting for these Chu bronzes was prompted by requirements of style. I have suggested that the spiraling, trumpet-like horns of the winged creatures at the corners of the larger Xinsheng *hu* (fig. 1) are a still earlier example of lost-wax casting in China (*The Great Bronze Age of China*, entry no. 67, with a reference, however, to the wrong illustration). Whatever the technique, these spiraling horns certainly recall the twisting forms of the drum base from the Sui Xian (fig. 7).

27. *Wenwu*, 1980, no. 10, pl. 1:1. The shape of the *ding* is a form well represented among the Cai Hou bronzes (*Shou-hsien Ts'ai Hou Mu*, pl. 4) and the Zeng Hou Yi bronzes (*Sui Xian*, pl. 40). The eighty-four character inscription on the Xichuan *ding* provides the basis for the mid sixth-century date offered for the burial (*Wenwu*, 1980, no. 10, pp. 19, 27–30).

28. The largest bell is 122 cm. tall and weighs 160.5 kg. (*Wenwu*, 1980, no. 10, pl. 1:3). The largest bell from the Zeng Hou Yi set is 153.4 cm. tall and 203.6 kg. in weight (*Sui Xian*, p. 3).

29. Apart from the stylistic and technological connections between the finds (see nn. 25–28), the occurrence of gold artifacts in the Xinzheng, Xichuan, and Sui Xian tombs forms another link. Gold sheets with intertwined serpentine motifs executed in repoussé are reported from the Xinzheng find (Carl W. Bishop, "The Bronzes from Hsin-cheng Hsien," *The Smithsonian Report for 1926*, pp. 457–68, Washington: The Smithsonian Institution, 1927). Similar gold sheets came from Xichuan (*Wenwu*, 1980, no. 10, p. 19, fig. 6). At Sui Xian, cast gold vessels were found (*Sui Xian*, pls. 94 and 96).

30. The finest example of this type comes from the fourth-century Chu tomb at Henan Xinyang Changtaiguan (Akiyama Teruka-zu et al., *Arts of China, Neolithic Cultures to the T'ang Dynasty: Recent Discoveries*, Tokyo and Palo Alto, 1968, pl. 98). For a discussion of the significance in Chu religion of these figures, which are usually considered grave guardians, see *Wenwu*, 1979, no. 6, pp. 85–87. It should be noted that the Changtaiguan creature bears a close resemblance to a bronze creature from Xinzheng now on display in the National Historical Museum in Taipei (Sun Haipo, *Hsin-cheng Yi-chi*, pp. 133–34; T'an Tan-chiung, *Hsin-cheng T'ung-ch'i*, pls. 35–36).

31. *Kaogu*, 1980, no. 5, pl. 4:7.

32. William Watson, *The Genius of China: An Exhibition of Archaeological Finds of the People's Republic of China*, London, 1973, no. 100; *The Great Bronze Age of China*, fig 90. The *hu* comes from Tomb 13 at Houma Shangmacun, which yielded also a pair of *ding* whose inscriptions suggest a burial date around the middle of the sixth century for the contents of the tomb (see *Kaogu*, 1963, no. 5, pp. 229–45; discussion of the inscriptions on pp. 270–72).

33. The find is reported in *Wenwu*, 1979, no. 1, pp. 1–31. A 450-word inscription is engraved on the four faces of the vessel (ibid., pp. 19–22, figs. 21–24; discussion of the inscription on pp. 47–49 and also in *Kaogu Xuebao*, 1979, no. 2, pp. 148–53 and 177–81).

An Archaeological Reconstruction of the Lishan Necropolis

Robert L. Thorp
Assistant Professor of Art and Archaeology
Princeton University

WHEN CHINESE ARCHAEOLOGISTS turn their attention from the underground army of life-size warriors more than a kilometer east of the tomb of the First Emperor of Qin (r. 246–210 B.C.) at Lishan to the tomb proper, what will they encounter? Historical accounts describe the burning and looting of the Qin capital region in 206 B.C., and we are well-advised to suppose that the Emperor's necropolis was subject to serious damage.[1] Even so, one might reasonably expect to find many remains of value and interest: the foundations of the aboveground components of the necropolis, the underground chambers, some of the tomb's furnishings, and the like. Given the quality of the artifacts that survived in the trenches to the east, one hopes all the more that excavations will begin soon.[2] However, even if large-scale excavations do commence in the near future, it will be several years before a complete picture can emerge. In the interim, what do we know of the site itself, what do textual sources have to say about it, and not least, what does comparative evidence suggest about the character of this most grand and famous burial? Weighing all these varieties of evidence allows us to anticipate the major features of this remarkable tomb prior to its excavation.

Were we entirely dependent on surveys or excavations conducted at the Lishan site, our ability to reconstruct the First Emperor's tomb would be extremely limited. In addition to the excavations at the several trenches with figures east of the funerary park, we can consult only a surface survey of 1962, a handful of random finds in and around the park area, the partial excavation of several foundations north of the mound and, most recently, a group of tombs and horse pits on the east flank of the necropolis. Several other discoveries have been announced, such as small-er-than-life-size bronze figures, horses, and chariots west of the mound, but as of this writing they have not appeared in archaeological journals. All of these finds have been plotted on the site map (Figure 1) and are considered below. Other comparative evidence is germane to this study: surveys and excavations of the Qin capital and its palaces, other Qin tombs, tombs of feudal lords contemporary with the First Emperor located outside the Qin domain, and finally, tombs of the subsequent Western Han (206 B.C.– 9 A.D.) period.

In employing such a wide variety of archaeological data, I assume that a tomb, however grand or unusual, represents a solution to certain specific problems.[3] Elements of the generic problems and of their solutions can be categorized and related one by one to the historical moment. Thus, while the First Emperor's tomb itself has not been opened, many tombs of periods before, during and after his lifetime are known through scientific excavations.[4] However much the First Emperor may have transcended the commonplace by virtue of his unique status and grand designs, some aspects of his burial must correspond in kind to those of lesser personages both in Qin and elsewhere. Analysis of the current archaeological data yields plausible notions of the range of options available to the master artisans charged with this task and of preferences then current among the elite. Such comparative evidence, moreover, underscores the distinctive scale and complexity of the tomb at Lishan.

Siting of the Tomb

Xianyang served as capital of Qin from 350 B.C. until the demise of the empire.[5] Its precise location, however, has been in dispute. Standard geographical reference works place the Qin capital approximately

30 *li* (15 kilometers or 9.3 miles) east of modern-day Xianyang City on the north bank of the Wei River.[6] The only published survey of sites associated with the Qin capital proposed a location near the Changling railroad station 10 kilometers east of the modern city.[7] A more recent treatment of the problem places the palace district of the capital farther east, suggesting that city walls may have enclosed an area some 15 *li* (7.5 kilometers or 4.6 miles) square.[8] The Qin city site would then straddle the present course of the Wei River and include high bluffs and terraces north of it where Qin palaces are now under excavation. If we adopt this placement, Han dynasty Chang'an stood almost due south, in an area that is today the northwestern suburbs of modern Xi'an.[9]

By contrast, the Lishan necropolis is over 35 kilometers east of Xi'an, east of Lintong District, well to the southeast of the Qin palaces on the north bank of the Wei. Traditional accounts describe the First Emperor's tomb as 80 *li* (40 kilometers or 24.6 miles) from the capital.[10] The siting of the tomb at such a great distance requires comment in light of the much closer proximity of important tombs to walled cities in other regions during this era. It was far more com-

mon in the centuries before unification to place royal and noble tombs within city walls or in sight of them. The position of Lishan can only be understood when the character of the Qin capital district as a whole is properly understood.

Literary sources make it clear that the capital district extended from Yueyang on the east westward even beyond the Xianyang palaces. Yueyang was also located north of the Wei River, roughly north of modern Lintong and the Lishan area.[11] Even in the reign of Duke Huiwen (r. 337–325 B.C.) construction had begun south of the river in the broad plain extending to the Zhongnan Mountain range.[12] In his twenty-sixth year (221 B.C.), the First Emperor moved 250,000 powerful and wealthy families to the capital, an infusion of population that must have placed great strains on existing facilities. We are told of this period that:

each time Qin smashed one of the various feudal lords, they imitated the [foe's] palaces and apartments and built [those imitations] on the terraces north of the Xianyang Palaces near the Wei River. These palaces extended from

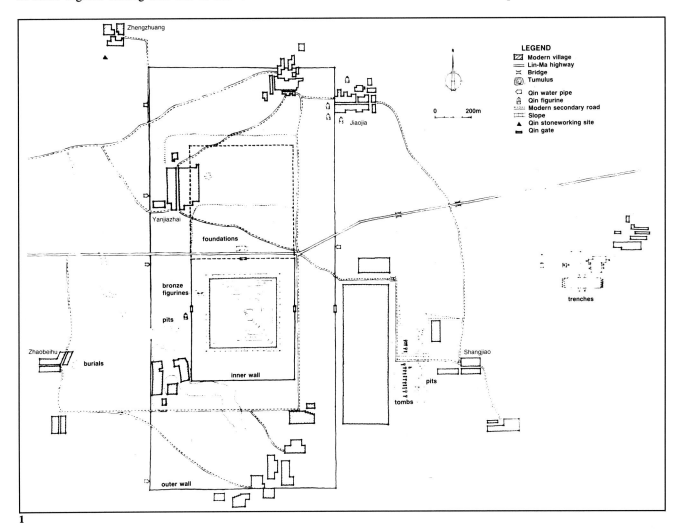

1

Figures

1. Plan of the Lishan necropolis. Rendering by Y.S. Huang.

the Yong Gate [on the west, eastward] to the confluence of the Jing with the Wei River.[13]

With the north bank so occupied, continued expansion south of the river was inevitable. In the First Emperor's twenty-seventh year (220 B.C.) work began on the Xin Palace, followed by renewed construction at the E Pang Palace in the immense Shanglin Park. Sima Qian's *Shi Ji* tells us:

> At this time the First Emperor considered the population of Xianyang too large and the palaces and compounds of the former kings [of Qin] too small. "I have heard," he said, "that King Wen of Zhou had his capital at Feng, and King Wu of Zhou has his capital at Hao. The area between Feng and Hao is a royal capital."[14]

Thus the sovereign intended to shift the nucleus of his capital to the plain south of the Wei. At the same time, he designed his new abode to be more grandiose than that of any Chinese ruler before him. The audience hall (*qian-dian*) of the E Pang Palace is described as 500 double paces (bu) wide and 500 feet deep (690 x 115 meters). Imperial thoroughfares and elevated roadways connected E Pang to the Xianyang Palaces north of the river, to the crest of the Zhongnan range to the south, and to Lishan on the east. Sima Qian claims that in the 200 *li* (100 kilometers) area around the capital, there were 270 palaces, many knit together by such thoroughfares and elevated ways.

Most of the tombs for the pre-unification kings of Qin who died after the capital was moved to Xianyang were sited in tracts east of modern Xi'an.[15] According to *Shi Ji* and its commentators, King Zhaoxiang (r. 306–251 B.C.) was interred at Zhiyangyi, an area identified with the Baling, tomb of Han Wendi (r. 180–157 B.C.) southeast of the modern city near the Chan and Ba Rivers.[16] This same Zhiyangyi was the locus of the tomb of the First Emperor's father, King Zhuangxiang (r. 249–247 B.C.). Located 25 *li* (12.5 kilometers or 7.7 miles) southwest of the First Emperor's own necropolis, it was known popularly as the "mound for viewing the son" (*jian zi ling*). Fu Su, eldest son of the First Emperor, was buried south of Lintong, while the ill-fated Second Emperor was laid to rest at a site south of modern Xi'an. When the burials of other consorts and heirs of the Qin kings are added, we see that Lishan was but one of at least eight royal or imperial tombs east of modern Xi'an. It becomes apparent that the Lishan necropolis was part of the royal Qin cemetery tracts southeast of the Xianyang Palaces and east of the First Emperor's new E Pang Palace. Secure in the "land between the passes," the Qin capital district embraced a broad area, its major edifices linked by arteries that facilitated rapid communication. Lishan was one of many nodes in the network of sites within this dispersed capital.[17]

Plan of the Necropolis

Today the funerary park of the First Emperor occupies a tract 5 kilometers east of Lintong on the level plain south of the Wei River, about one kilometer north of Mount Li from which we derive its name.[18] The necropolis is defined by a pair of walls that create two rectangular compounds oriented 10 degrees east of magnetic north (Figure 1). In 1962 after it had been designated an Important Cultural Site, the outer wall was measured as 2173 meters north-south by 974.2 meters east-west for a total perimeter of almost 6.3 kilometers. These figures are at best careful estimates since on the north and east sides no traces of the wall were visible aboveground and all corners save the northwest were in fragmentary condition. Where the foundations of the wall could be measured, they averaged about one meter in height and 6–7 meters wide. The inner wall was reported initially to be almost square, 684.5 meters north-south by 578 meters east-west, but recent reports suggest that it too was rectangular, perhaps as much as 1300 meters north-south.[19] The 1962 survey characterized the inner wall as somewhat better preserved, and noted that its north wall was as much as 10 meters wide at the base. If the inner wall was actually rectangular as the most recent reports indicated, this 10-meter-wide wall must be explained as something other than the north segment of the inner wall, perhaps as related to structures north of the mound. All of the walls were made by the technique of pounded earth.

At the center of the inner compound stands the tumulus (Figure 2), 350 meters north-south by 345 meters east-west at its base and about 43 meters in height. The original shape of the mound cannot be ascertained; today the tumulus appears less robust than such Han dynasty successors as the Maoling due to its sagging slopes and a cover of scrub trees. An early photograph (c. 1914) shows a profile with a clear break like a shoulder more than halfway up the mound; the summit appears better defined and smaller than today.[20] The survey of 1962 describes the mound as a rounded cone that has been squared off after centuries of plowing the fields that abut it. Nonetheless, personal inspection confirms that the mound has four distinct faces; it is best described as a truncated, four-sided pyramid. The sagging profile may result from erosion and settling, especially if the mound was built by adding pounded earth to a natural hill. By contrast, the Maoling of Han Wudi (r. 141–87 B.C.) presents a taut, sharply defined profile in spite of its smaller base dimensions.[21]

From its visible aboveground components, the Lishan necropolis appears then as essentially two rectangular compounds aligned on a north-south axis with the burial mound in the southern portion of the inner precinct. The position of Lishan may have been regarded as auspicious in relation to its natural setting: a sheltering range of mountains nearby on the south, the Wei River flowing to the north. These considerations may have contributed to siting the royal Qin cemetery tracts in this general area as well. Strategically, the tomb was protected within the passes equally as well as the capital and its palaces; the underground army, in any case, was placed on sentinel duty on the east flank. Jeffrey Riegel has suggested that the tomb was situated east of the capital as a reflection of the influence of the cult to Mount Tai and its associations with the pursuit of immortality.[22] Certainly the First Emperor was susceptible to the entreaties of many magicians including those from the Shandong region, and we know that he visited Mount Tai to conduct the venerable *feng* and *shan* sacrifices there. Han Wudi, equally attached to recipes for long life, however, sited his tomb west of his capital.[23]

The necropolis derives its plan from established forms known at several excavated sites in other regions. The royal tombs of the state of Zhongshan in Pingshan Xian, Hebei Province, were laid out as a row of mounds oriented east-west surrounded by double walls of rectangular plan.[24] Even more useful than the site itself is a measured drawing of the burial district *(zhao yu tu)* cast on a small plate of bronze about a meter in length and one-half meter wide (Figure 3). The drawing details the placement and dimensions of five mounds surmounted by mortuary temples, with accessory buildings, earthen terraces, double walls, and their gates. Plans of this type are mentioned in *Zhou Li* (*Institutes of Zhou*, a text of problematic date) as among the responsibilities of the court official in charge of burials *(zhong ren)*. Accord-

ing to this plan, the outer wall was to measure over 410 meters long by 176 meters deep, converting ancient units to modern metric form.[25] The inner wall, in turn, was to be 340 by 105 meters. Within that enclosure, the three largest mortuary temples were 200 meters square at their bases (Figure 4). In the event, the complete royal Zhongshan funerary park was never realized—only the two tombs excavated in recent years were constructed. A similar plan consisting of a row of three large tombs is known from Guweicun in Hui Xian, Henan Province.[26] There temples surmounted the burial shafts rather than being built around and atop burial mounds. Like the Zhongshan site, a terrace of earth contained the three tombs, but no remains of encircling walls have been reported at Guweicun.

The key element in both of these plans is the side-by-side placement of the burials, probably a lord and heirs or consorts interred together, the higher-ranking lord in a central location flanked by the others. Lishan does not follow this plan but rather isolates a single burial within its own compound. Unlike the feudal kings or lords of the other sites mentioned above, the First Emperor enjoyed a social-hierarchic position unequalled by any other mortal. His necropolis manifests that unique station. As unifier of all under Heaven, the First Emperor may also have been well aware of his exceptional historical status.

In scale, Lishan contrasts sharply with the compar-

2

Figures

2. The Lishan tumulus, c. 1914. After V. Segalen, *Mission archéologique,* vol. 1, 1924, pl. 1.

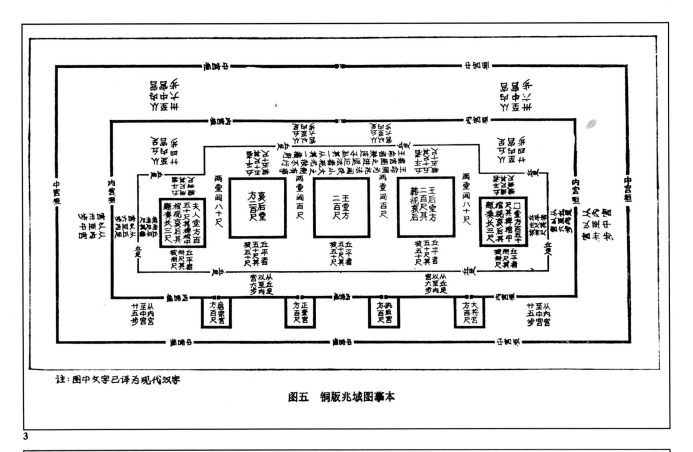

注：图中文字已译为现代汉字

图五　铜版兆域图摹本

3

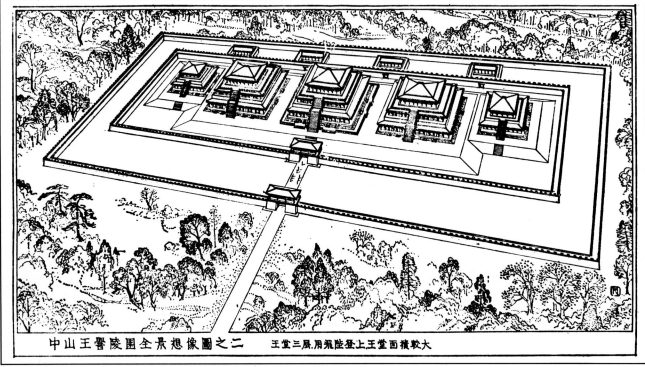

中山王䁝陵园全景想像图之二　王堂三层用飞陛登上王堂面积较大

4

Figures

3. "Burial district plan" *(zhao yu tu),* copy with graphs rewritten in modern forms. After *Kaogu,* 1980, no. 1, p. 125.

4. Reconstruction of "Burial district" at Pingshan, Hebei, by Fu Xinian. After *Kaogu,* 1980, no. 1, p. 110.

ative examples above. The outer wall of the First Emperor's precinct is more than five times longer than its counterpart on the Zhongshan plan. The inner walled area at Lishan is eight times longer than the terrace surrounding the tombs at Hui Xian. On the other hand, the proportions of the delimited areas are comparable, the ratio of length to width being roughly 2:1 in all cases.

If the Lishan necropolis far exceeds the burial sites of other feudal lords, how does it compare with tombs of the earlier kings of Qin? Information on the royal tombs near the earlier Qin capital of Yong in Fengxiang Xian has recently appeared.[27] While these data are given only in summary form, they suffice to allow a general comparison. Tomb 1 in Nanzhihui Commune, Fengxiang Xian, has been probed and measured with the following results: total length, 300 meters; length of the east ramp, 156 meters; dimensions of the burial shaft, 59 by 38 meters; length of the west ramp, 84 meters. If the figures supplied in this preliminary summary are accurate, Tomb 1 at Nanzhihui Commune is the largest tomb yet reported for ancient China. As the scion of the same royal house, the First Emperor may well have demanded that his burial be larger than that of any of his predecessors. Palaces of large scale are attributed to the pre-unification Qin kings in textual sources, so a tradition of grandiose designs may have been characteristic of Qin. The First Emperor's projects responded to that tradition.

Ascertaining the character of the necropolis during its lifetime depends in part on textual sources and in part on the exceedingly fragmentary evidence of chance finds and incomplete excavations within the walls. The most frequently quoted authority on these matters, the Eastern Han scholar Cai Yong (133–192 A.D.), states in his text *Du duan (Solitary judgments)* that:

the ancients did not sacrifice [in] the tomb. Funerary parks had compounds and retiring chambers; Qin followed this [practice]. Commentators have said that ancient ancestral temples consisted of a temple hall *(miao)* in front and retiring chambers *(qin)* in the rear, after the manner in which residences have a court in front and retiring chambers in the rear. The ancestral tablet is deposited in the temple hall for use in the seasonal sacrifices. The chambers have gowns, caps, armrests and staffs, like the paraphernalia of the living to be used when presenting offerings. The Qin first removed the retiring chambers to occupy a position at the flank of the tomb. Therefore the area above the mound is called the "Retiring Hall" *(qin-dian).*[28]

Cai Yong's comments require some revision in light of the evidence from the burial district plan found at Pingshan Xian, Hebei. Here, a century before the First Emperor, we see temples located at the burial site, literally atop the tombs. On the other hand, lik-

ening the functional divisions of a ritual complex to the different parts of a palace or residence does accord with our knowledge of ancient Chinese architecture, a tradition in which many functions could be performed in one common type of structure. This view agrees furthermore with the lack of distinctions between secular, religious and political activities on the part of lords and rulers who embodied what, from a modern point of view, are several different roles.[29]

Remains within the funerary park can be described at present as extremely fragmentary but nonetheless suggestive. One group of foundations has been properly excavated, that located about 150 meters due north of the mound near the modern highway that bisects the park (Figure 1).[30] If the inner wall was indeed rectangular in plan, these structures would have been within that compound. Four foundations in an east-west row have been identified, the largest almost 20 meters long and 3.4 meters wide. The largest foundation was also the most complex with an elaborate limestone doorway, walls of plastered stone, and walkways paved with stones. Two pairs of these foundations were connected by a common wall; they may represent chambers on the perimeter, possibly the south margin, of a compound directly north of the mound. Extensive areas of hard pounded earth are known to lie in this general area: south of Yanjiazhaicun (a section 250 meters in length) and east of that same village (a section 300 meters in length).[31] Both of these areas lie within the inner wall.

Remains of lesser structures, perhaps outbuildings like gate houses and galleries, have also been found. In every case the finds as published defy more than the general recognition that at one time a foundation, wall, path, or roof existed on the site. Underground water pipes of ceramic and stone are known, and may have been part of the drainage system for major buildings. Two groups of water pipes, for example, were found under the western walls in that northern area which includes the extensive tracts of pounded earth noted above.[32] Scattered sites within the walls have yielded a large quantity of architectural pottery, bricks, roof tiles and tile ends, and sometimes other ornaments such as a large bronze fitting weighing 150 kilograms covered with a kind of lightning design.[33] Inscriptions on some tiles name offices charged with their manufacture, offices probably subordinate to the Privy Treasury *(shaofu).* Inscriptions on objects found at sites near the east, south and west inner walls carry the name of the Right and Left Provisions Office *(zuo/you shi guan),* leading to the hypothesis that structures in that area supplied the victuals needed in the rites and ceremonies performed at Lishan. Several inscriptions moreover include the name "Lishan," testifying to the contemporary name of the funerary park.[34]

Kneeling figurines have been recovered from various sites near the outer wall of the park over the last several decades, and a recent excavation now makes their role in the necropolis clear. Four were found, it is said, near Jiaojiacun, thus in the area northeast of the mound near the outer wall; one is said to come

from the west flank of the mound itself. These figurines, one well known because it was displayed in
the Chinese Exhibition of 1973–75, have been found
at depths of about a meter, far shallower than the
better-known trenches with the underground army.[35]
Probing and partial excavations in 1976–77 identified
ninety-three pits in several rows in the vicinity of
Shangjiaocun. Some of these pits contained horses
(some buried alive); others held kneeling figurines of
the type known from the earlier, accidental discoveries. Nine kneeling figurines have been reported from
these new excavations, all virtually identical in dimensions and pose to the previous finds. We are thus
allowed to suppose that these small figures were buried with offerings in a fashion similar to that already
known from at least one Han imperial tomb.[36] Since
the earlier finds were said to originate near Jiaojiacun,
it is possible that such sacrificial pits extend along the
outer wall of the funerary park from Jiaojiacun to
Shangjiaocun.

Knowledge of areas outside the walls of the Lishan
funerary park is minimal but here, too, recent discoveries are promising. Some of these finds have been
mentioned only in passing, such as the burials of
some seventy convicts—some perhaps buried alive and
with crude epitaphs—said to lie 1600 meters west of
the park near Zhaobeihucun.[37] Perhaps the most intriguing of the recent finds is the remains of a stoneworking factory that may have produced stone building materials for the Lishan complex. Situated near
Zhengzhuangcun near the northwest corner of the
outer wall, this site consists of foundations, a large
work area, and sections with both unfinished and finished stone products.[38] Among these products are water pipes like those unearthed in several parts of the
park. Work here has only begun, but among the artifacts are iron chokers and shackles that must have
been worn by convicts assigned to this labor. In the
initial survey of Lishan in 1962, the authors took note
of the stone water pipes, suggesting that since this
kind of stone is not native to Lishan itself, the material may have been brought in from sources across the
Wei River, as the *Historical Records* mentions in relation to the E Pang Palace.[39] Stone slabs were used also for the doorway of one of the foundations north of
the mound. This new discovery helps complete the
picture, indicating that workshops on the site produced necessary material.

The last major report to date describes a cluster of
seventeen medium-scale tombs lying about 350 meters
east of the outer wall near Shangjiaocun.[40] Of that
group, eight have been excavated and the deceased
found to be men and women of twenty to thirty years
of age, all seemingly executed. While the tombs were
robbed, the remaining artifacts and the scale of these
burials strongly suggest these individuals were of noble rank, and the tombs contemporary in date with
both the necropolis and the trenches further east. The
preliminary report concludes that the deceased were
among those Qin high officials and princes put to
death in 208 B.C. at the behest of Zhao Gao, the
wicked eunuch serving the Second Emperor. Whether

or not that precise identification is accepted, these
burials are likely to be those of persons who followed
the First Emperor in death. *Historical Records* states
that women of the palace and master artisans responsible for the tomb were put to death after the First
Emperor's funeral; the Shangjiaocun tombs could be
among that group.

Such compromised sources as we have for recon-
structing the First Emperor's funerary park evoke a
complex establishment, far more impressive than its
present circumstances would indicate at first glance.
Extensive structures must have occupied the northern
half of the inner compound, and it is not impossible
that walkways and corridors, either above or below
ground, connected this zone to the mound and to other areas. Gates in the walls and galleries near some
portions of the walls are also likely. The narrow areas
flanking the mound on the east, south and west may
have been devoted to offices supplying the sacrifices
and ceremonies, while outside the walls themselves
service areas and factories may have been erected.
Given the profile of the tomb mound, some kind of
mortuary temple may have been placed there in the
fashion that is posited for the Zhongshan tombs in
Hebei (Figure 4).[41] The precinct must have resembled
many other walled compounds in the capital district,
yet one more node in a network that filled the plains
south of the Wei River.

Tomb Structure

I assume that the First Emperor's burial chamber
did not diverge in all particulars from the range of
plans and structures now attested for the late Zhou
and Western Han periods. The precise combination of
features cannot be predicted, although we can weigh
probabilities. As an ultimate expression of what was
possible in his day, it is likely in fact that no burial
yet excavated anticipates the First Emperor's tomb in
its entirety.

Sima Qian tells us that the First Emperor began
the construction of his mausoleum upon ascending
the throne in 246 B.C. and that work continued with
a larger force of laborers after unification in 221 B.C.
More than 700,000 convict laborers are said to have
toiled at the task, the same labor force set to work on
the E Pang Palace southwest of the capital. It appears
that this work force was shifted back and forth between the two projects. After the funeral, for example, the laborers were pulled from the E Pang site to
raise the burial mound.[42] The figure of 700,000
workers may be inflated but is not inherently incred-
ible. Multitudes of laborers were characteristic of ancient China from Shang times onward, and strict social regimentation was one reason for Qin's rise to
power.[43] During the five-year period (194–189 B.C.)
when Han Chang'an was being walled, forces of
145,000 persons were raised more than once.[44] We
have evidence of many large-scale undertakings in late
Zhou and early Han: the many state's walls, among
them that of Qin, the layout of regular tracts of land
for cultivation, and the many city walls.[45]

Sima Qian's texts describing the construction of Lishan focuses on its underground structure and furnishings, but is so terse and problematic that commentators and translators have had to exercise considerable ingenuity in elucidating it to their satisfaction.[46] The *Historical Records* account first uses two phrases, "pierced three springs" *(chuan san quan)* and "put down copper/bronze" *(xia tong)* that are not readily deciphered. Commentators suggest a variety of explanations for the former, tending toward the view that the site was purged of streams and underground water; but as Jeffrey Riegel has pointed out, the phrase may simply mean that the site was properly situated, deeply tied into its natural environment.[47] It seems unlikely that a cast-bronze chamber lies behind the enigmatic second phrase; the text here may be garbled and have to do with sealing the chamber or part of it. *Historical Records* mentions a chamber *(guo)* but does not describe it. For suggestions along that line we must rely on other Western and Eastern Han texts. Wei Hong (fl. 25–57 A.D.) states that the tomb was "sealed with patterned stones," while Liu Xiang (79–8 B.C.) wrote that the First Emperor's tomb was "a stone chamber like a detached palace."[48]

Many kinds of evidence fortify the hypothesis that the First Emperor's tomb chamber was built with stone. In addition to the textual sources, we have the evidence of the stoneworking site northwest of the park. If the chamber were located directly under the mound, as one would expect from later practice, a stone chamber would perhaps be a necessity to survive intact under the massive weight. Moreover, stone chambers were not uncommon in North China during this period. One of the Guweicun tombs mentioned above for their plan with temples aboveground was built with massive rubble walls on its north and south sides, and stone buttresses perpendicular to its east and west walls (Figure 5).[49] The north and south walls rose from a rubble foundation 1.6 meters thick to a height of 12 meters, almost to ground level. Other stone chambers are known from several regions of late Zhou China; the tomb at Sui Xian, Hubei Province, renowned for its chime of sixty-five musical bells, on the other hand, was set into sandstone bedrock which served much the same purpose as a rubble sheathing (Figure 6).[50] Such traditions of building tombs were known to the Qin court. A passage in *Lü Shi Chunqiu* (Mr. Lü's "Spring and Autumn," c. 235 B.C.), a text compiled for the Qin minister of that name, recommends piling up stone and charcoal around the burial chamber *(ji shi ji tan yi huan qi wai)* for protection against dampness and for strength.[51] The preliminary evidence from the royal Qin tombs near Fengxiang Xian also indicates the use of stone and charcoal around their wooden chambers. Whether or not the entire burial chamber was built with stone, it seems likely that stone was employed to sheath the chamber.

The more difficult question that remains concerns the actual plan of such a chamber: What type of structure was used and how was it realized? Since the great majority of late Zhou and early Western Han tombs excavated to date are representative of lower

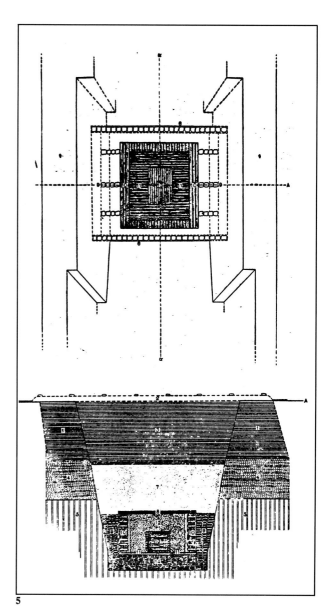

5

6

Figures

5. Plan (top) and section (bottom) of Tomb 2, Guwei Village, Hui Xian, Henan. After Kuo, *Hui Hsien*, p. 90.

6. Chamber of the Sui Xian tomb, Hubei. After *Sui Xian Zeng Hou Yi Mu*, Beijing: Wenwu Chubanshe, 1980, no. 2.

social strata, only a few sites offer positive clues to this puzzle. Liu Xiang's description of the chambers ("like a detached palace") may indicate that the tomb was divided into separate rooms with functions analogous to the various divisions of a palace. Such a plan has in fact been attested in the largest and best preserved late Zhou tombs known: the Sui Xian tomb in Hubei Province (Figure 6), and the Xinyang tomb located in nearby southern Henan (Figure 7). Both burials date from a period about two centuries earlier than the construction of Lishan. In each case, substantial wooden structures were assembled within the tomb shaft: The Sui Xian chamber was no less than 21 meters wide and 16.5 meters long, an irregular cruciform plan of four rooms. The central room held sacrificial vessels and musical instruments, perhaps analogous in function to the formal hall (chao) of a palace. The eastern room contained the coffin of the deceased, while members of his entourage who followed him in death were interred both there and in the western room. A rear room served as an arsenal. Thus four areas served at least three functions: formal hall, retiring quarters, and storage. Although smaller, the Xinyang tomb chamber was more regular and elaborate in plan; an anteroom stretching across the front held musical instruments and ritual equipment, while two rows of three rooms each stood behind (Figure 7). The central room of the first row contained the multiple coffins of the deceased; the five encircling rooms contained supplies and furnishings including a couch and palanquin.[52]

A central plan such as that seen at Xinyang became an important tomb chamber type in the third and second centuries. Tomb 2 at Guweicun, for example, while less elaborate, consisted of a central coffin chamber and a gallery on all four sides (Figure 5). This same tomb is an important early example of a mode of construction called by Zhou and Han texts "yellow core (timbers) aligned together" (huang chang ti zou). In Tomb 2, the inner chamber was built using timbers, either 1 or 4 meters in length and 20 or 30 centimeters square by stacking courses of the timbers in alternating orientations. Thus the lowest course was laid north-south using 4-meter-long timbers for the side walls and 1-meter-long timbers for the end walls. The second course was laid on an east-west axis, the side walls from 1-meter timbers and the end walls from 4-meter timbers. The process was repeated until a height of 4 meters was reached, for a total of 17 courses.[53] Liu Xiang's account of the Lishan tomb concludes with a story of how a shepherd accidentally set the plundered tomb afire while searching for a stray sheep, more circumstantial evidence for a wooden chamber or components. A number of Western Han tombs with this construction are known, including a pair of Han princely tombs near Beijing at Dabaotai (Figure 8). In Tomb 1 at Dabaotai, the timbers were stacked in courses "aligned together" to create a wall 3 meters tall and 1 meter thick. This wall delimited a rectangular chamber about 16 meters long and 10 meters wide; a pair of galleries, each 3 meters wide, encircled that chamber.[54]

Like the use of a sheathing of stone and charcoal, the "yellow core (timbers) aligned together" are mentioned by Lü Shi Chunqiu. The term, moreover, is a standard element in descriptions of imperial and princely burials throughout Western Han, when it appears that this inner chamber, like the lacquered coffins and jade burial shrouds, was prepared at the imperial Eastern Garden Workshop (Dongyuan jiang). At Lishan, a burial chamber built with a plan comparable to the Dabaotai tomb—an inner chamber of stacked timbers and an outer shell of ashlar masonry or rubble—would accord with our knowledge of late Zhou and Western Han burial practices.

The comparative evidence cited above allows us to assess some of the features of the underground components of the First Emperor's tomb. Much remains unanswerable. How large a tomb chamber might the First Emperor have had? The largest royal Qin tomb near Fengxiang Xian had a shaft 59 meters long by 38 meters wide at the mouth, i.e., ground level. The walls slanted inward, reducing these dimensions, but only the depth of the base, 24 meters, has been reported. The chamber itself is said to be 4.2 meters high. Whatever its dimensions, what kind of construction was employed to span the distance from wall to wall? The Qin trenches employ a simple post and beam system to roof their corridors, with baulks of earth between them.[55] The strength of wooden beams would probably determine some of the dimensions of the burial chamber. The Sui Xian chamber had rooms as large as 4.75 meters wide, but some of its roof beams were over 9 meters in length.

Assuming the tomb was looted and burned in 206 B.C., only a fraction of its decorations and furniture would have survived, and subsequent damage, natural or human, will probably have destroyed most of what was not burned initially. From the Sui Xian, Xinyang and Dabaotai tombs, one should probably expect lacquer-painted walls, possibly draped with textiles. Proper furniture would have been likely, such as the couches found both at Xinyang and Dabaotai. A set of nested coffins should have occupied an innermost area, but how they were built cannot be postulated. The ambiance created would probably evoke that of a palatial hall, for which the Qin palaces now under excavation supply some clues.[56] Architectural pottery, wall painting, and metal fixtures would not have been out of place.

When all is said and done, the primary limitations on anticipating the tomb of the First Qin Emperor are not a paucity of literary or archaeological evidence but the boundaries of our imagination and creativity. If one goal of modern archaeology is the recreation of the past, much of the burden falls on our capacity to integrate the evidence from all sources with analytical structures whose validity is continually tested and challenged.[57] This essay outlines plausible answers to the questions it addresses, but can stand only as a preliminary analysis. Irrespective of how much of this analysis remains valid once the tomb is opened, the effort of attempting such a study has much to commend it.

Since this paper was revised for publication in October 1981, several new reports of excavations at the Lishan site have appeared in the Chinese archaeological journals.

(1) It now appears that the tomb had two ramps, located on the east and west flanks of the burial mound respectively. This would imply that the proper orientation of the necropolis is not north-south—the long axis of the two walls—but rather east-west, highly unusual in relation to other sites of the period and subsequent eras. If this is the case, the mound in the southern half of the inner compound may well have been balanced by structures in the northern half of that area. This new information is mentioned only briefly in Xu Pingfang, "Funerary Parks and Burial Districts of the Qin, Han, Wei, Jin and Northern and Southern Dynasties," *Kaogu,* 1981, no. 6, p. 521.

(2) Two more kneeling figurines have been excavated from a group of burial pits between the outer and inner walls on the west flank. See "Brief Report of Probing and Clearing Burial Pits Within the Funerary Park of the Tomb of the Qin First Emperor," *Kaogu*

yu wenwu, 1982, no. 1, pp. 25–29.

(3) The convict burials first mentioned in a news item of April 19, 1980 have been reported in "Convict Tombs at Zhaobeihu Village on the West Flank of the Tomb of the Qin First Emperor," *Wenwu,* 1982, no. 3, pp. 1–11. In a subsequent article, Sun Yingmin questioned the identification of these graves as convicts; see *Wenwu,* 1982, no. 10, pp. 73–74.

Equally important, there has been considerable discussion and debate in recent writings of the early history of burial mounds and burial precincts. Since the Lishan site figures prominently in this topic, the reader is referred to the following articles: Huang Zhanyue, "Burial Mounds," *Wenwu,* 1981, no. 2, pp. 89–92; Wang Shimin, "Burial Mounds and Tombs of the Spring and Autumn and Warring States Eras in China," *Kaogu,* 1981, no. 5, pp. 459–66; Yang Kuan, "Architecture Above the Tomb and the Mound-and-Chamber System of the Pre-Qin period," *Wenwu,* 1982, no. 1, pp. 31–37; Yang Hongxun, "The Problem of Architecture Above the Tomb in the Period Before Qin," *Kaogu,* 1982, no. 4, pp. 402–6.

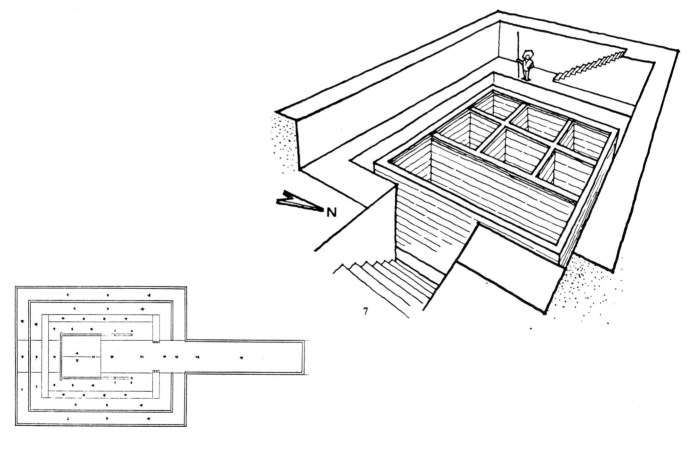

7

8

Figures

7. Chamber of the Xinyang tomb, Henan. Rendering by Y.S. Huang after *Wenwu,* 1957, no. 9, p. 23.

8. Plan (top) and section (bottom) of Tomb 1, Dabaotai, Hebei. After *Wenwu,* 1977, no. 6, pp. 24–25.

Notes

1. Ssu-ma Ch'ien (Sima Qian), *Shih Chi* [Historical records], Pe-king: Chūng-hua Shu-chü, 1959, chüan 6, p. 275 and chüan 7, p. 315.

2. For a general introduction to the tomb and underground army, see Maxwell Hearn, "The Terracotta Army of the First Emper-or of Qin," *The Great Bronze Age of China,* ed. Wen Fong, New York: Metropolitan Museum of Art, 1980, pp. 353–68. A more recent and popular account is Arthur Cotterell, *The First Emperor of China: The Greatest Archaeological Find of Our Time,* New York: Holt, Rinehart and Winston, 1981. Relevant Chinese sources are noted below.

3. George Kubler, *The Shape of Time: Remarks on the History of Things,* New Haven and London: Yale University Press, 1962, pp. 31–61.

4. Robert L. Thorp, *The Mortuary Art and Architecture of Early Imperial China,* Ph.D. dissertation, University of Kansas, 1979; "Burial Practices of Bronze Age China," *Great Bronze Age,* pp. 51–64.

5. Ssu-ma, *Shih Chi,* chüan 5, p. 203.

6. Ku Tsu-yü, *Tu Shih Fang-yü Chi-yao* [Essentials of geography for reading history], rpt. Taipei: Le-t'ien Ch'u-pan-she, 1973, chüan 53, p. 2329. The traditional gloss on the name is that the city was both "south of the mountains" *(shan yang)* and "north of the river" *(he yang),* hence, "all, both" *(xian) yang.*

7. "Investigation and Trial Digs at the Site of the Ancient Ch'in Capital Hsien-yang," *Kaogu,* 1962, no. 6, pp. 281–89.

8. Liu Ching-chu, "A Preliminary Study of Several Problems Concerning the Ch'in Capital Hsien-yang," *Wenwu,* 1976, no. 11, pp. 25–30.

9. Liu's placement of the capital requires careful scrutiny. Lacking any evidence of a walled city per se, it is more reasonable to suppose that the Xianyang Palaces were situated in the area north of the river but not that the entire capital can be deli-mited as Liu has suggested. See "Several Supplementary Cor-rections to the Report of Excavations at the Qin Capital Xianyang," *Wenwu,* 1979, no. 2, pp. 85–86. The author is at work on a study of the Qin and Han capitals.

10. Ku, *Tu Shih Fang-yü Chi-yao,* chüan 53, p. 2341.

11. "Record of Preliminary Probing at the Site of the Ch'in Capital Yueh-yang," *Wenwu,* 1966, no. 1, pp. 10–18. The remains of Yueyang are 10 km. northwest of the Yanliang railroad station and 2.5 km. north of the Wei River. The identification of Yueyang as a Qin capital site is probably mistaken.

12. Hsu Fü, *Ch'in Hui-yao Ting-pu* [Important documents of the Ch'in, supplemented], Shanghai: Ch'un-lien Ch'u-pan-she, 1955, p. 370.

13. Ssu-ma, *Shih Chi,* chüan 6, p. 239.

14. Ibid., chüan 6, p. 256.

15. Ibid., chüan 6, pp. 288–90; Hsü, *Ch'in Hui-yao Ting-pu,* pp. 104–7.

16. On the Baling, see Du Baoren, "The Positions of the Han Im-perial Tombs," *Kaogu yu Wenwu,* 1980, no. 1, pp. 29–33.

17. Yan Wenru has argued recently that the so-called Zhou tombs north of modern Xianyang are also royal Qin tombs; "A Criti-cal Case That the Zhou Tombs Are Qin Tombs," *Kaogu yu Wenwu,* 1980, no. 2, pp. 95–97. These sites have been published by Sekino Tadashi and Daijo Tokiwa, *Shina Bunka Shiseki* [Historical remains of Chinese culture], 12 vols., Tokyo: Hōzōkan, 1939–41, vol. 9, pp. 99–102 and pl. 91.

18. "Brief Report of an Investigation of the Tomb of the Ch'in First Emperor," *Kaogu,* 1962, no. 8, pp. 407–11. The author visited the site in Feb. 1979 and Oct. 1980. On the name Li-shan, see Zhao Kangmin, "The Qin First Emperor's Tomb Was Originally Named Lishan," *Kaogu yu Wenwu,* 1980, no. 3, pp. 34–35.

19. Zhao Kangmin, "Architectural Sites Nos. 2, 3, and 4 North of the Tomb of the Qin First Emperor," *Wenwu,* 1979, no. 12, pp. 13–16. In this report, the mound is described as 685 m. south of the north wall, 200 m. north of the south wall, and 125 m.

from both the east and west walls. Adding these figures to the base dimensions for the tumulus itself (350 m. by 345 m.), one can compute a total length north-south of 1235 m. and a width east-west of 595 m. for the inner wall. Other recent reports also imply that the inner wall was rectangular.

20. Victor Segalen, Gilbert de Voisins and Jean Lartigue, *Mission archéologique en Chine,* 2 vols., Paris: Librairie Orientaliste Paul Guethner, 1924, vol. 1, pl. 1.

21. "Survey of the Mao-ling, Hsing-ping District, Shensi," *Kaogu,* 1964, no. 2, pp. 86–89.

22. Personal communication. For the belief in immortality, see Yü Ying-shih, "Life and Immortality in the Mind of Han China," *Harvard Journal of Asiatic Studies,* vol. 25, 1964–65, pp. 80–122.

23. See nn. 16 and 21.

24. "Brief Excavation Report of Warring States Period Burials of the State of Zhongshan at Pingshan District, Hebei Province," *Wenwu,* 1979, no. 1, pp. 1–31. Tomb 1 at this site is assigned to King Cuo who died c. 310 B.C.; Tomb 2 is assigned to a consort who died somewhat earlier.

25. Fu Xinian, "Research on the 'Burial District Plan' from the Warring States Tomb of King Cuo of Zhongshan and the Plan of His Funerary Park," *Kaogu Xuebao,* 1980, no. 1, pp. 97–118; Yang Hongxun, "Research on the Warring States Royal Tombs of Zhongshan and the 'Burial District Plan,' " *Kaogu Xuebao,* 1980, no. 1, pp. 119–37. I follow Fu Xinian in equat-ing a double pace *(bu)* to 5 ft. *(chi).* To produce the figures cit-ed here, I use 23 cm. as the value of one foot.

26. Kuo Pao-chün, ed., *Hui Hsien Fa-chüeh Pao-kao* [Report of ex-cavations at Hui Hsien], Peking: K'o-hsüeh Ch'u-pan-she, 1956, pp. 69–109.

27. Han Wei, "A Brief Discussion of Spring and Autumn and Warring States Period Tombs in Shaanxi," *Kaogu yu Wenwu,* 1981, no. 1, pp. 83–93.

28. Hsü, *Ch'in Hui-yao Ting-pu,* pp. 107–8. The notes to the "An-nals of Han Mingdi" (r. 58–75 A.D.) cite *Han guan yi* [Han of-ficial observances] of Ying Shao (c. 140–206 A.D.) which relates that "The First Emperor of Qin first erected retiring chambers at the flank of the tomb. The Han followed this and did not al-ter it." See Fan Yeh, *Hou Han Shu* [History of Later Han], Peking: Chung-hua Shu-chü, 1965, no. 1, p. 99.

29. On this tradition, see my "Origins of Chinese Architectural Style: The Earliest Plans and Building Types," *Archives of Asian Art,* vol. 36, 1983.

30. See n. 19.

31. *Kaogu,* 1962, no. 8, p. 408.

32. Ibid.

33. "A Ch'in Dynasty Ceramic Figurine and Stone Plinths Unearthed Near the Tomb of the Ch'in First Emperor," *Wen-wu,* 1964, no. 9, pp. 55–56. This ornament is now displayed at the Lintong District Museum which the author visited in Oct. 1980.

34. See nn. 18 and 19. "Ch'in Dynasty Bronzes Unearthed Near Lin-t'ung District," *Wenwu,* 1965, no. 7, pp. 54–55. "Tile Ends Newly Unearthed at the Tomb of the Qin First Emperor," *Wenwu,* 1974, no. 12, p. 87.

35. *Kaogu,* 1962, no. 8, p. 410; *Wenwu,* 1964, no. 9, p. 55; *Wenwu,* 1973, no. 5, p. 66; *The Chinese Exhibition,* London: Times Newspapers, 1973, no. 136; Hou Chin-lang, "La sculpture des Ts'in," *Arts Asiatiques,* vol. 33, 1977, pp. 133–81.

36. "Brief Report of Probing and Clearing Horse Pits on the East Flank of the Tomb of the Qin First Emperor," *Kaogu yu Wen-wu,* 1980, no. 4, pp. 31–41; Thorp, *Mortuary Art and Architec-ture,* pp. 119–20.

37. "New Archaeological Discoveries at the Tomb of the First Em-peror of Qin," *Xinhua News Dispatch,* Apr. 19, 1980. More in-formation is found in "Bronze Chariots from Qin Emperor's Tomb," *China Reconstructs,* vol. 30, no. 5, May 1981, pp. 68–69.

38. "Brief Report of an Investigation of the Qin Stone Working Site at Zhengzhuang, Lintong," *Kaogu yu Wenwu,* 1981, no. 1,

pp. 39–43.

39. *Kaogu,* 1962, no. 8, p. 419.

40. "Brief Report of Clearing Qin Tombs at Shangjiao Village, Lintong," *Kaogu yu Wenwu,* 1980, no. 2, pp. 42–50.

41. See n. 25.

42. Ssu-ma Ch'ien, *Shih Chi,* chüan 6, p. 256; Hsu, *Ch'in Hui-yao Ting-pu,* pp. 107 and 376.

43. For Qin social structure, see Derk Bodde, *China's First Unifier,* Leiden: Brill, 1938; Li Yu-ning, *The First Emperor of China,* White Plains, New York: International Arts and Sciences Press, 1975.

44. Pan Ku, *Han Shu* [History of Former Han], Peking: Chunghua Shu-chü, 1962, no. 2, pp. 88–91.

45. Frank Leeming, "Official Landscapes in Traditional China," *Journal of the Economic and Social History of the Orient,* vol. 23, 1980, pp. 153–204, makes a case for extensive landscapes shaped by human labor before the Han. For late Zhou cities, see Kwang-chih Chang, *The Archaeology of Ancient China,* 3rd ed., New Haven: Yale University Press, 1977, pp. 321–50.

46. Ssu-ma, *Shih Chi,* chüan 6, p. 265. For a recent English rendering, see Hearn, "The Terracotta Army," pp. 356–57.

47. Ibid., chüan 6, p. 266; *Huang Lan* [Imperial survey, c. 220 A.D.], ed. Ts'ung-shu Chi-ch'eng Ch'ien-pien, Taipei: Shang-wu Yin-shu-kuan, 1965, p. 9, supplies such explanations.

48. Hsü, *Ch'in Hui-yao Ting-pu,* p. 107; Pan, *Han Shu,* chüan 36, p. 1954.

49. See n. 26.

50. Robert L. Thorp, "The Sui Xian Tomb: Re-thinking the Fifth Century," *Artibus Asiae,* vol. 43, nos. 1 and 2, 1982, p. 78.

51. *Lü Shih Ch'un-ch'iu* [Mr. Lü's Springs and Autumns], ed. Hsü Wei-yü, 2 vols., Peking: Wen-hsüeh Ku-chi K'an-hsing-she, 1955, chüan 10, p. 7b.

52. Thorp, "The Sui Xian Tomb," pp. 79–81.

53. Thorp, *Mortuary Art and Architecture,* pp. 141–47.

54. Ibid.

55. Hearn, "The Terracotta Army," pp. 362–63.

56. "Brief Report of Palace Architectural Site No. 1 at the Ch'in Capital Hsien-yang," *Wenwu,* 1976, no. 11, pp. 12–24; "Brief Excavation Report of Palace Architectural Site No. 3 at the Qin Capital Xianyang," *Kaogu yu Wenwu,* 1980, no. 2, pp. 34–41. Qin and Han architecture is the subject of a forthcoming study by the author.

57. Martha Joukowsky, *A Complete Manual of Field Archaeology,* Englewood Cliffs, New Jersey: Prentice-Hall, 1980, pp. 2–3.

Sources of Foreign Elements in the Culture of Eastern Zhou

Emma C. Bunker
Research Assistant

Denver Art Museum

THE MAJOR CHARACTERISTICS of Chinese civilization during the Eastern Zhou period were primarily indigenous developments, enriched occasionally by influences from beyond the frontiers. Most foreign contact came via the steppe zone of north Asia which stretches from Lake Baikal and the north border of China in the east to the Black Sea in the west. Sometime early in the first millennium B.C., the numerous pastoral tribes which occupied this area adopted large-scale transhumance and mounted warfare, creating a new society of semi-nomadic warrior-herdsmen with whom the Chinese had to contend.[1] Frequently these barbarian horsemen formed large confederacies, consisting of numerous tribes and subtribes, each possessing its own artistic vocabulary and customs. Ancient Chinese texts abound with references to the various equestrian tribes which inhabited southern Siberia, Mongolia, and what is now northern China in the region of the Great Wall, but little mention is made of their art and culture. In the past, the artistic remains of these northern mounted barbarians have been known primarily through chance finds and curiosity shop discoveries. Recently, major archaeological endeavors by the People's Republic of China and the Soviet Union have uncovered important sites belonging to these tribes which have yielded valuable information concerning their customs and artistic tastes, a few of which played a minor role in the development of Warring States culture.[2] The most obvious results of foreign contact with these steppe tribes were the adoption of horseback riding, the belt hook, and certain exotic animal motifs which intruded into the Chinese bronze vocabulary.

According to Sima Qian,[3] King Wu Ling of the state of Zhao in Shanxi adopted horseback riding, *hu fu* (barbarian riding clothes), and the art of mounted archery from the northern barbarians in the late fourth century B.C., while preparing for war against the state of Zhongshan in present-day Hebei province.[4] A comparison between the saddles and bridles depicted on the cavalry horses from Qin Shihuangdi's terra-cotta army[5] and those excavated with fifth-fourth centuries B.C. material at Pazyryk in the Altai mountains of southern Siberia[6] clearly demonstrates the Chinese debt to their northern barbarian neighbors. The Qin saddles are basically stirrupless pads with a slightly raised pommel and cantle secured by a girth and crupper atop a saddle blanket. The Qin and Pazyryk bridles which display sliding-cheek snaffle bit assemblies are also similar, with one exception.[7] The reins on the reconstructed Qin bridle terminate in bronze handgrip loops which would have been impossible horse gear for a mounted warrior who must be able to join the ends of his reins so that they will rest on the horse's neck and not fall to the ground when he drops them to shoot an arrow. The bronze loops may have belonged originally to one of the chariot bridles from the same pit, No. 2, since they are more typical of some driving reins.[8] The tails of the Qin cavalry horses are depicted as encased in leather sheaths that simulate a braid, another barbarian custom with a steppe priority found among the riding equipment from Pazyryk.[9] The roached mane on the Qin cavalry horse is interrupted halfway down the left side by a long strand of hair, a "mounting lock" frequently employed in the ancient world before the invention of stirrups, which do not occur in China until the fourth century A.D.[10]

Recent discoveries in China show that parts of the Great Wall were built as early as the seventh century B.C. to fend off barbarian tribes in the north,[11] but ancient Chinese literature specifically describes these tribes as foot soldiers as late as 541 B.C.[12] Horseback riding was present by the eighth-seventh centuries B.C. among the pastoral tribes of southern Siberia,[13] but apparently did not spread to the northern borders of China until the fifth century B.C., where it was illustrated on a bronze ornament found with late Spring and Autumn period ritual vessels in a barbarian grave at Nanshengan in the Liao Valley.[14] Horseback riding is not mentioned in any of the surviving Chinese literature before Sima Qian's discussion of Zhao's late fourth-century B.C. conversion to it. Nevertheless, the existence of the fifth-century B.C. bronze horsemen from Nanshengan,[14] and a fourth-century B.C. gold plaque from the Far Eastern steppes (Figure 1) which depicts a barbarian mounted hunter carrying a long sword in a scabbard of Chinese manufacture, clearly suggest that China must have had some knowledge of horseback riding long before the late fourth century B.C., perhaps alluded to in texts which have not survived the ravages of time.[15] Creel has suggested that "the Chinese resisted riding because . . . it required the wearing of a short jacket rather than the long gown which, in Chinese eyes, was obligatory for a man of status."[16]

Several scholars have suggested that the long iron sword and the scabbard slide (its attachment device) were also introduced into China by the horse-riding tribes of the steppes.[17] However, recent archaeological finds indicate an indigenous Chinese non-equestrian development without foreign stimulus in the fifth century B.C. for both. In Europe, the long iron sword developed naturally from the dagger and short bronze sword by the end of the second millennium B.C., long before the introduction of mounted warfare in the seventh century B.C.[18] In the ancient Near East, warriors depicted with long swords in ninth-century B.C. Assyrian reliefs ride in chariots,[19] while the mounted contingents carry bows and arrows, the horseman's weaponry par excellence.[20] A baldric slung over the right shoulder attached to the scabbard served as a suspension device in both areas.[21] The Scythians, primarily known for their mastery of mounted archery, carried only short swords, the *akinakes,* suspended from their garment belts by cords attached to extensions of their scabbards.[22] Fighting with a long sword on horseback would have been extremely hazardous without stirrups, with a missed mark resulting in an horrendous spill.[23] "Of all Xerxes' mounted contingents, only the Caspians had some form of sword," and there is no reason to believe that it was a long one.[24]

Trousdale hypothesized that a long sword should have been present among the finds at Pazyryk, attributing its absence to robbers who had desecrated the tombs in antiquity.[25] The recent archaeological investigations in the Borotal and Alagil Valleys of undisturbed culturally related barrows yielded plenty of evidence for mounted warfare, but no long swords.[26]

According to Loehr[27] and Watson,[28] the long iron sword evolved in China from the short bronze sword, as a weapon first wielded by a man on foot. The Chinese certainly possessed the technology to produce

such a weapon. "He Lu, the King of Wu who reigned from 514 to 496 B.C., invited Gan Jiang to . . . make two swords which would be famous . . . . To make these swords Gan Jiang collected refined iron from the five mountains, the best metal in the world. . . . "[29] This is recorded in the Spring and Autumn Annals of the States of Wu and Yue which were not written down in their present form until the second century B.C., yet, as Needham points out, "it certainly embodies many local traditions."[30] These two swords must have been long, as the Chinese never made short swords of iron, only of bronze.[31] Such an early date for a long iron sword is confirmed by the recently discovered long steel (forged from iron) sword at Changsha associated with late Spring and Autumn period material.[32]

Two dagger sheaths dated seventh-sixth centuries B.C. reportedly from the northern zone of China display rings on their sides.[33] The recently excavated barbarian tombs at Xigou in western Inner Mongolia dated fourth-third centuries B.C. revealed an iron sword blade with a superb gold scabbard.[34] The scabbard has a pierced extension a third of the way down the side by which it was hung, just like the Scythian *akinakes* mentioned earlier, not the more sophisticated scabbard slide, which, if it were a steppe invention, would surely have been utilized.

A sixth-century B.C. ivory dagger sheath found near Luoyang displays on its wall a long rectangular form pierced with three small holes which must have served to secure it to the owner's belt.[35] A bronze kneeling figure from Henan in the Nelson Gallery wears a dagger tucked into his belt secured from slipping by a loop on the scabbard wall facing away from the body of the wearer.[36] A fifth-century B.C. mold from Houma shows the same attachment method.[37] The fifth-century B.C. figures which support a bell stand excavated at Sui Xian in Hubei province wear short swords attached by their scabbard loops to their garment belts.[38] The earliest extant Chinese jade scabbard slides date to the fifth century B.C.,[39] which suggests that some time during the century the scabbard loop had developed and evolved into a separate entity, i.e., the Chinese scabbard slide, frequently made of richly decorated jade or lacquered wood during the Warring States and Han periods. The earliest scabbard slides found in China were associated with short bronze swords, and only later with long iron ones.[40]

Anyone who has ever ridden a galloping horse should recognize immediately the inefficiency and awkwardness of carrying a long sword suspended by a scabbard slide from a low-slung belt. Unattended, it would bang against the horse with an unnerving clatter, since it would have no fixed position as did the later cavalry sabers with their two-point suspension device. The famous gold belt plaque (Figure 1) from the Far Eastern steppes dated fourth century B.C. in the Siberian Treasure of Peter the Great shows a barbarian rider galloping at full tilt while attempting to shoot a fleeing boar.[41] His long sword suspended by a scabbard slide from a low-slung belt is obviously incompatible with the motion of the horse, so that the rider has been forced to hold the scabbard tightly against the horse's side with his leg to prevent it from flying around uncontrollably—hardly a comfortable position for a rider while gripping his mount with his thighs without the aid of stirrups. This plaque was produced by one of the equestrian pastoral groups of the Far Eastern Steppes and displays horsegear similar to that found in the fourth-century B.C. Pazyryk kurgans, but a close examination of it reveals a typical Warring States chape on the scabbard.[41] The long iron swords excavated at Xichagou in Liaoning associated with Xiongnu expansion during the second century B.C. are also of Chinese manufacture,[42] suggesting that the northern nomads did not have the technology to create an iron sword of great length. Why else would the Xiongnu have desired to purchase iron weapons from the Han soldiers so much that a law was enacted to prevent their sale?[43] It was always archery that was important for the mounted Inner Asian warrior.[44] The Qin cavalry was certainly not armed with long iron swords, whose rarity among the finds from Xi'an has already been discussed at length by Barnard and Keightley.[45] The mounted warrior attacking a tiger on a third-century B.C. mirror from Jincun in the Hosokawa Collection brandishes a typical bronze short sword,[46] as does the mounted barbarian on a second-century B.C. Xiongnu plaque in the Los Angeles County Museum,[47] while the two figures on the Warring States Winthrop Mirror who hold long swords are pictured on foot.[48]

The majority of reliefs and paintings from ancient China which illustrate the long iron sword carried on a scabbard slide show it worn by nobles and courtiers on foot dressed in long, flowing robes,[49] suggesting that it was a prestige symbol of rank and authority.[50] The first Han emperor Gaozi wielded a three-foot iron sword, the technically superior weapon of a conqueror.[51] The Han noble depicted in the murals from the Shaogou cemetery near Luoyang handles his long sword suspended by a slide with great ease on foot (Figure 2).[52] When inactive, he holds it in front of him, as does a small jade man in the Raphael Collection.[53]

The hypothesis proposed by Maenchen-Helfen and perpetuated by Trousdale was that the scabbard slide was invented in the Priural Steppes in the seventh-sixth centuries B.C., and brought east along with the long iron sword by the Yueji, a tribe considered by Tolstov to have moved from southern Kazakhstan to the northern border of China during the sixth century B.C.[54] Furthermore, Pulleyblank has convincingly shown by linguistic evidence that the Yueji, who spoke an Indo-European dialect called Tocharian, were descendants of peoples already on the northwestern border of China by late Shang times; they would therefore have been geographically unavailable in the sixth century B.C. to have brought the slide and the long iron sword from the west to China.[55] Historically, there is no other tribal group who could have accomplished this feat either. Also, there is no evidence that the slide as a separate entity ever existed in the Ural area until much later as a result of influ-

ence from the Far East.[56] Unless future excavations prove otherwise, it would seem that a Chinese priority exists for both the long iron sword and the scabbard slide in the Far East.[57]

This does not negate Maenchen-Helfen's theory that the belt hook, whose Chinese name is etimologically Indo-European, was introduced into China by barbarian tribes from beyond the northern frontiers, where belt clasps were significant items of a mounted warrior's regalia.[58] In spite of its outside origin, the belt hook quickly became a vehicle for Chinese taste and decoration from the fifth century B.C. on, with little remaining to indicate its barbarian ancestry.

Recently, it has been suggested that one type of Chinese Han armor "may reflect influences received from the northern nomads."[59] This is way off the mark, since there is absolutely no archaeological evidence for any sort of armor in the Far Eastern steppes, not even at Pazyryk where so much material has survived. Sima Qian describes the Xiongnu as armed, not armored.[60] If, by chance, the Xiongnu did have some sort of armor by the first century B.C., they must have acquired it from the Chinese and not vice versa, as there is no earlier precedent for it among the northern barbarians. The Scythians in the west wore armor derived from Greek and Iranian sources, yet its use did not spread eastwards across the steppes.

In the past, scholars dealing with the Eastern Zhou period have attempted to explain many animal features which appeared to be unusual in the bronze decor as influence from the art of the steppes, frequently described as "Animal Style"[61]—an obsolete, misleading term that should be discarded. There never was any general steppe "style." Each of the numerous Eurasian steppe tribes had its own artistic repertoire and taste, in spite of the remarkable cultural homogeneity that had developed among them. Before a northern source can be recognized for an Eastern Zhou motif, a steppe priority or even existence must first be established.

When Karlgren wrote his classic, *Ordos and Huai*, in 1939,[62] scientifically excavated and dated finds in the Far Eastern steppes were extremely scarce. Numerous prominent motifs in Eastern Zhou art then considered barbarian loans have since been shown to have a Chinese priority, thanks to recent archaeological discoveries in East Asia and Charles Weber's masterful study "Chinese Pictorial Bronze Vessels of the Late Zhou Period."[63]

"The surprisingly foreign note of the eight felines crouching with dropped heads around the foot" of the Xinzheng *fang hu* in the exhibition *The Great Bronze Age of China* is stressed in the catalogue where the vessel is dated late seventh-sixth centuries B.C.[64] The decoration of this spectacular *fang hu* is far more compatible with a mid-sixth-century B.C. date,[65] and the felines are not really foreign motifs at all. Their poses, curled up snouts, and slightly heart-shaped ears continue Shang and Western Zhou stylistic conventions (Figure 3)[66] as seen on the Qingjiang Xian *ding* felines.[67] Barbarian plaques in similar feline form col-

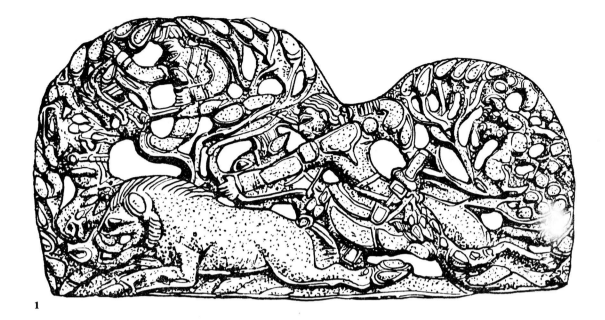

1

2

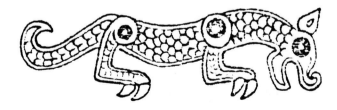

3

Figures

1. Hunting plaque, 4th century B.C. Gold inlaid with semi-precious stones. Length 19 cm. Siberian Collection of Peter I, Hermitage.

2. Western Han Tomb Mural, Shaogou, Luoyang (after *Kaogu Xuebao,* 1964, no. 2, p. 115, pl. 1).

3. Comparison of three felines from Shang-Early Zhou, Middle Zhou, and the Xinzheng *Fang Hu* (after C. Weber, *Artibus Asiae,* vol. 28, nos. 2 and 3, fig. 16).

lected at Xuanhua in Hebei can be considered late sixth-fifth centuries B.C.[68] Their perforated eyes, shoulders, and haunches are vestigial reminders of the inlay cell tradition found on the Xinzheng *fang hu*. A feline-shaped plaque (Figure 4) in the Los Angeles County Museum displays a stylistic stage intermediary between the Xinzheng *fang hu* and the Xuanhua plaques.[69] The late seventh-century B.C. Scythian feline with its highly stylized heart-shaped ear and curled up snout from Ziwiyé in northern Iran,[70] suggested as a parallel to the Xinzheng felines,[71] must also derive ultimately from a Chinese source, since the motif has no earlier tradition in western Asia.[72]

The realism displayed by certain animals depicted on fifth-century B.C. Liyu vessels often attributed to steppe influence occurs only on objects made for Scythian taste in the Black Sea area by the Greeks from the fifth century B.C. on.[73] There is nothing in the earlier art of the Far Eastern steppes which could have inspired such realism. It must therefore have been an impulse within the Chinese Eastern Zhou tradition. Several other elements of Eastern Zhou art, erroneously credited to foreign influence are the rope pattern,[74] granulation,[75] inter-lace animal forms,[76] hunting scenes,[77] and the technique of inlaying one metal with another[78]—none of which has earlier traditions in the artistic vocabularies of the Eastern steppe barbarians than they do in China. The rope patterns on sixth-fifth century B.C. Chinese vessels are merely translations into metal of a rope sling. Granulation was probably a Chinese invention for creating texture, as it was not employed in the steppes. The inlaying of one metal with another must be a variation of an already highly developed Chinese metallurgical tradition which had produced bronze inlaid with turquoise since the Shang period. The inlaying of gold plaques with semiprecious stones, not another metal, from the fourth century B.C. onward in the Eastern steppes was far less technically advanced than in China.[79]

Nevertheless, there is a distinctly foreign flavor about a fifth-century B.C. copper inlaid *dou*,[80] as pointed out by Jenny So.[81] The vessel shape is Chinese, but the randomly placed inlaid animals, treated as curvilinear silhouettes with spiral shoulder and haunch markings, are extremely unChinese.

The earliest vessels which depict animals by such decorative, graceful silhouettes are Weber's Group VI, made in the Hui Xian area of northern Henan in the late sixth and early fifth centuries B.C.[82] The main motifs were silhouettes of birds, felines, and deer in various combinations. A glance at Weber's chronological motif charts show that these creatures begin to intrude into the Chinese bronze decor without earlier prototypes late in the sixth century B.C.[83] The method of manufacture of these vessels was an extremely complex one which also appeared suddenly in China in the late sixth century B.C., and died out in the fifth century B.C. According to a recent technical study by Pieter Meyers, "Scholars had never fully understood how the copper figures that decorate the surface of [this type of] Chinese vessel of the [Eastern] Zhou dynasty were applied; 'inlaid' hardly appears to be a satisfactory description . . . . The figures and decorations, visible on the surface of the bronze, were probably cut out of copper sheet, (or precast before attachment) . . . . The figures with their supports were carefully placed between the inner and outer molds, with the copper figures inserted into or resting against the outer mold while the rods rested against the inner mold."[84] Then the molten bronze was poured into the mold, and solidified around the relatively cool copper animal and bird figures. Postcast polishing would have ensured a smooth surface.

Numerous scholars have remarked on the non-Chinese character of these vessels, but none has provided a satisfactory explanation.[85] I would like to suggest a possible source of inspiration for this unusual inlay technique and the weird creatures on some of these vessels, like those on the *dou*. Beasts and birds conceived in curvilinear silhouettes of felt and leather cutouts applied to cloth, ceramics, and wood (Figures 5A and 5B) abound among the finds from the sixth- and fifth-century B.C. kurgans at Tuekta and Pazyryk in the Altai Mountains of southern Siberia.[86] Fantastic animals, some whose antlers terminate in birds' heads,[87] cervids represented with all four legs shown, sometimes with a triangular opening in the tops of the thighs,[88] a bird attacking its prey,[89] animal combat,[90] shoulder and haunch markings are all motifs common to the Altai, and found again as intrusive conventions on the early copper-applied pictorial vessels of north China.[91]

The northern Chinese must have seen or even acquired some appliqué work of the tribes who buried their dead in the frozen kurgans of the Altai in southern Siberia. That trade existed between southern Siberia and China through Mongolia is evidenced by the presence of Chinese silk and mirrors among the Pazyryk finds.[92] Actually, a lively trade between Mongolia and Siberia, and Mongolia and China, was still the norm when the great Russian scholar Radloff surveyed the area in the nineteenth century A.D.[93] The short-lived inlay technique used in these vessels must be a translation of appliqué work into metal, a far more convenient method than laboriously hammering rows of metal wire to fill depressed areas. It is interesting here to note an earthenware bottle from Pazyryk decorated with leather cutouts pasted on its surface (Figure 5C). Further research and more archaeological discoveries are needed to fill in the many gaps in this theory. The similarities between the silhouette treatment of the animals and birds, their weird appendages, and their appliqué effect on the Chinese vessels and the leather and felt cutouts excavated in the Altai of southern Siberia are too tantalizing to ignore.

Weber has also demonstrated a few other stylized steppe motifs, such as an animal with a returned head, a deer with folded legs and its head thrown up, a coiled feline, and an animal in a "flying gallup" which penetrated the otherwise typically Chinese character of the early pictorial vessels by the early fifth century B.C.[94] These minor intrusions did not last

4

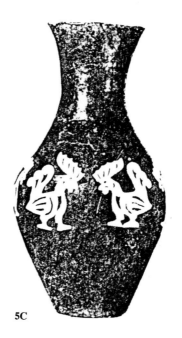

5A

5B

5C

Figures

4. Feline-shaped plaque, 6th–5th centuries B.C. The Nasli M. Heera-
maneck Collection of Ancient Near Eastern Art, gift of the Ah-
manson Foundation, Los Angeles County Museum of Art.

5A. Bird, leather cutout, Pazyryk, barrow 2, 5th century B.C.

5B. Feline with antlers, leather cutout, Tuekta, barrow 1, 6th century
B.C.

5C. Bottle, earthenware decorated with pasted-on leather cutouts, Pazyryk, barrow 2, 5th century B.C.

long in the bronze vocabulary and were shortly replaced by the more rational Chinese scenes of ritual, archery contests, and chariot hunts. There are no hunting scenes either on foot or in chariots among the known examples of Far Eastern steppe art, so the representations on the fifth-century B.C. "Hunting hu" must belong to a growing Chinese pictorial tradition.

The narrow dividing bands on a fifth-century B.C. Liyu hu display rather harmless reclining animals interspersed with ferocious ones which clamp other animals as well as a human in their jaws.[95] This kind of hostility between beast and beast, or beast and man, is not typical of Chinese taste, although it enjoyed a long tradition in the art of the ancient Near East from the third millennium B.C. onwards. Animal combat occurs in the art of southern Siberia by the sixth-fifth centuries B.C.,[96] but the attack of man by beast is yet unknown in the art of the Far Eastern steppes. Why would the ancient Chinese borrow such barbarian motifs?[97] Perhaps to personify demons, just as the medieval world in Europe used pagan imagery to illustrate evil in Christian art.

Stimulus from beyond the northern frontiers must have been ultimately, if not immediately, responsible for the subject matter of the extraordinary fourth-century B.C. animal attack sculpture from Lingshuo, Pingshan Xian, Hebei, the capital of the ancient state of Zhongshan.[98] Here an extremely vigorous tiger is represented crunching a writhing cervid in its jaws. This is a far more animated rendition than would have been found in any example from the Far Eastern steppes, which would have been extremely stylized and static. The Zhongshan artist has transformed a steppe theme into an extremely realistic tour de force, replacing the mystery of the steppes with rationalism. Zhongshan was a small state founded by the last Xianyu ruler after his escape from the Chu, which had conquered his state between 515 and 510 B.C. The Xianyu, a tribe of the White Di, had moved eastward from northern Shaanxi in the seventh century B.C., and founded a little known state in west-central Hebei province in 530 B.C. They are recorded in ancient Chinese texts as foot soldiers with no evidence of any steppe cultural background.[99] The Zhongshan culture was similar to that of the Chinese of the Central Plains, not a horse-riding steppe one,[100] but its geographic location could easily have resulted in contact with the mounted, semi-nomadic tribes of Mongolia and southern Siberia, where animal combat was an extremely popular artistic subject. Nevertheless, the rendering of the Zhongshan animal combat continues a realism already employed earlier in depicting the same theme on a fifth-century B.C. Liyu hu,[101] suggesting that the Zhongshan animal attack was a second generation motif which needed no immediate steppe stimulus for its theme. The huge awe-inspiring standard tops also found at the ancient Zhongshan capital may be considered to reflect a nomadic barbarian steppe heritage.[102] The regalia of a nomadic barbarian chieftain, which would have had to be easily portable out of necessity, would hardly have included six almost five-foot-tall bronze standards, for

which no prototypes have ever been found in the steppes.

A steppe priority does exist though for the posture of the animal portrayed with its hindquarters twisted at a 180-degree angle on one of the Chu coffins from Tomb No. 1 at Mawangdui in Hunan.[103] A gold plaque in the Treasure of Peter I shows a horse in the same position. The plaque—erroneously dated fifth-fourth centuries B.C. in *The Great Bronze Age of China* catalogue[104]—belongs to the late second-first centuries B.C., evidenced by a recently excavated Sarmation first-century B.C. plaque from the Volgorad region which displays the same "floppy triangle and circle" design on its shoulder and haunch.[105] This twisted posture is also found on some first-century B.C. gold pieces recently discovered at Shibergan in ancient Bactria,[106] an area with which the Han Chinese had much contact after the opening up of the Silk Route by Wu Di.

The Han Chinese also came in contact with numerous barbarian tribes in the southwest, whose rich culture has been revealed in the last few decades by extensive excavations at Dabona, Shizhaishan, Taijishan, and Lijiashan in Yunnan province.[107] Dabona appears to be the earliest site to yield the bronze kettledrum so distinctive of this area and ultimately one of the hallmarks of the "so-called" Dongson culture of southeast Asia. Dabona is regarded as the culture of the Kunming, one of the tribes mentioned in the Shi Ji. The other sites apparently pertain mainly to the kingdom of Dian during the second and first centuries B.C.[108] The archaeological remains suggest a village society practicing agriculture and animal husbandry with a knowledge of mounted warfare.

According to the Shi Ji, the royal house of Dian claimed ancient descent from the princely house of Chu through a General Zhuang Qiao who, during an expedition to the southwest for King Wei of Chu sometime between 339 and 329 B.C., conquered the barbarian tribe of Dian.[109] When he attempted to return to Chu he was cut off by Qin forces, so returned with his army to Dian where he established himself as the ruler, adopting native customs. This claim of ancient Chu descent on the part of the Dian appears to have been a conceit fabricated to enhance their dynastic status in the eyes of the Han Chinese court with whom they came into direct contact late in the second century B.C. Why this myth was pepetuated by Sima Qian in his Shi Ji remains a mystery. In a remarkably complex study, William Watson[110] has shown that the Qin campaign southward took place in 277 B.C., which would have meant that Zhuang Qiao languished in Dian for at least fifty-two years before attempting to report back to Chu. Further research results in the fact that Zhuang Qiao apparently was not a Chu general during the reign of King Wei, but some sort of legendary bandit—if, in fact, he was a historical figure at all and not a pastiche of many.[111] This myth has perhaps influenced some scholars in suggesting a Warring States date for the earliest Shizhaishan material, which cannot be earlier than the second century B.C. Many of the Dian weapons derive from late Shang and Western Zhou types rather than later Eastern Zhou ones. This precludes the arrival in Dian of a princely Chu general, whose army would certainly have been equipped with the latest Warring States' weapon models. The dismissal of Chu descent does not negate the abundance of Chu ancestry, whether direct or indirect, for numerous artistic motifs in Dian art, in particular the Bird and Snake theme.

On the other hand, the numerous plaques depicting mounted hunting scenes and animal combat with great vigor and naturalism suggest some affinity with northwestern Asia. The comparison cited between a Lijiashan tiger biting the bull's rump and a similar motif found at Persepolis is most apt.[112] Two bronze caskets from Tombs 11 and 12 at Shizhaishan[113] have repoussé lobed surfaces quite reminiscent of Achaemenid metalwork[114] and are not at all Chinese. An etched carnelian bead found at Shizhaishan prompted K.C. Chang to suggest trade with the ancient Near East.[115] Any similarities between the art of the Black Sea region and the animal combat plaques from Shizhaishan must be due to a common source. Scythian art from the fourth century B.C. on was basically Hellenistic Greek. Therefore, a similarity between the Scythian horsemen on the Solokha comb[116] and a Shizhaishan plaque[117] is not surprising and does not need influence from the Far Eastern or Western steppes to account for it, only trade from Bactria, which was loaded with Hellenistic influence. The body decoration of the animals which adorn the bronze armor plates (Figure 6) from Lijiashan[118] ap-

pear to have been influenced by embroidery, where thread would have been laid or applied and held firm by couching. The random placing of the animals is similar to those on an imported Bactrian embroidery found at Noinula,[119] a Xiongnu site in Outer Mongolia.[120] The Lijiashan conception is much closer to second-century B.C. Hellenistic genre painting as reflected in a Pompeiian mosaic, which displays aquatic creatures scattered in a very orderly fashion.[121] The explanation may be the exotic intrusion into Yunnan by trade of a foreign textile tradition via Bactria or northern India.

Sources for the ubiquitous geometric decor among the Dian and later Dongson art need no longer be sought in a pontic migration bringing designs of Bronze and Iron Age European origin, a favorite theory popularized by the late Heine-Geldern.[122] K.C. Chang has already pointed out the existence of many of these motifs in Eastern Zhou-early Han finds at Lifan and Ganzi in nearby Sichuan.[123] Now, the recent discoveries in southeast Asia, represented by the superb ceramics from Ban Chiang, provide a far earlier ample geometric vocabulary.[124]

The Eurasian steppes was a cultural crossroad of crucial importance through which many customs and art motifs were transmitted east and west during antiquity. Many of the intermediary stages of influence are still unknown; hopefully future archaeological discoveries will uncover new material that will help answer the innumerable questions still remaining about the equestrian tribes from this area and their influence on ancient China.

6

Figures

6. Bronze armor plate from Lijiashan tomb, Yunnan (from *Kaogu Xuebao*, 1975, no. 2, p. 121).

Notes

1. I wish to take this opportunity to express my appreciation to Mary Littauer for all her advice and editing of the section of this paper dealing with horseback riding and horse gear. Any remaining mistakes are my own. According to Mrs. Littauer, riding began as early as the late third millennium B.C. in the ancient Near East, but organized riding with the ability to handle weapons from horseback did not occur until the first millennium B.C.; see M.A. Littauer and J.H. Crouwel, *Wheeled Vehicles and Ridden Animals in the Ancient Near East,* Leiden/Cologne, 1979, pp. 43–44 and 65–68.

2. See P.R.S. Moorey et al., *Ancient Bronzes, Ceramics, and Seals,* Los Angeles County Museum of Art, Los Angeles, 1981, Emma C. Bunker, "Ancient Art of Central Asia, Mongolia, and Siberia," pp. 140–76, for an extensive discussion of these tribes, their culture, and the most pertinent sites.

3. Burton Watson, *Records of the Grand Historian of China,* translated from the Shi Ji of Sima Qian, New York and London, 1961, vol. 2, p. 159.

4. Qian Hao, Chen Heyi, and Ru Suichu, *Out of China's Earth,* New York and Beijing, 1981, p. 33.

5. Wen Fong, ed., *The Great Bronze Age of China,* New York, 1980, pp. 342–43.

6. John Haskins, "Targhyn—The Hero, Aq-Zhunus—The Beautiful, and Peter's Siberian Gold," *Ars Orientalis,* vol. 4, 1961, pp. 153–69, fig. 2. The breastplate employed by the Pazyryk peoples was not adopted by the Qin.

7. Haskins, "Targhyn," fig. 3.

8. I am very grateful to Mrs. Littauer for pointing out this problem and providing me with the Louvre reference, CA 616, Attic, c. 570–560 B.C., by the "C" painter, and another published Greek piece, Payne Humfry, *Necrocorinthia,* 1931, no. 1494, pl. 42:1. The Greek rein terminates were probably leather. Why the Chinese ones are metal is yet unknown.

9. Haskins, "Targhyn," p. 163.

10. Mary Aiken Littauer, "Early Stirrups," *Antiquity,* vol. 55, no. 214, July 1981, pp. 99–105.

11. *China Reconstructs,* vol. 30, no. 11, Nov. 1981, p. 34.

12. H.G. Creel, "The Role of the Horse in Chinese History," *American Historical Review,* vol. 70, no. 3, Apr. 1965, pp. 651–52.

13. M. Griaznov, "Horses for the Hereafter," in *The Scythians,* Unesco Courier, Dec. 1976, pp. 38–41. The author describes 138 saddled and bridled horses excavated at Arzhan in the eastern Sayan mountains of southern Siberia dated eighth-seventh centuries B.C. by carbon-14 and dendrochronology.

14. *Kaogu Xuebao,* 1954, no. 1, p. 137, no. 12.

15. Jaroslav Prusek, *Chinese Statelets and the Northern Barbarians in the Period 1400–1300 B.C.,* Dordrecht, 1971, p. 131; and Creel, "The Role," p. 656.

16. Creel, "The Role," p. 651.

17. William M. McGovern, *The Early Empires of Central Asia,* Chapel Hill, 1939, p. 101; O.J. Maenchen-Helfen, "Crenelated Mane and Scabbard Slide," *Central Asiatic Journal,* vol. 3, no. 2, 1957, pp. 85–138; William Samolin, "Western Elements in the Art of Chu," ed. Noel Barnard, *Early Chinese Art and Its Possible Influence in the Pacific Basin,* New York, 1972, vol. 1, pp. 187–96; and William Trousdale, *The Long Sword and Scabbard Slide in Asia,* Washington, D.C., 1975, p. 118.

18. Col. D.H. Gordon, "Swords, Rapiers and Horse-riders," *Antiquity,* no. 106, 1963, pp. 67–87; Stuart Piggott, *Ancient Europe,* Edinburgh, 1965, pp. 145 and 181; and Creel, "The Role," p. 650.

19. E. Ewart Oakeshott, *The Archaeology of Weapons,* New York and London, 1960, fig. 18.

20. R.D. Barnett, *Assyrian Palace Reliefs,* London, n.d., pl. 147.

21. Oakeshott, *The Archaeology,* p. 56.

22. Renate Rolle, *Die Welt der Skythen,* Lucerne and Frankfurt, 1980, p. 77.

23. Gordon, "Swords, Rapiers," p. 73. Some riders are depicted as brandishing long swords on a few ancient monuments, but my guess is that they dismounted and fought with them only on foot.

24. Ibid., p. 77.

25. Trousdale, *Long Sword,* p. 116.

26. *Sovetskaia arkheologia,* 1980, no. 2, p. 191.

27. M. Loehr, *Chinese Bronze Age Weapons,* Ann Arbor and London, 1956, p. 72.

28. William Watson, *China,* London, 1961, pp. 84 and 139.

29. Theodore A. Wertime and James Muhly, eds., *The Coming of the Age of Iron,* New Haven and London, 1980, Joseph Needham, "The Evolution of Iron and Steel Technology in East and Southeast Asia," p. 516.

30. Ibid., p. 515.

31. Trousdale, *Long Sword,* p. 54.

32. *China Pictorial,* no. 11, 1978. This sword is steel, which is an alloy essentially of iron and varying amounts of carbon.

33. William Watson, *Cultural Frontiers in Ancient East Asia,* Edinburgh, 1971, fig. 46.

34. *Wenwu,* 1980, no. 7, p. 6.

35. George W. Weber, *The Ornaments of Late Zhou Bronzes,* New Brunswick, 1973, p. 106. The three holes were personally observed on a recent visit to the museum in Luoyang.

36. *Handbook of the Collections in the William Rockhill Nelson Gallery of Art and Mary Atkins Museum of Fine Arts,* Kansas City, 1959, p. 174.

37. *Wenwu,* 1961, no. 10, p. 32.

38. Qian Hao, Chen Heyi, and Ru Suichu, *Out of China's Earth,* fig. 57.

39. Trousdale, *Long Sword,* p. 67.

40. Ibid., pp. 55–57.

41. Philip Denwood, ed., *Arts of the Eurasian Steppelands,* London, 1978, Emma C. Bunker, "The Anecdotal Plaques of the Eastern Steppe Regions," pp. 122 and 126 and pl. 2a, for a discussion of this plaque. There I erroneously thought the sword was of barbarian manufacture and did not recognize its Chinese characteristics.

42. Trousdale, *Long Sword,* p. 67.

43. Denis Sinor, "The Inner Asian Warriors," *Journal of the American Oriental Society,* vol. 101, no. 2, Apr.–June 1981, p. 142.

44. Ibid., pp. 133–44.

45. David N. Keightley, "Where Have All the Swords Gone? Reflections on the Unification of China," *Early China,* vol. 2, fall, 1976, pp. 31–34; and Noel Barnard, "Did the Swords Exist?," *Early China,* vol. 4, 1978–79, pp. 60–65.

46. Sherman E. Lee, *The History of Far Eastern Art,* New York, 1973, color pl. 5.

47. Moorey, et al., *Ancient Bronzes,* p. 167.

48. Bernhard Karlgren, "Huai and Han," *Bulletin of the Museum of Far Eastern Antiquities,* no. 13, 1941, pl. 26, D 1.

49. Trousdale, *Long Sword,* figs. 21–23, 28 and 30.

50. Loehr, *Chinese Bronze,* no. 102. Loehr considers a long bronze rapier in the Jannings Collection as a prestige weapon, as it is too brittle to be functional.

51. Trousdale, *Long Sword,* p 65.

52. *Kaogu Xuebao,* 1964, no. 2, p. 115, pl. 1.

53. Trousdale, *Long Sword,* fig. 20.

54. Ibid., pp. 113 and 116–19.

55. Edward G. Pulleyblank, "Chinese and Indo-Europeans," *Journal of The Royal Asiatic Society,* Apr. 1966, pp. 3–39.

56. Trousdale, *Long Sword,* p. 102. A loop appears on the scabbard wall of a sword on a fourth-century B.C. Greek amphora, but this is not a proper slide. There is no archaeological evidence in the Urals for a separate scabbard slide either.

57. This supersedes my agreement with Trousdale in my review of *Long Sword* in *Oriental Art,* autumn, 1978, p. 331–32.

58. O.J. Maenchen-Helfen, "Are Chinese Hsi-p'i and kuo-lo Indo-

European Words?", *Language,* vol. 21, pp. 256–60; and Trousdale, *Long Sword,* p. 68.

59. Al Dien, "A Study of Early Chinese Armor," *Artibus Asiae,* vol. 43, nos. 1 and 2, p. 13.

60. Watson, *Records of the Grand Historian,* vol. 2, p. 155.

61. Moorey, et al., *Ancient Bronze,* p. 140.

62. B. Karlgren, "Ordos and Huai," *Bulletin of the Museum of Far Eastern Antiquities,* vol. 9, 1939, pp. 97–112.

63. C.D. Weber, "Chinese Pictorial Bronze Vessels of the Late Zhou Period," *Artibus Asiae,* vols. 28, nos. 2 and 3, 1966, pp. 107–40; vol. 28, no. 4, 1966, pp. 271–302; vol. 29, nos. 2 and 3, 1967, pp. 115–74; and vol. 30, nos. 2 and 3, 1968, pp. 145–213.

64. Fong, *Great Bronze Age,* no. 67.

65. Weber, "Chinese Pictorial," *A.A.,* vol. 30, nos. 2 and 3, p. 155 and fig. 70. The surface treatment of scales on the felines is typical of sixth-century B.C. Chu workmanship.

66. Weber, "Chinese Pictorial," *A.A.,* vol. 28, nos. 2 and 3, pp. 112–13, fig. 16.

67. Fong, *Great Bronze Age,* no. 17.

68. T.J. Arne, *Bulletin of the Museum of Far Eastern Antiquities,* "Die Funde von L'uan-ping and Hsuan-hua," no. 5, 1933, pl. 10.

69. Moorey, et al., *Ancient Bronzes,* no. 798.

70. Emma C. Bunker, A. Farkas, and B. Chatwin, "Animal Style from East to West," New York, 1970, no. 17.

71. Fong, *Great Bronze Age,* p. 266.

72. Denwood, ed., *Arts of the Eurasian,* Rose Kerr, "The Tiger Motif: Cultural Transference in the Steppes," pp. 74–87.

73. Weber, "Chinese Pictorial," *A.A.,* vol. 28, nos. 2 and 3, pl. 32.

74. Ibid., vol. 30, nos. 2 and 3, pp. 202–3.

75. Ibid., p. 203.

76. Michael Sullivan, *The Arts of China,* Berkeley, Los Angeles, and London, 1977, p. 47, and W. Watson, *China,* New York, 1961, p. 162.

77. Ibid., pp. 56–57.

78. Fong, *Great Bronze Age,* p. 306.

79. Denwood, ed., *Arts of the Eurasian,* Bunker, pl. 2a (see n. 41).

80. Fong, *Great Bronze Age,* no. 70.

81. Ibid., p. 268.

82. Weber, "Chinese Pictorial," *A.A.,* vol. 29, nos. 2 and 3, pp. 123–36, and figs. 36–39.

83. Ibid., vol. 30, nos. 2 and 3, figs. 70 and 71.

84. Pieter Meyers, "Applications of X-Ray Radiography in the Study of Archaeological Objects," *Advances in Chemistry Series,* no. 171, Archaeological Chemistry II, 1978, p. 90. In a recent conversation with Dr. Meyers, he said that some vessel fragments he had examined showed that the copper figures were cast, not cutouts.

85. Watson, *China,* p. 167.

86. *Frozen Tombs,* published for the Trustees of the British Museum, 1978, figs. 22, 37, 38, 40 and 43–51.; and S.I. Rudenko, *The Frozen Tombs of Siberia,* London, 1970, pp. 229–78 and figs. 108–17.

87. Rudenko, ibid., p. 263.

88. Ibid., p. 270.

89. Ibid., pl. 139L.

90. Ibid., pls. 169–70.

91. Weber, "Chinese Pictorial," *A.A.,* vol. 30, nos. 2 and 3, figs. 79, 62 and 63.

92. Rudenko, *The Frozen Tombs,* figs. 55 and 89.

93. Ibid., p. XXII.

94. Weber, "Chinese Pictorial," *A.A.,* vol. 30, nos. 2 and 3, pp. 205–6 and 212.

95. Fong, *Great Bronze Age,* no. 69.

96. Rudenko, *The Frozen Tombs,* p. 268–69.

97. The two tigers flanking a human head on an Anyang *ding* handle are protective, not hostile, while the human on the Liyu *hu* is in a distinctively uncomfortable position, and not a continuation of a Shang motif.

98. Fong, *Great Bronze Age,* fig. 101.

99. Prusek, *Chinese Statelets,* pp. 184–88.

100. Qian Hao, Chen Heyi, and Ru Suichu, *Out of China's Earth,* pp. 29–31.

101. Fong, *Great Bronze Age,* no. 69.

102. Ibid., pp. 318–19.

103. Ibid., p. 326.

104. Ibid., fig. 102.

105. Mr. Artamonov, ed., *The Dawn of Art,* Leningrad, 1974, no. 71.

106. Viktor Sarianidi, "The Treasure of the Golden Mound," *Archaeology,* vol. 33, no. 3, May/June 1980, p. 39.

107. K.C. Chang, *The Archaeology of Ancient China,* New Haven and London, 1977, pp. 453–70.

108. Noel Barnard, ed., *Early Chinese Art and Its Possible Influence in the Pacific Basin,* New York, 1972, Emma C. Bunker, "The Tien Culture and Some Aspects of Its Relationship to the Dong-son Culture," pp. 291–328.

109. Fong, *Great Bronze Age,* p. 327.

110. William Watson, "Dongson and the Kingdom of Tien," *Readings in Asian Topics,* Scandinavian Institute of Asian Studies, Monograph Series, vol. 1, Lund, 1970, pp. 45–71.

111. Ibid., p. 51.

112. Fong, *Great Bronze Age,* p. 327.

113. *Yunnan Chin-ning Shi-chai-shan Ku Mu Ch'un Fa-chueh Pao-kao,* Peking, 1959, vol. 2, p. 43, 4 and 5.

114. L. Vanden Berghe, *Archéologie de l'Iran Ancien,* Leiden, 1959, pl. 136.

115. Chang, *The Archaeology,* p. 467, n. 110.

116. Karl Jettmar, *Art of the Steppes,* trans. Ann E. Keep, New York: Crown Publishers, 1964, pl. 4.

117. Michele Pirazzoli-t'Sertevens, *La Civilization du Royaume de Dian a l'époque Han,* 1974, fig. 31.

118. Chang, *The Archaeology,* fig. 220.

119. R.D. Barnett, "The Art of Bactria and the Treasure of the Oxus," *Iranica Antiqua,* Leiden, 1968, vol. 8, p. 51.

120. Umehara Sueji, *Studies of Noinula Finds in North Mongolia,* Tokyo, 1960.

121. *Pompeii A.D. 79,* essay and cat., John Ward-Perkins and Amanda Claridge, Museum of Fine Arts, Boston, 1979, vol. 1, pl. 238. This mosaic derives from a second-century B.C. Hellenistic trend in genre painting and preoccupation with observation of fauna that began at Pergamum in the work of Sosus during the second century B.C.; see Jean Charbonneaux, Roland Martin, and Francois Villard, *Hellenistic Art,* New York, 1973, pp. 182–84.

122. Chang, *The Archaeology,* p. 467.

123. Ibid.

124. Chin You-di, *Ban Chiang Prehistoric Cultures,* Bangkok, 1975.

The Beginnings of Metallurgy in China: A Comparative Approach

Ursula Martius Franklin
Professor of Metallurgy and Materials Science
University of Toronto

THE BASIC APPROACH that underlies all presented in this paper can be stated briefly as follows: Ancient objects—vessels or weapons, molds, furnaces or slags—are looked upon as primary historical sources. Within them is contained much information on skills, resources, and values of the societies from which these artifacts have come. I regard ancient objects as equivalent to literary sources in the sense that artifacts too can be read and evaluated using a variety of techniques based on modern materials science. The information content of objects can be related to and compared with evidence gained from the study of artifacts of different types, styles, historical periods, or localities.

Just as literary sources have to be critically assessed and interpreted in the larger context of their time, so do the materials sources. While much care and scholarly effort have been devoted to the preservation, translation, and interpretation of written sources, indepth technical studies of the materials evidence of history are only beginning to make an impact on our understanding of the past. It is, of course, quite clear that the materials evidence cannot stand by itself just as literary evidence cannot. Only by considering the total human, economic, political, and technological context can we arrive at a reasonably trustworthy reconstruction of the past.

Perspectives on Copper and Bronze in China

This paper will focus on insights gained from the recent studies of Chinese bronzes and related objects which, I suggest, can throw new light on some of the most interesting historical questions, such as the beginning of the Bronze Age in China.

When speaking about Chinese bronzes, it is well to remember that the West's interest in them started only during this century. The travelers' accounts of old, even the detailed reports of the Jesuits, make no mention of bronze. This fact stands in stark contrast to the fame of Chinese silk or to Europe's attitude towards Chinese porcelain. The latter was not only well known and treasured but became the object of intense curiosity, leading to much study and experimentation in an effort to replicate this particular Chinese achievement.

Chinese bronzes do not have a similar long history of appreciation, study, and scrutiny. Furthermore, while porcelain or silks have always been looked upon as commodities—as items of trade (silkroad)—bronze is not regarded merely as a commodity. At least since the turn of this century, the presence of copper and/or bronze has been considered as a benchmark in the development of any society; occasionally bronze has become part of the very definition of civilization itself, thus assuming an almost symbolic value. Consequently when discussing the development of bronze, its technology and its applications, one is inevitably touching on aspects of social and cultural evolution and with it on the diverse theories in this field.

Underlying all theories of social development is the belief that there exists an evolutionary sequence that governs the broad temporal phases in the development of all societies. This assumption of the universal development sequence is also the common base of the two modern theoretical prototypes: those theories that regard the forces and relations of production as the activators of all social development, and those models that look at society essentially as an organic entity growing with time toward levels of greater and greater internal complexity.[1,2]

It may be of interest to note in passing the growing realization within the scholarly community that, while general models and theories may contain valuable guidelines, their application to any specific situation requires a much more complex and sophisticated approach. Nowhere is this insight more applicable than in the study of ancient technologies and their role in the evolution of society.[3]

If one were to fit what is known today about bronze and other metals in early China into the standard global picture of the evolution of metallurgy—a picture outlined, for instance, recently again by J.A. Charles[4]—one would find three apparent contradictions:

(1) In time, i.e., when bronze began to occur.

(2) In application, i.e., how early metals were used.

(3) In technology, i.e., how bronze objects were made.

These contradictions are not independent of each other but interrelated. Their interrelatedness provides, in fact, the key to an interpretation that transcends and resolves them.

Ma Chengyuan[5] and Xia Nai[6] have recently summarized details regarding the copper and bronze objects that have been excavated from late neolithic contexts in China, some originating well before 2000 B.C. Chinese archaeologists confidently expect to come across more extensive evidence of the beginning of metalworking in neolithic China in the future.

However, even taking this into account, it seems on first impression striking and somehow inconsistent that the great artistic and technical achievement that constitutes the bronzes of China seem to reveal such slender roots.

The Problem of Personal Ornaments

On closer inspection one may find an explanation of this situation in a very ancient and uniquely Chinese preference—or better non-preference—in the use of metal.[7]

When one looks at the global repertoire of ancient metal objects, one realizes how many of the earliest metal artifacts were used for personal decoration. This is quite understandable; the novelty of the material and its strikingly different color and texture can account partly for this decorative use. Furthermore, ornaments pose only minimal requirements as to mechanical strength, shape, and form. Thus the application to ornaments lends itself well to the introduction of new materials. Many of the early pieces found in other than Chinese cultural contexts are beads or small hammered and pierced fragments; necklaces or bracelets have accompanied their owners into the grave. For instance, bronze from Ban Chiang, Thailand, contained a bracelet of cast tin-bronze, found on the wrist of a skeleton.[8] Most of the graves of the Minusinsk Basin as well as those of the steppe people in the Ordos contain a sizeable number of hammered personal ornaments made of copper and/or bronze.

However, for reasons not known to me, there are no personal ornaments made of metal among the finds from early Chinese sites. While many personal ornaments are found in tombs from the neolithic on, the ornaments are made of bone, stone, antler or jade; they are not made of metal. Even after the ritual

bronze vessels began to appear in the tombs of Erlitou as well as during subsequent periods, when tombs were most richly endowed, copper and bronze were not used for personal ornaments either for the rich or the poor (buckles must be considered as articles of dress, rather than as personal ornamentation).

I suspect that the view of what does or does not constitute an appropriate use of metal—which seems so deeply imbedded in the Chinese tradition—may relate to the fact that metals, with the exception of gold, are man made, i.e., derived materials, in contrast to the natural and unaltered materials such as stone, bone, teeth, pearls or jade.

The preference for non-metallic materials for personal ornamentation has deprived the archaeologist of a major source of evidence for the earliest metal use in China. While habitation sites may yield from time to time ornamental copper or bronze fragments used in the decoration of wood (for furniture, standards or insignias, similar to the use of the gold foils occasionally reported), one has to accept the fact that one mode of early metal use will remain absent in China. This is particularly regrettable since the basic burial customs have remained unchanged from neolithic through Shang into early Zhou.[9] Had the early Chinese preferred metal for personal ornamentation, these graves would have been a marvelous source of evidence for the beginning of copper and bronze in China.

In summary: When discussing archaeological inventory in China, serious attention has to be paid to the culturally determined absence of personal decoration made of metal. This fact has to be considered when comparing and contrasting the Chinese situation with that of other civilizations. It may well account for some of the apparent contradictions in time and application mentioned above. For those who are looking for "proof" of the indigenous nature of Chinese metallurgy, this very characteristic idiosyncrasy should be another indication that there were no metal-using outsiders who brought the knowledge of copper and bronze work into China. The people to the west, north, and south of the Chinese heartland used metal extensively for personal ornamentation and would have brought this application to them.

China's Approach to Metallurgy

Let us now discuss the technology of metalworking used in China in order to see what the development of this technology might imply in a larger context.

While some hammered copper and bronze objects have been reported from early Chinese sites, the artifacts excavated at Erlitou contained already tin-bronzes cast in piece molds. Attention has been drawn by scholars to the intimate relationship between ceramic and metals technology in China.[10,11] The ceramic achievements made piece-mold techniques possible, and the management of elevated kiln temperatures a prerequisite for subsequent metallurgical development.

Regarding smelting of ores, we should not forget Tylecote's reminder of the essential difference between a pottery kiln and a smelting furnace.[12] The chemistry of smelting requires that the charge and the fuel remain intimately mixed and in contact with each other. In the case of pottery, the development of kilns is directed toward separating the source of fuel and heat from the pots, leading to multi-chamber kilns.

But the relationships between ceramics and metallurgy in China goes well behyond this, because the whole Chinese approach to metal and alloys is essentially a "chemical" rather than a "physical" one. Properties of metal and alloys can, in principle, be varied by either changing the composition—i.e., the proportions and nature of the alloying elements—or by mechanically altering the microstructure of the metal/alloy through working or heat treatment. In the case of ceramics, of course, the properties of the final objects are varied by changing the nature and the properties of the constituents of the ceramic mix (clay, sand, temper, water, etc.).

From its beginning, Chinese metallurgy seems to have followed this ceramic pattern. The importance of the often discussed passage from the *Kaogongji* seems to lie in the confirmation and regularization of this approach. It is expressed by specifying the ratios of copper and tin for various applications of bronze. Whether these specifications were exactly adhered to and whether they, in fact, applied to weight or volume appears to me less important than the documentation of this essential chemical (ceramic) approach to the structure and property relationships in alloys.

This discussion should again remind us that in any society the metallurgical techniques will develop along the path that is internally consistent with the manner in which other materials are being treated.

Implications of the Piece-Mold Technology

In addition to setting the pattern for the approach to the structure and property relationship of metals, the intimate connection between ceramic and metal technology has resulted in the evolution of a uniquely Chinese system of casting bronze into piece molds. This system, in turn, has had profound consequences on the mode of bronze production, on the division of labor, and on the organization and coordination of bronze manufacturing.

In the second half of this paper I would like to outline these concepts in some detail in order to show what the study of Chinese bronze vessels beyond composition and style can tell us about their production. The discussion, then, will address a third contradiction mentioned above—the contradiction in technology.

Holistic and Prescriptive Processes

In order to analyze technological processes in a historical perspective, it is helpful to introduce two classifications: that of a holistic process and that of a prescriptive process. These processes have to be seen as end-members of a spectrum of making things; in reality, most practical processes will have holistic as well as prescriptive components.

A holistic process, such as fashioning stone tools,

making a wrought iron sword or a bronze bowl by raising and chasing, involves basically a single, stepwise approximation toward the final object. The craftsman, starting with a selection of suitable raw materials, must know intimately the whole sequence of steps necessary to produce the object. The artisan's knowledge and judgment determines the sequence of the process as well as its end—the moment when one says, "This is as good as I can make it."

The element of judgment at every step of the continuing work sequence is characteristic of holistic processes, which are one-of-a-kind processes. Each small step depends on and is determined by the preceding step. The holistic process is essentially a sequential, linear development.

Prescriptive processes, on the other hand, are different in kind. Casting bronze into piece molds may serve as an example: Here a model of the final shape is made first, either in wood, clay or maybe leather. The mold is fashioned from the model, sectioned and then fired and reassembled around the core that may or may not be made from the original model. The object is cast from an alloy of predetermined composition. The final success depends just as much on the quality of the model, on the mold-making and on the mold-assembly as it depends on the appropriateness of the alloy and the soundness of the casting. Beyond small repairs, the final product cannot be improved by extending or altering the last phase of the production sequence. The final shape of the vessel is determined by the initial model. The whole casting process can be viewed as a sequence of unit processes (to use the modern engineering term). The outcome of the production depends entirely on the competence of the execution of each unit. I have called this type of subdivided or subdividable process "prescriptive" in order to indicate the characteristic external pre-ordering and normalizing inherent in it. The making of textiles or pottery could provide similar examples.

The perceptions underlying a prescriptive manufacturing process are different in kind from those on which holistic production is based. In the prescriptive case the image of the final product stands at the beginning of the production process. A considerable degree of abstraction and a thorough technical understanding is required to perceive a division of the process into unit processes dictated by the technical requirements of production. It has to be seen that each unit represents an autonomous skill, thus drawing on different groups of workers. The founder need not know how to make molds; the mold maker does not have to be competent enough to make an alloy or to cast a vessel.

Inherent in the prescriptive process, therefore, is an essential predictability; there is no room for surprise. Prescriptive processes can be perceived only when the full sequence of technical events is understood and in hand. In practice the process as a whole can work only if there is overall coordination, strict adherence to procedure at every step, and an effective oversight of the entire operation.

The formalization of a prescriptive process has a

profound influence on the direction of subsequent development and experimentation. However varied different prescriptive processes may be, there is a certain production-related standardization of form and material in all of them. The scope of experimentation becomes limited to what is possible within the technology of the process; the direction of technological innovation is biased toward improvement of the existing procedure. The feedback loop between trying and finding out is long and indirect, since changes in one of the unit processes will affect all other units in the production system.

The holistic processes, on the other hand, consist of sequences of directly related steps. They are the perfect vehicle for the increasingly expert artisan, whose products are never completely predictable and whose knowledge and experience encompasses all phases of the work. Here experimentation is almost inevitable, the feedback loop between trying and finding out is short and direct. This does not mean that holistic processes are simple or unsophisticated, but rather that the situational judgment of the artisan, exercised at every step of the work, provides the internal unity of the process.

All beginning technology is holistic. Only after extensive understanding and knowledge has been accumulated can generalization and abstraction take place. Only then can one envisage a prescriptive process and be able to arrive at the necessary standardization and organization.

Divisions of Labor

Anthropologists frequently speak of division of labor and craft specialization. As simple societies become more complex, divisions of labor according to age, sex, rank or skill become more pronounced. Special skills can become the exclusive prerogatives of specific families, groups or clans. Such craft specialization occurs usually according to the type of product. Herskovits remarks after a discussion on the division of labor between men and women:[13]

> In still other non-literate societies, certain men and women specialize not only in one technique but in a certain type of product, as for instance when one woman will devote her time to the production of pots for everyday use and another will make pottery exclusively for religious rites. It must also be stressed that except under the most unusual circumstances we do not find the kind of organization where one woman characteristically specializes in the gathering of the clay, another in the fashioning of it, a third in the firing of the pots; or, where one man devotes himself to the getting of wood, another to roughly blocking it out into the proportions of a stool or a figure, and a third to finishing it.

Generally in the types of craft specialization or divisions of labor that has been documented by anthropologists or archaeologists, the processes themselves remain holistic. Though the differentiation along product lines can be quite detailed, it does not seem to lead to changes or modification in the organization of the production processes themselves.

In contrast to the interest in craft specialization, the anthropological and archaeological literature does not dwell on prescriptive processes, although Roman technology provides some fine examples of them. Most historians of technology speak of the division of labor according to the needs of the manufacturing process only in connection with mechanization and with the introduction of factories or factory-like establishments. The weavers of Florence in the Middle Ages or the British metalworkers during the Industrial Revolution are frequently cited as examples of trades impacted by the new organization of work. In each case, crafts are seen to give way to manufacturing, the holistic turns into the prescriptive.

In 1682 Sir William Petty wrote as a new dictum:

> Manufacture will be divided into as many parts as possible, whereby the work of each artisan will be simple and easy. As for example in the making of a watch, if one shall make the wheels, another the spring, another shall engrave the dial plate and another make the case, then the watch will be better and cheaper than if the whole work be put upon one man.[14]

In spite of our habit of linking the beginning of the process-related division of labor to mechanization, the presence of machines is not a prerequisite of this development. The essential requirement for a prescriptive process is *control,* i.e., being in command of material resources, knowledge, and people. If, in addition to the technical knowledge, the instrumentalities of control such as coordination, regulation, supervision, and enforcement are present, prescriptive processes are possible.

While prescriptive processes, which are usually associated with industrialization and the factory system, are manifestations of sophisticated technical knowledge, they are most of all important social inventions. Their presence in a certain historical setting is a diagnostic indication of the social order of the society that employed such production methods. The requirement of control, in terms of human and material resources and of organization and supervision, defines a "milieu" without which a prescriptive technology cannot develop or thrive.[15]

A Fresh Look at Chinese Bronze Casting

Applying the general consideration previously outlined to the piece-mold casting technology, we see that many aspects of the process—such as the standardization of form and decor, and the incorporation of precast parts—are consistent with the nature of prescriptive production. Furthermore, one finds that as experience and skills of the artisans increased, the technology itself seems to guide innovation and development. The objects become more ornate and complex, they become much larger, finally representing tremendous technical accomplishments. The large objects were made by the same techniques as the small ones—a fact that is remarkable in itself—and no radically new metallurgical techniques seem to occur for some time. (The apparent absence of drawn wire is particularly intriguing in this context.) Clearly, while the prescriptive process itself and the social order that sustained it facilitated the expansion and the extension of the production, it also directed innovation toward improvement and elaboration of the existing system.

Considering the nature and the prerequisites of the prescriptive technology, and recognizing Shang bronze casting as such a technology, one may want to address again the question of the beginning of metalworking in China.

There is no doubt in my mind that there must have existed in China earlier, holistic methods of metalworking. The new excavations have shown the occasional indication of such products, and more evidence might be preserved in isolated pockets still to be discovered; but we may never be able to reconstruct the full extent of the earlier phases of metalworking in China. Just as the factory destroyed the crafts of Europe, Shang bronze industry may have almost totally eliminated the evidence of the holistic copper and bronze production in China. The detailed analysis of the modes of bronze production outlined above should explain and resolve the third contradiction mentioned.

Possible Future Research

There may be an indirect way to obtain further light on the question of the earlier phases of Chinese metalworking. One may wish to link for this purpose two separate observations; one is the intimate relationship between ceramic and metal technology in early China, the second is the realization that the setting up of prescriptive processes required the good prior knowledge of the basic technology of all phases of the process. Moreover, it is unlikely that bronze casting was the only prescriptive production in Shang China. It is probable that the ceramic production went through a development similar to that of the bronze industry at approximately the same time. Consequently, a good technical analysis, that takes style and form as well as raw materials and production methods into account, may detect the times and places where pottery production underwent a transition from the holistic to the prescriptive processes.

Since ceramics cannot be remelted and the raw materials for pottery production cannot be monopolized in the way metal production can, it is likely that early holistic pottery has had a better chance of survival than had the metal artifacts. In fact, prescriptive production of pottery may have never completely replaced the holistic processes. The study of the geographic, technological, and stylistic features of early Chinese ceramic production may provide, therefore, suitable analogues to the evolution of Chinese metal technology. It should also be noted that the textile technology of China is likely to show noticeable transitions from holistic to prescriptive production.

Taking a process-oriented perspective, one should also reflect on the skill and competence of the labor force involved in such a production. Although prescriptive processes subdivide process knowledge and thus provide opportunities for the utilization of less broadly skilled labor, the products of Shang bronze industry bespeak of highly developed artistic, technological, and organizational skills. The artifacts we see today do not look like products of unwilling minds and forced hands. There is an evolution of tradition, ability, and assurance in them that indicate imagination, pride, and continuity. Researchers might one day want to ask how these skills were developed, taught, and transmitted, how technical talent was recognized and rewarded, and how the continuation and extension of this tradition was assured.[16]

Notes

1. L.S. Klejn, "A Panorama of Theoretical Archaeology," *Current Anthropology,* vol. 18, 1977, pp. 1–43.
   B. O'Laughlin, "Marxist Approaches to Anthropology," *Advances in Anthropology,* vol. 3, 1975, pp. 341–87.
   M. Godelier, "Infrastructure, Societies and History," *Current Anthropology,* vol. 19, 1978, pp. 763–71.

2. Elman Service, *Origins of State and Civilization: An Evolutionary Perspective,* New York: Norton, 1974.
   Bruce Trigger, *Time and Tradition: Essays in Archaeological Interpretation,* Edinburgh University Press, 1978.
   For the theoretical framework of Chinese archaeology, see the discussion by K.C. Chang in *Shang Civilization,* New Haven and London: Yale University Press, 1980, p. 60 ff.

3. Heather Lechtman has outlined a most perceptive critique of the traditional approach to prehistoric technology in her essay "The Central Andes, Metallurgy Without Iron," in *The Coming of the Age of Iron,* ed. T.A. Wertime and J.D. Muhly, New Haven and London: Yale University Press, 1980.

4. J.A. Charles, "The Coming of Cu and Cu-Base Alloys: A Metallurgical Sequence," in *The Coming of the Age of Iron,* see n. 3.

5. Ma Chengyuan, "The Splendor of Chinese Bronzes," in *The Great Bronze Age of China,* ed. Wen Fong, The Metropolitan Museum of Art, New York: Alfred A. Knopf, 1980.

6. Hsia Nai (Xia Nai), "Archaeology and the History of Technology," *Kaogu,* vol. 2, 1977, pp. 81–91.

7. U.M. Franklin, "On Bronze and Other Materials in Early China," Proceedings of Conference "On the Origins of Chinese Civilization," Berkeley, 1978.

8. C. Gorman and P. Charoenwongsa, "Ban Chiang: A Mosaic of Impressions from the First Two Years," *Expedition,* vol. 18, no. 4, 1976, pp. 14–26.
   T.S. Wheeler and R. Maddin, "The Techniques of Early Thai Metalsmith," *Expedition,* vol. 18, no. 4, 1976, pp. 38–47.
   D.T. Bayard, "Early Thai Bronze Analysis and New Data," *Science,* vol. 176, 1972, pp. 1411–12.

9. R.L. Thorp, "Burial Practices of Bronze Age China," in *The Great Bronze Age of China,* see n. 5.

10. Li Chi, *The Beginnings of Chinese Civilization,* University of Washington Press, 1957.

11. N. Barnard, "Bronze Casting and Bronze Alloys in Ancient China," *Monumenta Serica Monograph XIV,* 1961.

12. R.F. Tylecote, "Furnaces, Crucibles and Slags," in *The Coming of the Age of Iron,* see n. 3.

13. M.J. Herskovits, *Economic Anthropology,* New York: A.E. Knopf, 1952, p. 126.

14. Sir William Patty, "Concerning the Growth of the City of London" in *Economic Writings of Sir William Patty,* vol. 2, 1682; ed. C.H. Hull, Cambridge, 1899, p. 287.

15. U.M. Franklin, "The Potential of Technical Studies," paper read at Symposium on the Great Bronze Age of China, Metropolitan Museum, New York, June 1980.

16. The work reported here is part of a larger study into the history of metallurgy as well as into the social impact of technology supported by both the Natural Sciences and Engineering Research Council of Canada and the Social Sciences and Humanities Research Council of Canada. I wish to express my thankfulness for encouragement and support to them, as well as to my own university.

Bronze Casting in China: A Short Technical History

W.T. Chase
Head Conservator, Technical Laboratory
Freer Gallery of Art

THE STUDY OF THE HISTORY of bronze casting in China is at present in a very interesting phase. To use a metallurgical analogy, solid centers are beginning to crystallize out from a fluid state. Archaeologists in the People's Republic of China yearly make new and startling discoveries—discoveries which constantly force us to revise our preconceived notions about metal crafts and, indeed all aspects of early China.[1]

In addition to the increasing pace of archaeological discovery in The People's Republic of China, the finds are being studied extensively, carefully, and thoroughly. Between the May 1981 date of the Los Angeles Symposium and the time of writing of this paper, a pioneering international conference in archaeometallurgy was held in Beijing, with the title "Early Metallurgy in China and Possible External Influences."[2] One can easily see that the study of early Chinese metallurgy is an active field at the present time.

In this paper we will attempt to summarize what we know about the technical history of bronze casting in China, to point out the gaps in our knowledge, and to see what sort of a general picture we can discern from the evidence to date.

Why should the history of Chinese bronze casting be of unusual interest? For those of us who have been involved with the study, the question is easy to answer; ancient Chinese bronzes have a unique beauty and power, and we would like to know how they were made. The ancient foundryman knew empirically how to make the metal do exactly what he wanted. In trying to understand the technical history, we can see the problems he faced and how he went about solving them. The evolution of foundry practice—along with all the allied crafts such as ceramics, mold-making, refining of metal, finishing and machining, etc.—can

help us to trace the development of technology in general.

Metallurgical technology in China is intertwined with economics, supply and demand, trade, and in the case of Chinese bronzes, the mandate of heaven, the rise and fall of royal houses, and the origin of the state.[3] This sort of study may also have some useful practical applications, such as the detection of fakes and forgeries, the definition of long-term corrosion mechanisms, and the rediscovery of forgotten useful techniques.[4] Understanding of the bronzes will also aid in their long-term preservation.

As in any historical study, we must examine the nature of our evidence. Each bronze (and each of the materials contained in it) has its own history. It is useful to consider an ancient Chinese bronze ceremonial vessel, not as a static object in a display case, but as a process (Figure 1). The bronze is still deteriorating, corroding, etc., and may at some point receive treatment from a conservator to improve its appearance or strength. One can trace the process back to the original emplacement of the ores which yielded the metal for the bronze, especially in the case of lead, which has different isotopic ratios due to its mode of geologic formation. Lead isotope ratios should make it possible for us to assign the lead in a particular artifact to its ore source.[5] One can also project the process forward to the eventual disintegration of the bronze.

Alternatively, a Chinese bronze can be seen as a sequence of events (Figure 2). In this paper we will consider with some care the alloying, casting, and finishing of Chinese ceremonial bronze vessels. While the questions of use, patination, burial, long-term corrosion, archaeological recovery, repair, etc., are very important in considering a Chinese bronze, we simply do not have the space to deal with them here. Correct answers to the questions of patination at the time of manufacture and long-term corrosion should allow us to infer what the bronzes must have looked like when new. The patination and corrosion story is, however, very complex;[6] in this paper we will concentrate on what the bronzes were made from and how they were made.

The Copper-Tin-Lead Ternary Bronze Alloy System and Its Properties

Bronze alloys were employed almost to the exclusion of any other alloys for approximately a thousand years in China; even after the introduction of iron, bronze was employed for weapons, vessels, coinage, and statuary. Tin bronzes served the ancient Chinese foundryman very well, and no other metals appear in consequential amounts from c. 1600 B.C. to about 500 B.C. Tin bronzes have remained in currency up until modern times.

The ancient Chinese were masters of cast bronze foundry technology. To make a bronze fit a specific application they did not rely on hardening by cold-working or on softening by annealing, but rather on the changes of the physical properties of the metal with changes in composition.[7] To appreciate the development of bronze alloys in China we must first ex-amine the fundamental properties of the copper-tin-lead ternary system.[8]

These properties of the system (along with the distributions of alloy compositions from various ancient bronzes) can best be visualized with the aid of triangular ternary diagrams. Figure 3 will serve as an introduction. We usually draw just the top half of the diagram, showing only that portion of the diagram where copper makes up more than half of the alloy; the lower boundary represents a composition with 50 percent copper. Tin increases toward the right of the diagram, and lead toward the left. The vertical median line of the triangle represents compositions with equal parts by weight of tin and lead. At the center of the lower boundary, the composition represented would be 50 percent copper, 25 percent tin, and 25 percent lead, shown as "50–25–25." Other compositions have been indicated as examples in Figure 3.

What are the properties that make the copper-tin-lead system so attractive and useful to the foundryman? The first, its ready availability, needs no illustration here. Copper, both in the native state and in ores, is easy to recognize in nature. The same is true of cassiterite (tin oxide) and galena (lead sulfide). Ores for copper, tin, and lead exist within easy transportation distance of the "nuclear area" of Chinese civilization.[9]

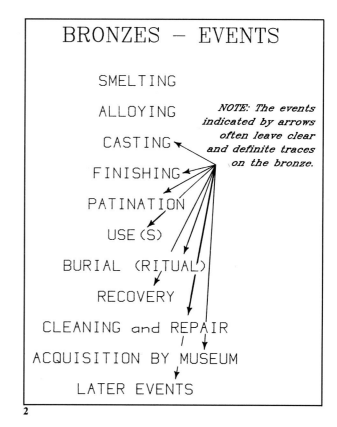

1

2

Figures

1. Schematic diagram showing bronzes as a process, from the formation of the materials used to make the bronze, through manufacture, use, burial, recovery, and display in a museum. The process will continue until the bronze eventually disintegrates.

2. Schematic diagram showing bronzes as a series of events.

The second is the range of colors available in the various alloys. While the change in color of the various copper-tin-lead alloys with composition has not yet been quantified, a general idea of the range of colors can be gained from Figure 4.[10] The color of a polished surface of the alloy goes from copper-red through orange and yellow to white as tin is added to the pure copper. Lead does not enter into the copper- and tin-containing phases to any great extent, but rather forms discontinuous spheres of nearly pure lead in the solid metal. The addition of lead, therefore, tends to add grey to the metal color, decreasing the intensity rather than changing the hue.[11]

From the available evidence it appears that the ancient Chinese formulated their alloys, at least in some cases, with color in mind. In Figure 4 we have indicated the compositions of three groups of bronzes. The mirrors, a group analyzed by R.J. Gettens and his students in the 1930s,[12] center nicely around a composition of silvery-grey color, as do the mirrors analyzed more recently by Riederer and Tien.[13] In fact, the composition of 71 percent copper, 26 percent tin, and 3 percent lead is just about the lowest-tin composition that can be called "white"; with less than 26 or 25 percent tin, the metal assumes a definite yellow tone. The ceremonial vessels shown in Figure 4 were analyzed at the Freer Gallery of Art; from our

full list of ceremonial vessels we have selected those tested by thermoluminescence for authenticity.[14] Their colors are in the orange to light-yellow range. The Mingdao coinage (also analyzed at the Freer) has a remarkably high lead content, and would have looked light pink to perhaps light yellow when newly cast and polished. These three types of bronzes form distinctly different compositional groups, a theme to which we will return below.

The third helpful feature of the copper-tin-lead system is that it exhibits a great range of physical properties which depend on composition. The hardness varies with tin (and lead) content, as can be seen in Figure 5, which has the mirrors again superimposed. One feels that the mirror alloy was chosen for its color and that the hardness was only a useful dividend; it does tend to minimize scratching, and allows the mirrors to take a high polish. On the other hand, the mirrors are extremely brittle, as can be seen by the elongation value for this composition, which ranges between 2 percent and 0 percent. While the coins fall in the same region of elongation values, we have not seen as many broken coins as mirrors, and the extrapolated values for elongation (dotted lines) may not be correct in this area. More work is needed in the high-tin and high-lead regions to pin down the exact value for the physical parameters.

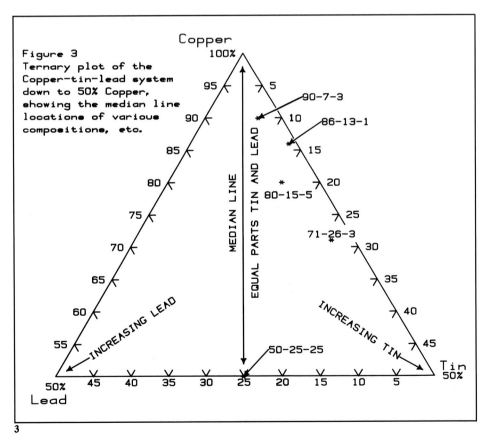

Figures

3. A ternary plot of the copper-tin-lead system down to 50 percent copper. The median line with compositions of equal tin and lead is shown, along with the directions of increasing tin and lead, and various compositional points.

Tensile strength is shown in Figure 6, along with analyses for some weapons. Many of the weapons have compositions which lie in the area of greatest tensile strength. The well-known quote from a swordsmith in the *Lü Shi Chunqiu,* saying that copper makes a sword elastic and tin makes it hard and easily broken, shows the kind of empirical knowledge of physical properties that was at the disposal of the ancient founder.[15] Figure 6 shows, by the tight grouping of the bladed weapons in the area of highest tensile strength, that the ancient Chinese foundryman put this empirical knowledge to good use.

One other helpful property of the copper-tin-lead system should be mentioned; the alloys lend themselves to casting. The highest-copper alloys (more than 97–98 percent copper) can be difficult to cast due to high gas absorption and medium (less than high) fluidity. Tin acts as a deoxidizer, decreases gas absorption, and promotes fluidity. Alloys with more than 6–7 percent tin tend to cast well, and those with 10 percent tin or more are highly fluid and cast very well. Lead (up to 3 percent) increases the fluidity of the melt, and in any amount improves the ease of finishing of the solidified casting.[16]

It is interesting, however, that for the most part the alloys represented in the copper-tin-lead ternary diagram do not lend themselves to hot-working or cold-working in the solid state. They are difficult or impossible to shape by hammering. Two important exceptions should be noted; alloys with high copper and low lead content, with tin less than 10 percent, can be hammered out to sheet, with frequent anneals. Bronzes with a tin content upwards of 20 percent, and no lead, can be hot forged, or quenched from a temperature above 550 degrees Celsius and cold-worked.[17] If any lead is present, these high-tin bronzes are unworkable. The high-tin composition forms the basis of modern cymbals, Asian Gongs, some early Korean and Thai metalwork, and the "white bronzes" of medieval Iran.[18]

Over the whole field of the ternary copper-tin-lead diagram, lead in amounts over 4 percent makes the alloys difficult to work. As we will see below, the Chinese came early to the use of leaded alloys. Some of the earlier finds from Gansu are alloys of lead and copper, with very little tin. Lead persists as an alloy constituent throughout the pre-Han period. One wonders if the exclusive use of casting by the early Chi-

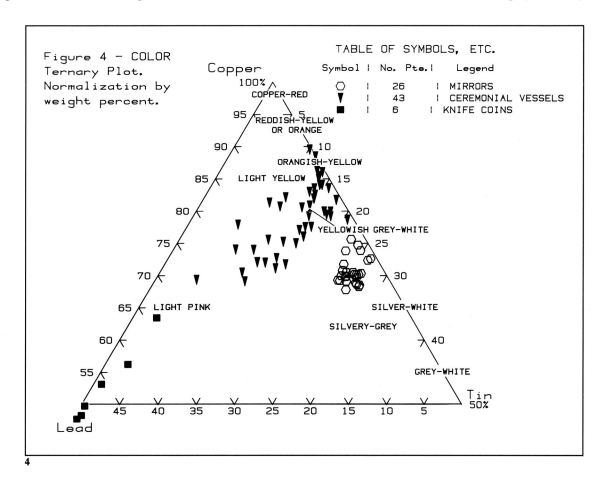

4

Figures

4. A ternary plot of the copper-tin-lead system, showing the colors in different compositional areas, with three groups of analyzed bronzes superimposed: ceremonial vessels are the descending triangles; mirrors are the open hexagons; *mingdao* knife coins are the filled squares.

nese metalworker could be caused not only by preferences or conservative workshop practice, but also by the fact that most of the alloys he dealt with simply *could not* be worked by hammering?

All of the alloys in the ternary field are castable, but some require particular attention to casting temperature. To produce metals on the scale that bronzes were produced in ancient China, copper would have had to be melted in refining or in casting of ingots for transport. Pure copper melts at 1083 degrees Celsius, so this temperature is, in a way, an absolute minimum which would have been reached for any metal production to take place.

Although the melting point of pure copper is higher than that of its alloys, modern practice requires that the bronzes be given some degree of superheat when casting, so that the metal will have time to flow into the mold before it solidifies. The amount of superheat required to cast a bronze of the size of the Si Mu Mou *fang ding* (about nineteen hundred pounds) would be rather high, especially if one considers that the modern techniques and machinery for handling large hot crucibles were not available. Table 1 shows melting points and recommended casting temperatures

for some of the tin bronze alloys. The degree of superheat used in normal casting practice can be seen by comparing the "melting point" with the "casting temperature." Note that the highly leaded bronzes require a high degree of superheat, and also that bronze, being an alloy, has a freezing or solidification range, rather than a freezing point. The beginning of freezing is shown by the "liquidus" temperature, and the end by the "solidus" temperature. In any case, the temperatures needed for successful casting did not strain the capabilities of the ancient Chinese, who were the world's most accomplished pyrotechnologists. The famous Anyang white pottery was fired at temperatures of 1200 degrees Celsius.[19] The highly-leaded alloys, which require a high degree of superheat, seem to come into use for coinage only after the large-scale casting of iron, at which time methods for running furnaces at higher temperatures would have become available.

It is clear from the data presented above and in Table 1 that more work remains to be done on the copper-tin-lead alloy system, its behavior and properties; nevertheless, we do understand enough about the general features of the system to make some sense out of

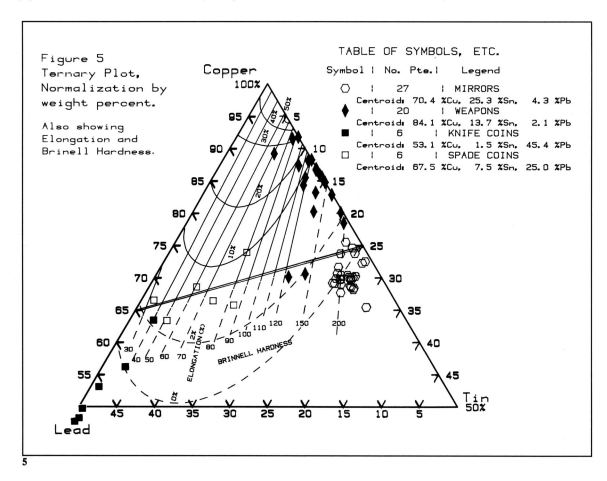

5

Figures

5. A ternary plot of the copper-tin-lead system with some of the same compositional groups of bronzes as fig. 4 superimposed. In addition, some weapons (filled diamonds) and a few late Zhou spade coins (open squares) have been added. The contours for elongation (in percent) and hardness (BHN value) have been drawn.

Table 1: Bronze Alloys—Melting Points and Recommended Casting Temperatures

Alloy Cu: Sn: Pb			Melting Point* Liquidus	Solidus	Casting Temperature* Thick Sections	Thin Sections	Alloy Designation
100:	0:	0	1083	1083	–	–	C80100
95:	5:	0	1040	appx. 960	–	–	95/5 R
93:	7:	0	1045	875	–	–	C90200
90:	10:	0	1000	832	980–1040	1040–1090	C90700 (205)
88:	10:	2	982	848	1066–1177	1177–1260	C92700 (206)
85:	15:	0	950	798	–	–	C91100
84:	8:	8	–	–	1010–1093	1093–1177	C93400 (311)
80:	20:	0	890	798	982–1038	1038–1093	C91300 (194)
80:	10:	0	928	762	1010–1177	1090–1232	C93700 (305)
80:	10:	10	(M.P. 960–965)		1010–1149	1093–1232	ASTM B30–51, alloy #3A
78:	7:	15	(M.P. 909–954)		1038–1149	1093–1232	ASTM B30–51, alloy #3D
75:	25:	0	795	760	–	–	75/25 R
71:	13:	16	950	–	995–1080	1080–1160	C94000 (296)
71:	26:	3	appx. 800	755	850– 950	900–1000	Chinese mirror alloy
70:	5:	25	(M.P. 899–909)		1010–1093	1093–1204	ASTM B30–51, alloy #3E

Notes:
*All temperatures in degrees Celsius.
Data from Gettens, 1969, p. 3 (after T.A. Rickard [alloys marked "R"]); Copper Development Association [alloys beginning with C]; Solymos [alloy designations in parentheses]; Romanoff, et. al. [alloy designations beginning with ASTM]; see also Hanson and Pell-Walpole, and Smithells.

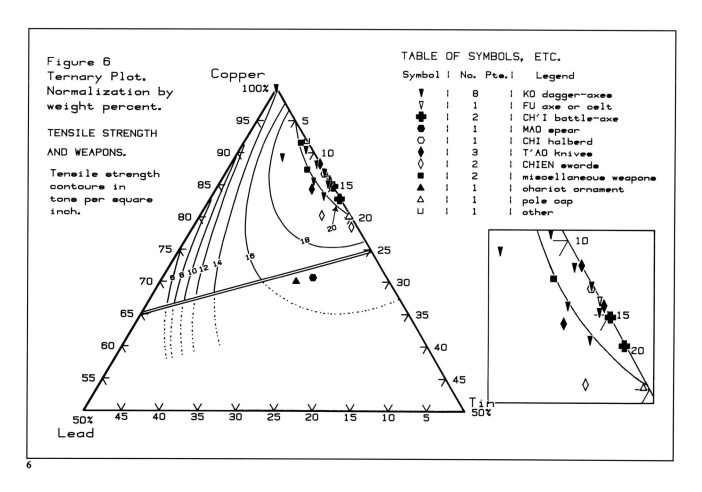

Figures

6. A ternary plot of the copper-tin-lead system showing compositions of weapons (from fig. 5), subdivided into weapon types, along with contours for tensile strength (tons per square inch). Note how the edged weapons tend to group in the area of highest tensile strength.

the development of bronze alloys in China.

The First Bronzes in China

In China, the early development of bronze alloys is still shrouded in mystery. Before the first piece-mold cast vessel from Erlitou (see next section), there are a few instances of earlier metalworking which give us tantalizing but fragmentary glimpses of possible origins for Chinese metalwork. Questions concerning beginnings are among the most controversial of any dealing with ancient Chinese metallurgy, and differing views have recently appeared in the archaeological literature.[20] Let us look briefly at the evidence to date, keeping in mind that new discoveries may well render what we are about to say obsolete by tomorrow.

One would like to start by citing the earliest metal artifact yet excavated in China; there are, however, a number of contenders for this title. Let's look at them in turn.

A fragment of bronze was excavated at the Neolithic Site of Banpo in Xian, Shaanxi Province. If this were actually to date from the Neolithic (c. 5000–4500 B.C.) it would easily be the earliest Chinese metal object. An Zhimin, however, cites the fact that it is made from copper-nickel alloy and dismisses it as an intrusive artifact, having nothing to do with the Yangshao culture.[21]

Possibly the earliest metal objects from China are two copper pendants dating from a Longshan culture level at Dachengshan, Tangshan, in Hebei Province. These pendants probably date to about 2000 B.C., and are made from quite pure copper, 99.33 and 99.97 percent respectively. The smaller of the two also contains 0.17 percent tin.[22] Remains of copper smelting have also been found in Longshan levels in Henan Province.

Another object from Longshan culture levels is a broken awl, now two broken pieces of brass rod, found at Sanlihe, Jiao Xian, Shandong Province, in 1974–75. The object has been analyzed by the Archaeometallurgy Group at the Beijing University of Iron and Steel Technology (BUIST), found to contain 23.2 percent zinc with traces of tin (0.36–2.15 percent), lead (1.77–4.26 percent) and iron (appx. 0.1 percent), along with sulfur and other impurities. An Zhimin also dismisses this piece as an intrusive, because of its high zinc content; the BUIST Group contends that the piece is genuinely of the Longshan Period and that it was smelted by primitive methods from an impure copper-lead-zinc ore. Deposits of this type of ore still exist at Qixia and Fushan in Shandong, less than 180 kilometers from Sanlihe. The BUIST Group has made experimental smelts of the ores and found that a brass can be obtained at 950–960 degrees Celsius (below the melting point of copper) in a reducing atmosphere. They also contend that this brass would only have been produced using primitive techniques. Once large-scale refining of copper—with higher temperatures and easy access of gases—had begun, the ancient founder would not have understood the need for a closed system running at a lower temperature to produce brass. The secret was

rediscovered by the Romans (and by the Indians), sometime around the first century.[23]

As the fourth contender for the earliest Chinese metal object, we have an early knife dating from Majiayao culture levels (c. 3000 B.C.) at a site in Linjia, Dongxiang, Gansu Province. It is made from a tin bronze (probably 6–10 percent tin, judging from the metallographic appearance). "The grains of the metal are aligned perpendicular to the edge, a structure which could be produced only by hammering."[24] The knife was accompanied by metalworking residues containing copper, malachite, and limonite; both the knife and the residues have been dated to 2750 B.C. by radiocarbon dating.

A large number of early copper-alloy objects have been found in Gansu Province.[25] Another knife, dated to the Machang Period (2200 B.C.) was also made from tin bronze. Twenty-five artifacts from Qijia culture levels in Gansu were mostly made of copper (sixteen objects), with three each of tin bronze, leaded copper, and leaded tin bronze. Fabrication techniques included cold-working by hammering, casting pure copper, and hot forging copper to make a fine awl 2 millimeters in diameter and less than 10 millimeters in length.

The complicated picture of various alloys and methods of working persists in the Huoshaogou culture levels (c. 2100–1600 B.C.) in Gansu; here a greater percentage of the metal artifacts (especially ornaments, studs, nose-rings, and earrings) were made from tin bronze. A mace or crosier head with four goats on the outside was made by casting the mace head onto the goats; this is a very early example of casting-on. Cold-working and hot forging also appear among this material, as do gold and silver nose-rings and earrings.

One of the most striking features of all of the material cited above is the total lack of vessels made of metal. This material is all weapons, tools, or items for personal adornment (including mirrors, in the case of the Gansu finds). There is something about all of these finds, and especially those from Gansu, that reminds us of the hoards and grave goods found on the steppes of central Asia. In fact, some of the later Gansu material has a definite stylistic affinity to central Asian decorative bosses and belt plaques. The shapes of the early knives, especially that from the Majiayao Culture (3000 B.C.), are very close to the Shang knives found at Anyang which show Siberian influence, and the Gansu macehead is closely paralleled by stone maceheads from South Russia and the Caucasus, suggesting a central Asian affinity.[26]

Taken all together, it is rather hard to make sense of these almost random finds of early metals in China as yet. For some of them, the associations and dating are unclear. There is a wide variation in alloy constituents, even including the substantial zinc in the Longshan awl. While no vessels made of metal have been found in Longshan cultural contexts, one should remember that some of the pottery vessels look as if they could be derived from metallic (sheet) prototypes.[27] Pottery vessels that may be derived from sheet-metal prototypes also appear in Gansu in the Qijia Culture. Our inclination at this stage would be to say that these early metal objects, especially those from Gansu, show the progress of the introduction of metal into China from the West. It comes in slowly, with poor control of alloys, and is used primarily for its decorative effect or as small tools. At these early stages, there is nothing (except, possibly, the use of leaded bronze at such an early time) that strikes us as indigenously Chinese in these objects. In fact, the occurrence of personal jewelry in this Gansu material seems not to connect at all with later Chinese metalwork, where jewelry simply does not occur (until the rise of sumptuary art in the Eastern Zhou).[28] Cold-worked and hot forged bronze also seems strange. The whole complexion of these finds suggests small-scale metalworking in the context of nomadic tribes (or local villages), and not the larger-scale, state-supported metalworking industry of the Shang Dynasty, making ceremonial vessels for the nobles and weapons for their armies.

The First Bronze Vessels in China

The earliest bronzes yet found in the classical Chinese bronze casting tradition are the four *jue* from Erlitou, one of which was exhibited in the recent Chinese Bronze Exhibition.[29] At the present time we have no data as to the alloy composition of this vessel. Another of the *jue* from Erlitou was reported to be composed of 92 percent copper and 7 percent tin.[30] This analysis was done by electron probe. The composition is very close to that of modern "statuary bronze," and would give a nice, tough bronze with reddish-yellow color. The tin is lower than the normal percentage found in later Shang vessels, and the absence of lead is very interesting. Yet another *jue* from Erlitou was found to contain 91.9 percent copper, 2.6 percent tin, and 2.34 percent lead. This analysis was done by chemical techniques (I believe, wet chemical techniques) at the Chemical Laboratory of the Institute of Archaeology, Beijing.[31] It should be noted that an adze from Erlitou (No. IIIT21F2) was analyzed by both methods: electron probe gave 98 percent copper, 1 percent tin; chemical analysis yielded 91.7 percent copper, 7 percent tin, 1.23 percent lead. The electron probe analysis could have been affected by segregation in the metal, compounded with inherently low detection limits. Analytical problems aside, these are all fairly high-copper bronzes; the adze should have been quite suitable for use in carpentry work.

The vessels from Panlongcheng, of which a selection is illustrated in *The Great Bronze Age of China Catalogue*,[32] have been analyzed in part for their alloy composition. One of those analyzed is the *li ho* #5.[33] It contains 6 percent tin and 22 percent lead; the patina is called grey-green, although we do not remember any peculiar coloration to the patina from seeing the vessel. A vessel with this composition would have been rather brittle, and the *jia* (Li M1:12) with 24.45 percent lead even more so. Two similar *jia* from the excavation were broken; this suggests both that the

brittleness of this high-lead composition has a real consequence in terms of the archaeological evidence, and that care must be taken in selecting objects to be analyzed; if broken pieces are chosen exclusively, one may overestimate the very elements that make these particular bronzes brittle, tin and lead.

Nevertheless, the analyses show the same picture as that revealed in some analyses done in the early 1960s by Ursula Martius Franklin which I have added to Table 2.[34] These bronzes, although not from archaeological excavations, seem to be of early types similar to those from Panlongcheng. Both sets of analyses show highly variable lead contents. One wonders if the lead could have come in from the use of a mixed copper-lead ore, which was not refined in the correct manner to separate the lead from the copper? Such ores do exist in north China, and in fact Sung mentions them in the *Tiangong Kaiwu*.[35] If the furnace had not been allowed to settle and the mixed refined copper and lead from the smelter had been used for casting, perhaps one would get lead results as variable as these. We hope that the use of lead isotope ratios to define lead sources (or at least to tell us if the lead in all these vessels came from the same place) may be of some help in unraveling the puzzle.

With the moving of the center of Shang civilization to Anyang, bronze metallurgy took a big step forward in sophistication, both in terms of design (to which we will return later) and in terms of alloy control. The first analyses of properly attested Shang bronzes, made during the 1930s, did not show differences in alloys between types of objects; on the other hand, very few bronzes were analyzed, and some of them were much corroded. Lead only shows as a trace element in one of the six bronzes analyzed, although the analytical total for this object was only about 40 percent, and of this about 6 percent is made up of Fe and SiO_2. The metallographic structures show possible lead above 3 percent only in the case of a bronze arrowhead, and here again the structure is so corroded that the possible lead globules have been replaced by what is probably cuprite.[36]

Liang and Zhang (Chang), in their pioneering analyses of bronzes including some from the Anyang site, noted that no zinc was present in the Shang bronzes, and that lead generally occurred in quantities less than 3 percent. In the later bronzes they analyzed, zinc was generally absent, but lead tended to increase with the passage of time.[37] While this picture seemed to be confirmed by later analyses of properly attested material,[38] analyses of material from museum collections in the West did turn up some bronze vessels thought to date from the Shang Dynasty with higher lead contents, although still mostly without zinc.[39]

Recently some very interesting new data on bronzes excavated from the Tomb of Fu Hao at Anyang has become available, data which suggest that the picture may not be as simple as we had thought.[40] These bronzes contain small but detectable amounts of zinc, ranging from 0.16 percent to 0.47 percent. The excavators say that there seem to be two separate groups of vessels, a low-lead group and a high-lead

Table 2: Analyses of Pre-Anyang Chinese Ceremonial Vessels

Object Analyzed and Sample	Copper	Tin	Lead	Total	Patination	Item No.
Erlitou						
jue						*Kaogu*, 1975,
Stratum 3	92.	7.	0.	99.	Not avail.	no. 5, pl. 9:2.
jue	91.9	2.6	2.34	96.8		An Zhimin
Panlongcheng						
jia						
leg	81.82	8.41	6.78	97.0	Blue-green	Li M2:19
ding						
leg	88.68	5.54	1.38	95.6	Blue-green	Li M2:55
jia						
leg	71.59	3.92	24.45	99.96	Grey-green	Li M1:12
lei						
foot	70.76	6.16	21.76	98.68	Grey-green	Li M1:8
Royal Ontario Museum						
jue						
body	–	5	8		–	Stephen, fig. 1.
repair		5	6		–	same
jue						
body (?)	–	2–3	5–6	(Zn 0.1–0.2)	–	Stephen, fig. 2.
jue						
body (?)	–	12	1–2		–	Stephen, fig. 3.
jia						
body	–	7–8	26–28		–	Stephen, fig. 4.
repair	–	5	5		–	same
jia						
body (?)	–	8	20–22		–	Stephen, fig. 5.
jia						
body	–	3–4	18		–	Stephen, fig. 6.
repair	–	5–6	16		–	same
li						
body	–	8	15		–	Stephen, fig. 7.
repair	–	8	15		–	same
li						
body	–	10	12		–	Stephen, fig. 8.
repair	–	<2	10–12	(trace of zinc)	–	same

Notes:
Data from An Zhimin; Bagley, p. 176; analyses originally published in *Kaogu*, 1975, no. 5, p. 304 and *Wenwu*, 1976, no. 2, p. 37; Stephen, pp. 62–67.

group. Forty-seven vessels have an average composition of 80.48 percent Cu, 16.14 percent Sn, and 0.89 percent Pb, while eighteen have an average composition of 79.02 percent Cu, 15.39 percent Sn, and 4.09 percent Pb—rather more than the 3 percent maximum referred to above. Large ritual vessels have low tin contents, possibly from deliberate saving of tin. Pairs of vessels have similar tin contents, and the tin contents of weapons differ from those of vessels. Only a summary of results was published in the excavation report; a fuller discussion was scheduled to appear in 1982.[41]

A ternary plot of the analyses mentioned above appears in Figure 7. The close grouping of the analyses from the Fu Hao Tomb material is easily seen; the Panlongcheng bronzes and the early bronzes in the collection at the Royal Ontario Museum can be seen to form a much more varied (perhaps uncontrolled) group of compositions.

The varied picture of Chinese alloying after Shang is too complicated to treat satisfactorily in this paper. Data is becoming available so that one can carefully follow the trends.[42] We should, however, look briefly at the question of alloying practice in China in general, as well as the famous *Zhou Li* "Six Formulas" in particular.[43]

In the *Kaogongqi* section of the *Zhou Li* (The Rites of Chou), the formulas for various types of bronzes are recorded in terms of proportions. If we take all of the vessels and bells plotted in Figure 8, we can see that for those without much lead, the average tin content falls at about 15 percent, close to the 14.3 percent specified in the *Zhou Li*. If lead is added as a diluent to an 85–15 (copper-tin) bronze, we would generate a series of compositions on a line intersecting the right-hand axis at 85–15, and running downwards to the left, through the points 76.5–13.5–10, 68–12–20, and 59.5–10.5–30, with lead additions of 10 percent, 20 percent, and 30 percent, respectively. This falls close to the center of the distribution in Figure 8. Due to the usual problems in measuring the constituents of the alloy and in losses during heating, etc., the copper-tin ratio is not exactly 85–15 (or 84.7–14.3), but forms a distribution around the mean.

Let us try to simulate the distribution we see with a mathematical model. If we suppose that the founder was aiming for about 15 percent tin in the bronze, and that he would then add lead as a diluent, we get the model shown in Figure 9, with its distribution compared to that of the actual bronze vessels; there is very little difference between the mathematical model and the actual distribution. For this reason, I think that we are justified in postulating the hypothesis that the 85–15 bronze composition was an aim point and the foundryman would add some lead to this, at times as much as he could possibly add. I have no figures on the price of lead and tin in ancient China, but I would guess that if lead was a by-product of copper smelting, it would be somewhat cheaper, and the reasons for lead additions would be economic. For a further instance of control of lead, weapons—which require higher tensile strength than vessels—are, for the most part, nearly lead free (see Figure 6).

We have seen above that the mirrors center tightly in one area on the ternary diagram, i.e., they have a consistent composition, appx. 71 percent Cu, 26 percent Sn, 3 percent Pb. The question of interpreting the *Zhou Li* formulas has long been debated, and one of the most difficult problems in interpretation is that the *Zhou Li* formula for mirrors is 50 percent copper and 50 percent tin. Rather than look at the discrepancy between the *Zhou Li* formula and the actual mirror analyses, perhaps we should assume that the ancient Chinese methods of formulation and foundry practice would cause the tin content to drop during the manufacture of bronzes, and that a starting composition of 50 percent Cu–50 percent Sn would yield a finished mirror with about 73 percent Cu–27 percent Sn (71–26–3 minus the lead, which we will assume to be an extra addition).

Thus, we have the two end points of the continuum represented by the *Zhou Li* formulas. The lower end point (vessels and bells) can be taken to represent the actual composition found in the objects. The upper end point (mirrors) is, for some presently unknown reason, offset from the actual composition by a considerable extent. If we assume that the formulas between the two end points are proportionally affected by the same unknown mechanism as the mirrors, we can simply draw a straight line between the two end points and use it to adjust the *Zhou Li* formula percentages to what the actual compositions should be.

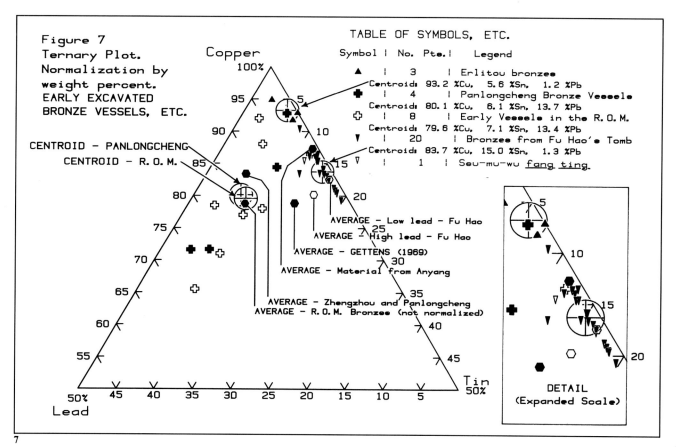

Figures

7. A ternary plot of compositions of early excavated bronze vessels, along with some vessels without provenance. The averages for various groups are also indicated, along with centroids of the distributions.

This has been done in Figure 10, and the results are shown in Table 3. The resulting proportions look much more reasonable than any we have yet seen for the various types of bronzes defined in the *Zhou Li,* even though they do not agree exactly with the proportions we have at present from analyses of groups of actual objects. We must also always remember that lead is left out of the *Zhou Li* formulas, and should probably be considered as a separate addition to the bronze formulation, both for reasons from the examination of the distribution above and for reasons of color.

In the future, we expect to see many interesting analytical results from newly excavated material in the People's Republic of China which will make it possible to flesh out this history of bronze alloys with more detail. One thing, however, emerges clearly; the ancient Chinese foundryman had a real mastery of his material, and could make and control bronze alloys to produce objects which exploited the full range of possibilities of cast bronze.

Early Chinese Casting

In China, casting in ceramic piece molds (or occasionally in stone molds) was the exclusive method of bronze fabrication from the beginning down to the mid-to-late Zhou Period, when lost-wax casting begins in the Chinese area. Then, in the Han Dynasty, we begin to see hammered bronze come in, to be supplemented by spinning and other techniques in the later periods. As an aside, gold was probably fabricated by other techniques [hammering, swaging, granulation],[44] but it was also used for exquisite castings such as the Eumofourpolos Dagger Handle[45] and the gold-handled and bronze-bladed dagger in the Museum of Chinese History, Taipei.[46]

In many other cultures, metalworking begins with sheet metal, usually in the form of native copper or gold or electrum.[47] Native copper, gold, or electrum can either be found in a sheet-like habit, or the material can be beaten into a sheet. On the other hand, if one starts with smelted metal, to work it in the sheet form the metal sheet must first be made, which involves casting a billet or ingot that can be hammered flat. In the simplest type of casting one simply digs out a concave depression in the ground and pours the metal into it; a round, concave depression will yield a bun-shaped or plano-convex metal ingot like those found from the Late Bronze Age in Europe.[48]

Working sheet has certain limitations, which, while

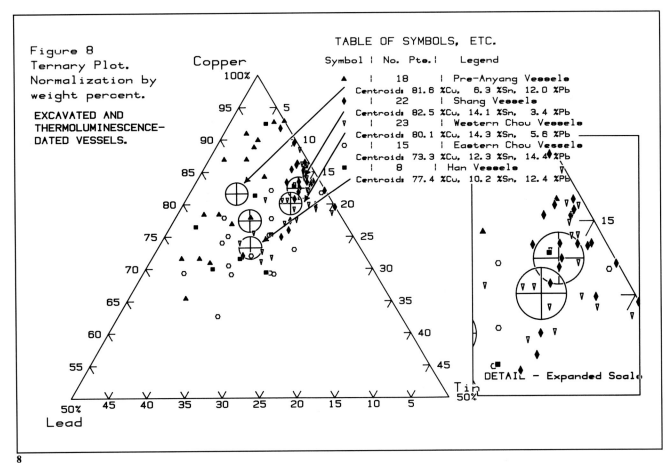

Figures

8. A ternary plot showing all of the reliable analyses we have for Chinese bronze ceremonial vessels and bells. The vessels are either from archaeological excavations or have passed a thermoluminescence test for authenticity. The objects have been grouped by date, and a centroid for each group is shown.

they can be overcome by a competent metalsmith, must be taken into account. The sheet can be bent, hammered up (or down; i.e., raised or sunk) into a round shape; formed by repoussé, joined by riveting, soldering, or lapping; pierced, deformed, etc.[49] The metal can be changed in thickness from one place on the sheet to another.[50] If the initial sheet is thick enough, metal can be removed to show relief, or added in the form of inlay.[51] Nevertheless, to be worked as sheet, the metal must be somewhat malleable and ductile. The process of annealing, i.e., softening the metal by heating to a temperature below its melting

point, must also be known and used to go very far in sheet-working.[52] In fact, a whole series of processes had to be in the "tool kit" of the ancient smith so that he could make the metal do what he wanted; some of these processes required a very specific series of steps, including intermediate anneals, to attain the final product. As suggested above, some of the bronze compositions simply cannot be handled as sheet.

In casting, however, the metalworker treats metal not as a deformable plane, but as a liquid. It is poured into a suitable container, a refractory void of the correct dimensions, configuration, surface finish,

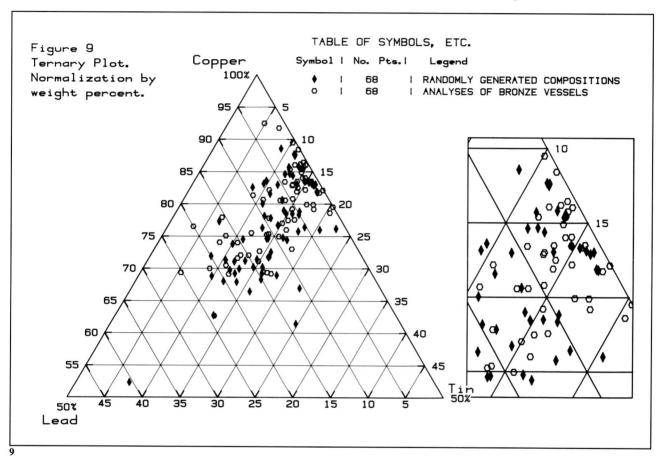

Figure 9
Ternary Plot.
Normalization by weight percent.

9

Figures

9. A ternary plot of the distribution from fig. 8 compared with a distribution derived from a mathematical model. In the model, the mean of the copper contents is set at 85 percent, and the mean of the tin contents at 15 percent. The tin contents were normally distributed around the mean with a standard deviation of 3 percent. By using computer-generated random numbers, a tin content was derived for each of the sixty-eight points. Lead contents were normally distributed with a mean of 3 percent and a standard deviation of 10 percent. This gave a normal distribution truncated at 0 percent lead. Computer-generated random numbers were again used to calculate a lead content for each point, and the final composition derived from the formulas: $Cu_2 = Cu_1 (100-Pb)$ and $Sn_2 = Sn_1 (100-Pb)$, where Pb is the derived lead content, Cu_1 and Sn_1 are the derived copper and tin contents, and Cu_2 and Sn_2 are the final copper and tin contents. Note that $Pb + Cu_2 + Sn_2 = 100$ percent. The actual distribution and the derived distribution are very similar, as can be confirmed by counting the number of points in each triangular (5 percent) cell on the diagram. A detail of the cells in the area of 10–20 percent tin and 0–10 percent lead can be seen on the lower right.

etc., and then allowed to harden (cool, solidify). The actual casting, while quite thrilling, is one of the simplest steps in the process; much more time is spent in making of the refractory void, and in cleaning up and finishing the casting after the mold is removed.

Many difficulties must be overcome in the casting process, such as the absorption of gases in the hot metal, shrinkage, hot tearing, cold shuts, insufficient penetration of the metal into the mold cavity, supporting the mold and core (chapletting), etc. The experienced craftsman learns what to do to avoid the problems and to make the metal do just what he wants it to, so that he can obtain a satisfactory casting. Most of the difficulties can be solved by trial and error, which can lead to a very conservative approach. To put it another way, if the craftsman's customary series of steps usually yields a satisfactory casting, he will be very reluctant to change his method. Generally he will have to be convinced by demonstration that another method will yield superior results or simplify his work. One wonders if the ancient Chinese foundryman's absolute technical mastery of casting in ceramic piece molds would not have been the greatest barrier to the introduction of the lost-wax process? Perhaps the lost-wax method was available

or even known but simply not of any interest to him, as he could obtain the results he wanted with his existing methods.

It seems from the evidence now available that the lost-wax process was known in China at about 500 B.C.[53] One of the best examples of a piece-mold casting foundry—the foundry complex at Houma—dates from slightly after this period, and no evidence of lost-wax casting is seen among the thousands and thousands of piece-mold fragments found here.[54] The vessels which may have been produced in Houma are exquisitely detailed and finished; if one could make vessels this good by piece-mold methods, one would probably feel there was no reason to switch to any other technique.[55]

We should also point out that the Chinese method, applied as we think it was done, was a direct method; instead of making the detail in the mold from a wax or a model, the ancient Chinese foundryman worked directly in the mold surface. Even in the late Zhou, when pattern-stamps were used, the craftsman still retouched the mold surface before casting. In my view, direct working in the mold, coupled with the very skillful abrasive finishing technique, are what give the ancient Chinese bronzes their exquisite surfaces, with

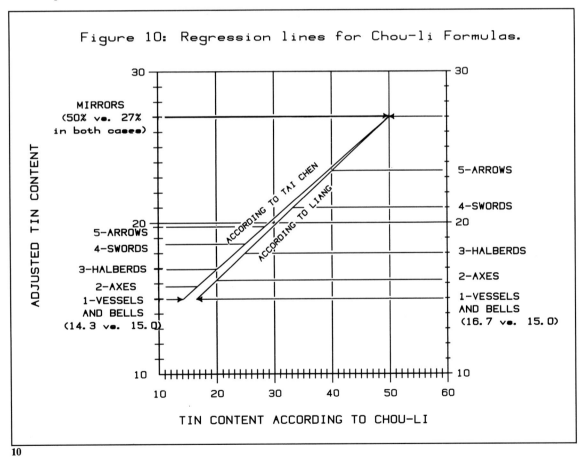

10

Figures

10. Regression lines to be used for prorating the *zhouli* "Six Formulas." Two methods for obtaining percentages from the original formulas have been incorporated here, that of Daizhen and that of Liang (see Barnard, 1961, p. 7 ff.). The resulting percentages for each of the formulas can be seen on the left and right axes respectively. See also Table 3.

Table 3: Various Interpretations of the Zhouli Formulas

	1 Vessels and Bells	2 Axes	3 Halberds and Spears	4 Swords and Knives	5 Pen-knives and Arrows	6 Mirrors
			Formula number and types of objects			
According to Liang*						
Sn (%)	16.66	20.00	25.00	33.33	40.00	50.00
Cu:Sn Ratio	5:1	4:1	3:1	2:1	3:2	1:1
Adjusted** Sn	15.00	16.20	18.00	21.00	23.40	27.00
Hardness (BHN)†	150	160	180	210	240(?)	300(?)
Elongation	7%	5.6%	5%	2%	1%	0%
Tensile strength (tons/in.²)	21	20	20	20	19	17
According to Daizhen*						
Sn (%)	14.29	16.67	20.00	25.00	28.57	50.00
Cu:Sn Ratio	6:1	5:1	4:1	3:1	5:2	1:1
Adjusted†† Sn	15.00	15.80	16.92	18.60	19.80	27.00
Hardness (BHN)†	150	160	170	185	200	300(?)
Elongation	7%	6.2%	5.1%	4.5%	2.5%	0%
Tensile strength (tons/in.²)	21	21	20	20	20	17
Actual values:						
Chase and Ziebold§	13.61	16.22	12.56	13.52	12.96	26.03
Barnard§§	13.6	13.6	19.5	16.3	16.1	23.2
Objects from Ebla§§§	10	10	13.5 (lances)	10.5–12.7 (daggers)	14–20 (razors)	16.6 (green-eyes?)

Notes:
* See Barnard, 1961, p. 6.
** See fig. 10; equation of line: Adjusted % Sn = 0.36004 (Formula % Sn) + 8.9982
† From ternary graphs; see Chase and Ziebold, figs. 6, 7, 8.
†† See fig. 10; equation of line: Adjusted % Sn = 0.33599 (Formula % Sn) + 10.2003
§ See Chase and Ziebold, Table 3; lead was ignored, and the Cu+Sn values normalized to 100%.
§§ See Barnard, 1961, Table 12; lead was ignored, and the Cu+Sn values normalized to 100%.
§§§ Pettinato, p. 173.

magnificently sharp decor.

Much has been written about ancient Chinese piece-mold casting, and how it was done.[56] Let us attempt to reconstruct the procedure for casting a *fang ding* like the Freer Gallery of Art's member of the Cuozhe *fang ding* set and see how it might have been done. Then we can briefly discuss the history of casting in China, mention casting problems and the relationship of the ancient Chinese methods to modern methods, and pose a few unanswered questions.

The vessel in question is shown in Figure 11. It is a square, four-legged *ding* of moderate size, and one of a set of four; two are owned by the Palace Museum in Taipei, and one is in the collection of the Hermitage Foundation in Norfolk, Virginia.[57] The vessel has a rather normal composition, 77.7 percent Cu, 14.9 percent Sn, and 5.5 percent Pb, a composition that would cast well and would be easy to finish. It weighs 3.77 kilograms (8 pounds, 5 ounces), and stands 26.7 centimeters (10½ inches) high.

The manufacture of this vessel probably started with a model, possibly made from the local earth. There might have been some clay added to the model to give it cohesion, and it might have been fired, although few models or model fragments survive.[58] The model would have been solid, and might have had the legs modeled in high relief against a block which stood in the place of the inter-leg core piece. The only way we can conceive of making the intaglio lines on the single-headed and double-bodied snakes is that they would have been sunken lines in a positive model. The intaglio lines on the flanges, handles, and the *taotie* masks on the legs may have been made the same way. The rest of the decoration, however, differs greatly among the four vessels of this set (as does the inscription rendering), and we think that the decoration must have been incised into the mold; this includes especially the *leiwen* patterns which form the background for the snakes, the circular protrusions on the *leiwen* ground, and the nipples or "hobnails" in the lower register.

The question of mold material is not a trivial one, but we cannot take it up in detail here. Suffice it to say that we think that the Chinese in the central area used the local earthy material, perhaps more or less levigated to remove coarse particles and to increase

11

Figures

11. A *fang ding* from the collection of the Freer Gallery of Art, Smithsonian Institution (FGA #50.7). The vessel stands 26.7 cm. (10½
in.) high and weighs 3.77 kilograms (8 pounds, 5 ounces). Chaplets
can be seen in the center of the undecorated areas on the side and
end.

the clay content and heighten the plasticity in some cases. Most of the mold fragments we have seen have at least two layers, a finer layer inside and a coarser layer outside.[59] We think that the finer clay must have been pressed into the surface detail of the model and allowed to harden, then the coarser layer applied to the outside; after drying, the whole outer mold, with sectional joins at the corners of the vessel, would have been taken apart and removed from the model.

At this time, while it was in a leather-hard state, the inside of the mold would have received its decoration. The craftsman must have spent many hours in careful tooling with fine points (perhaps bone needles and gouges). After tooling was complete, the mold would be reassembled and fired, perhaps with a charcoal fire inside it, until it became a hard ceramic.

Next, the interior core and the inter-leg core piece would have to be made. It is possible that the model might have served as the basis for one of the core pieces. Let us assume that the model was used for the interior core of the vessel. It would then have been scraped away to make the casting space for the metal to run in. This idea of an expendable model may show us the reason why the four vessels in this set differ in size, shape, and decoration. Four separate models would have had to be made, and then scraped down. After the model had been scraped down to make the casting space and had been cut off at the top of the legs to delineate the upper surface of the vessel bottom, the model and the mold could be reassembled and earthy material packed in to form the inter-leg core piece. The molds would again be disassembled, and the inter-leg core piece would be dressed in the area of the legs, and possibly scraped a little more where it would form the outside of the vessel bottom. The lines often seen in vessel bottoms (and seen in all four of this set) would have been incised at this time.

Formation of the inscription is somewhat of a puzzle. The inscription is on the inside of one of the side walls of the vessel. It would have been in relief on the interior core piece. The relief lines might conceivably have been made by careful removal of the core material, especially if a thin, even layer had been left in the inscription area, which could have then been cut away carefully to an even depth surrounding the reversed characters. It seems more likely that the inscription was taken as an impression from a positively incised inscription, and that the block would have been inserted into a recess carefully cut for it in the interior core. The edge of the inscription block would have been luted with core material, and any discontinuity smoothed over. It would be nice to have a little more proof of inscription production methods from surviving foundry waste than we have at present.

The interior core and inter-leg core piece would probably have been lightly baked to dry them, but not fired as strongly as the mold. These pieces do not need as much strength as the mold; they do not have as fine detail; and further, the major firing shrinkage has already taken place in the mold before the interior pieces were scraped down to make the casting

space. Exact register between the core and mold had to be maintained to cast such thin bronzes, and we think that the register was established by firing the mold first, then making and scraping the core pieces, and then assembling them without further heavy firing.

After the core pieces were lightly baked, chaplets would have been applied, using a clay slip. The chaplets could have been made from bronze scrap from earlier miscast vessels; due to the hot-shortness of this bronze composition, it could have been broken up into nice little squarish pieces of the correct thickness when hot. The main chaplets in the sides and the bottom would be easy to place in undecorated areas. The only place where chaplet positioning would be difficult is in the area of the inscription; here the chaplet was set carefully between two characters at the center of the inscription, which made it fall near the lower edge of the undecorated area on the outside of the *ding* (see Figure 12).

The sequence of assembly of the mold would probably have been as follows; the interior core, with the lower ledge containing the backs of the handles, the upper portion of the lip, and the core-extensions for the insides of the handles, would have been placed upside-down. Small chaplets were applied with slip to the vertical surfaces, using special care in placing the chaplet in the inscription. Larger chaplets (to prevent the core from floating upward with hydrostatic pressure) were applied to the horizontal surface. A mold dressing of finely powdered charcoal or lampblack was probably applied. (Remains of a thin, black layer can be seen under the remnant core inside the foot of some bronzes, although this has not, to our knowledge, been analyzed.)

Then the mold pieces would have been set lightly in place around the core; mortise-and-tenon joints on the mating surfaces would have assured correct register. The inter-leg core piece would have been carefully slid in to sit on the top of the large chaplets in the area which would become the bottom of the vessel. During the whole procedure, great care and watchfulness would be exercised by the foundryman to make sure that everything was going together right. After the mold assembly was complete, it was then probably bound with ropes or buried (or both) to hold it together.

During the mold assembly, the metal was probably being heated. Our knowledge of how the metal might have been heated and poured is well summarized by Barnard and Sato.[60] Let us simply say that the molten metal was introduced into the mold through one of the open leg holes and then allowed to solidify. After a fairly short time (possibly an hour or less in the case of such a small bronze), the mold would be broken off, and the foundryman would see his handiwork. In the case of this vessel, one leg did not fill out, and he saw a three-legged vessel. The missing leg was then cast on separately, around a core.[61]

The earliest vessels in China (those from Erlitou see above) were cast in a similar way, although it is still unclear whether chaplets were used. One of the *jue* from Erlitou that the author examined in the Museum of the Institute of Archaeology, Beijing, in 1981, had visible mold flash running around the upper flat portion of the base and down the outer edges of the legs. This would suggest that the mold was set up with a solid inter-leg core piece which touched the outer mold at the outside of the legs and at the bottom of the vessel itself. This *jue* is undecorated.

As vessels became more decorated, new methods of making decoration evolve. The evolution of decoration is well-known by Barnard and Sato,[62] and the stylistic evolution has been defined by Loehr.[63] The earliest decoration on bronzes is very simple, just bosses or large incised lozenges.[64] Then monster masks occur, in a thin thread relief, which later thickens to well-defined, swelling areas. Circular relief elements appear which look as if they were cut into the mold with a bamboo tube. Next, larger relief fields with intaglio lines appear. This stage is the one where it is almost impossible to conceive of manufacture without starting from a model with positive decoration, and the play of areas of relief with intaglio lines against fine areas of *leiwen,* etc., continues through the Late Shang and into the Zhou.

Later, in Middle and Late Zhou, bronze molds begin to be produced by pattern-stamping, and other techniques begin to come in, including lost-wax as mentioned above. Multiple-mold casting, and permanent-mold casting (in iron molds produced from iron mother molds) are in full swing in the Former Han Dynasty.[65]

The salient features of the casting description above have been combined from many sources. Descriptions of modern Japanese casting practice have been especially helpful. These include a movie made some years ago on casting by the *morokome* process,[66] another movie on the *sogata* process for casting iron teakettles,[67] and a thesis by Jim Stewart on modern Japanese casting by the *komegata* process.[68] In all three processes, a template is used to define the shape of the object to be cast. The *morokome* and *sogata* processes employ flasks, made either of ceramic or stone, to contain the mold (Figure 13). The inside of the flask is faced with the mold material, using a template (Figure 14). The mold is then decorated by means of stamps or tooling (Figure 15). The mold material in the flask is then fired to incandescence with charcoal (Figure 16). After it has cooled, the interior is filled with the core material (Figure 17). The mold is disassembled and removed, leaving the core material as a representation of what the finished object will look like. The core is then filed down to produce the casting space (Figure 18), and things proceed as outlined above (Figure 19). In the *sogata* process, iron chaplets are used exactly as bronze ones were used in ancient China. We should also point out that in modern Japanese bell casting, inscriptions and some decorations are made as separate blocks which are then luted into the mold.

None of the three Japanese processes requires a model, and in fact, the question of how and when models were employed in ancient Chinese casting is

12

13

14

116

15

16

17

18

Figures

12. A radiograph of the inscribed sidewall in the *fang ding* shown in fig. 11. A triangular chaplet can be seen in the center of the inscription area, between two characters. This chaplet shows dark on the radiograph, and can also be seen on the outside of the bronze, just above the lower border of the undecorated area.

13. Three stone flasks for the casting of a square *hibachi* (similar to a *fang ding*) laid on the foundry floor of the Enjo Foundry, Matsue, Japan, 1964. The flask for the bottom of the vessel is at left; the decorated central band of the vessel will be cast in the central flask, and the handles and rim in the flask at right. In the front is a flask for casting the base of a round, three-legged vessel. Photograph by Robert Debold, 1964.

14. A template being used to apply an even layer of fine clay mold material to the inside of the central flask from fig. 13. The template guide on one side can be seen as the square form by the founder's left hand. He is holding the template. Enjo Foundry, photograph by Robert Debold, 1964.

15. Stamping the design into the still-plastic mold material, using a brass stamp and a small hammer. Most of the design has already been stamped in. Enjo Foundry, photograph by Edward Yates, 1964.

16. Beginning the firing of the outer molds for the square *hibachi* at the Enjo Foundry. A bundle of rice straw is used to start the charcoal which is packed into the flasks next to the mold material. Photograph by Robert Debold, 1964.

17. After the outer molds have been fired and cooled, they are packed with core material, incorporating iron pieces for reinforcement. When the core material has dried, the outer molds will be disassembled and the core removed. Enjo Foundry, photograph by Edward Yates, 1964.

18. After removal from the mold, the core material is an exact reproduction of what the vessel will look like. The core is then filed down methodically to establish the casting space. The tube in the worker's left hand is used to blow away the dust. Enjo Foundry, photograph by Robert Debold, 1964.

still an active issue (see the paper by Meyers and Holmes in this volume). One of the hardest questions to answer is how the intaglio lines so often seen in Late Shang bronzes could be formed without starting from a model. It is possible that the mold material could have been cut away, leaving the lines in relief, which would then form an intaglio line in the final bronze. In fact, one of the Anyang mold pieces from the Academia Sinica (Figure 20), seems to show this sort of construction. We should point out that it is clearly evident from the surfaces of the bronzes that they received extensive finishing after casting. This finishing has removed the evidence of exactly what the mold surface was like, although some vessels, such as the lead *jue* in the Freer Gallery of Art Study Collection, did not receive any finishing and have preserved the evidence of the mold surface. A detail of the surface of the *jue* reveals that "the design was first outlined in the mold with a sharp tool, then the surplus material between the lines was removed."[69] Cutting in the mold is also clearly shown in the case

of *leiwen* in the Anyang mold fragment from the Academia Sinica (Figures 21 and 22).

We wish that we could review in more detail here the evidence for casting methods and the ways that the ancient Chinese solved the problems inherent in casting bronze. The questions of whether the bronzes were cast into hot or cold molds, casting positions for the various types of bronzes, segregation of lead in the melt, problems of turbulent flow and absorbed gases in the metal, the registration between the various pieces of the mold assembly, etc., should all be considered. A careful chronology of casting methods based on actual examples should also be compiled, but the time may be premature for such an effort. All of these would extend this paper far beyond a "short history."

From the evidence recounted above, however, and especially the Gansu and Erlitou material, it seems to us that the best hypothesis at present is that metallurgy was introduced into China from the West at about the beginning of the second millennium B.C. Soon af-

19

20

Figures

19. The reassembly of the core and molds just prior to casting. Both surfaces have been coated with lampblack. The founder is blowing dust off the mold surface prior to setting the second half of the central flask into position. Enjo Foundry, photograph by Robert Debold, 1964.

20. A mold fragment from Anyang, now in the collection of the Institute of History and Philology, Academia Sinica, Nankang, Taipei, showing scrape marks around what will be a wide intaglio line in the final bronze. The mold also has a fine *leiwen* pattern at the top. The fragment is a little over 5 cm. wide. Photographed by the author, 1980, reproduced by courtesy of the Academia Sinica.

21. A side view of the mold fragment shown in fig. 20. The sectioned bubbles in the side walls of the *leiwen* pattern are clearly visible. These indicate that the *leiwen* were cut into already-solidified mold material. Photograph by the author, 1980, reproduced by courtesy of the Academia Sinica.

ter its introduction, bronze casting in ceramic piece molds began, a method with a definite affinity to ceramic production using molds, which had been going on for a long time in the Chinese sphere.[70] We see the early stages of bronze vessel production at Erlitou. Once bronze production had begun, the development was independent of outside influences—through the bronzes of Zhengzhou to those of Anyang, then with the elaboration of early Chou, the pattern-stamping techniques of the Spring and Autumn Period, and the sumptuary inlay and gilding techniques of late Zhou, along with the development and large-scale production of iron. It seems, in fact, that the influences driving metal production and innovation in China can be more easily explained by the development and needs of the state; but the social development of metallurgy in China is another topic that needs more space than we can give it here. Our working hypothesis for the moment is the introduction of metallurgy from outside, followed by independent development.

The history of casting and alloys in China will be put on an increasingly more secure footing with new archaeological discoveries in the years to come and with extended technical research into the bronzes already unearthed. We can look forward to many more exciting revelations in the future.

Let us close with a quotation from Needham's translation of the *Mengqi Bitan* by Shen Gua, the eleventh-century Chinese scholar, talking of the repolishing of old bronze mirrors:

> The ingenious workmanship of the ancients has not been equaled by subsequent generations. Nowadays, when people get hold of ancient mirrors, they actually have all surfaces ground flat. So perishes not only ancient skill but even the appreciation of ancient skill.

We hope that our recounting of our researches into alloys and casting methods has given you a little more appreciation for the ancient skills of the Chinese foundrymen; our appreciation of their skills increases with every new discovery.

22

Figures

22. A photomicrograph of the *leiwen* shown in figs. 20 and 21. An area of unremoved clay can be seen at the corner of the middle groove in the photograph. The first tool-stroke removed part of the clay in this area, but the second started not at the corner, but rather a little past it. The tool can be seen to have had a rounded edge. Multiple tool-strokes can also be seen in the other *leiwen* grooves, along with a slight rounding of the bottoms of the grooves. In the final bronze, these slightly rounded parts would form the tops of the cast *leiwen* pattern, and would be finished off flat. Photograph by the author, 1980, reproduced by courtesy of the Academia Sinica.

Notes

1. For example, the discovery of half-life-size bronze statues at the tomb of Qin Shihuang di as reported in the popular press, and the discovery of ten tons of bronzes in the tomb of Marquis Yi of Zheng in Sui Xian, Hubei Province. Some of the latter show evidence of lost-wax casting and the use of soft solder; see Hua Jueming, 1981, "... Lost-wax Process," also K.C. Chang, 1977, 1980, 1981.

2. Proceedings to be published by Science Press, Beijing, in 1983.

3. K.C. Chang, 1977, p. 204.

4. Chase and Franklin, p. 215; Johnson and Francis, p. 2.9.

5. Brill, et al., p. 93; a collaborative project to study further lead isotope ratios in Chinese bronzes and other materials is now in its second year: it is a joint venture of the Freer Gallery of Art and the U.S. National Bureau of Standards, and is funded by the Smithsonian Scholarly Studies Program, with aid from the Conservation-Analytical Laboratory.

6. Brown, et al., pp. 213–14 inter alia; Chase, 1975, 1978.

7. Chase and Ziebold, p. 300 ff.

8. Ibid., also Hanson and Pell-Walpole, p. 300 ff.

9. Barnard and Sato, p. 24–25.

10. Redrafted from Chase and Ziebold, figs. 5, 10, and 13.

11. Experiments to quantify the color changes in cast tin-lead bronzes are currently in progress as a joint project between the Center for the Study of Artist's Materials, Carnegie-Mellon University, and the Freer Gallery Technical Laboratory.

12. Gettens, 1934; Vandenbelt.

13. Riederer, Abb. 3; Dian Zhanghu.

14. Chase, 1973, p. 88.

15. Needham, 1964 and 1975, p. 1; see also Chase and Franklin, p. 243, note 67.

16. Copper Development Association, p. 20 ff.

17. Hanson and Pell-Walpole, p. 241 ff.; Matsuda, p. 85 ff.; Chadwick, p. 336.

18. Coghlan, p. 110; Melikian; Smith; Bayard; Wheeler and Maddin, p. 39.

19. Tichane, p. 14; Pope, 1949, p. 53.

20. An Zhimin, p. 269; Archaeometallurgy Group, B.U.I.S.T., p. 287.

21. An, p. 270.

22. An, p. 274; Archaeometallurgy Group, p. 298, table 6, nos. 6, 7; see also Li Xueqin, p. 3.

23. Han Rubin, et al., p. 2; Craddock, p. 11.

24. Zhang Xuezheng, et al., p. 3.

25. Ibid., Archaeometallurgy Group, passim.

26. Loehr, 1956, pp. 65 and 97.

27. Bagley, p. 197.

28. Franklin, p. 3; on the social climate of Eastern Zhou leading to increased personal adornment, see Gale and Hsü.

29. Fong, p. 74; An, p. 280.

30. An, p. 280.

31. Ibid.

32. Fong, p. 103 ff.

33. Number Li M1:8 in Bagley.

34. Stephen, passim.

35. Sung, p. 244; on the variability of the metal compositions of pre-Anyang versus Anyang bronzes see also Wan Chia-pao, 1975, p. 9.

36. Carpenter, pl. 3; see also p. 692.

37. Liang and Chang.

38. Barnard and Soto, p. 19.

39. Gettens, 1969, pp. 54 and 42–44.

40. Institute of Archaeology, 1980, p. 16.

41. In *Papers on Chinese Archaeology,* no. 2, 1982, in press.

42. Institute of Archaeology and the Hebei Committee for the Preservation of Archaeological Monuments, p. 378 ff.

43. Biot, vol. 2, p. 491 (bk. 41, fol. 3); on the interpretation of the formulas see Barnard, 1961, pp. 6–12; Gettens, 1969, p. 22; Chase and Ziebold, p. 314 ff.; for copper-tin formulas in other early cultures, see (inter alia) Pettinato, p. 175.

44. The author's examination of the famous gold dragon buckle from Tomb No. 9 in Pyongyang, Korea (now in the Korean National Museum, Seoul) revealed beyond any doubt that it had been decorated with real granulation and filigree.

45. Jenyns and Watson, p. 31, pl. 9.

46. Barnard, 1976, p. 68.

47. Gettens, 1969, p. 4 ff.

48. Tylecote, p. 31.

49. Untracht, passim.

50. Maryon, passim.

51. Meyers (in Harper and Meyers), p. 147; Gibbons and Ruhl, p. 181; Gibbons, Ruhl, and Shepherd, p. 166.

52. Untracht, pp. 246 and 481.

53. See n. 1; on general history and descriptions of lost-wax casting see Donaldson, Griswold, Hunt, Rich, and Young.

54. Gettens, 1969, p. 29.

55. For example, see the Freer Gallery of Art's Late Zhou *jian* basin (FGA #39.5) and its counterpart; Keyser, passim.

56. Barnard, 1961, p. 48 ff.; Gettens, 1969, p. 57 ff.; Keyser; Barnard and Sato, p. 53 ff.; Zhang Wanzhong; Wan Chia-pao, 1964, 1966, 1968, 1970, 1972; Fong, p. 71; Institute of Archaeology, p. 16 ff.; Hua Jueming, et al., 1981; Fairbank; Knauth, p. 116; Feng Fugen, et al.; for general information on modern and Western casting methods see Rich, Young, Clarke, and Flemings.

57. Pope, et al., 1967, p. 190 (no. 38; FGA #50.7); the author hopes to write the description of a complete examination of the set of four vessels for the Proceedings of the 1981 Canberra Conference on the Application of Scientifically Derived Data in Archaeological and Historical Research.

58. See, however, Barnard, 1961, pl. 13 and fig. 23, for a picture of a fragment of a model for a vessel not dissimilar to this one.

59. On the question of mold material, see Gettens, 1969, p. 107, and Zhang Wanzhong.

60. Barnard and Sato, p. 27 ff.

61. Gettens, 1969, p. 164.

62. Barnard and Sato, p. 5, fig. 2.

63. Loehr, 1953; see also Soper.

64. Fong, p. 74, no. 1; Bagley, figs. 22 and 23.

65. Barnard and Sato, pp. 52, 65–66; Li Ching-hua.

66. *The Enjo Foundry,* made in Matsue, Japan, by Robert Debold and Ed Yates with the assistance of the Desert Research Institute, Reno, Nevada, and Bill Bleachner of Bleachner Films, Reno.

67. Seen by the author at Tokyo Gedai University in 1979.

68. See bibliography; further, see Savage and Smith, pp. 291–92.

69. Gettens, 1969, p. 117, fig. 147; note that a relief line shows prominently in the vertical element on the viewer's right in the figure.

70. Ho Ping-ti, p. 199 ff.

71. Needham, 1962, sec. 26, p. 93.

Bibliography

An Zhimin, "Some Problems Concerning China's Early Copper and Bronze Artefacts" (in Chinese), *Kaogu Xuebao,* 1981, no. 3, pp. 269–85.

Archaeometallurgy Group, Beijing University of Iron and Steel Technology, "A Preliminary Study of Early Bronze Artefacts" (in Chinese), *Kaogu Xuebao,* 1981, no. 3, pp. 287–302.

Bagley, Robert W., "P'an-lung-ch'eng: A Shang City in Hupei," *Artibus Asiae,* vol. 39, nos. 3 and 4, 1977, pp. 165–219.

Barnard, Noel, *Bronze Casting and Bronze Alloys in Ancient China,* Monumenta Serica Monograph XIV, Tokyo: Nippon Oyo Printing Co., 1961.

Barnard, Noel, "Notes on Selected Bronze Artifacts in the National Palace Museum, the Historical Museum, and Academia Sinica," in *Proceedings of a Symposium on Scientific Methods of Research in the Study of Ancient Chinese Bronzes and Southeast Asian Metal and Other Archaeological Artifacts,* ed. N. Barnard, Melbourne, Australia: National Gallery of Victoria, 1976, pp. 47–82.

Barnard, Noel, and Sato Tamotsu, *Metallurgical Remains of Ancient China,* Tokyo: Nichiosha, 1975.

Bayard, Donn, "Temporal Distribution and Alloy Variation in Early Bronzes from Non Nok Tha," *Current Anthropology,* vol. 22, no. 6, Dec. 1981, pp. 697–99.

Biot, Edward, trans., *Le Tcheou-li ou Rites des Tcheou,* 2 vols., Paris: Imprimerie Nationale, 1851.

Brill, Robert H., Kazuo Yamasaki, I. Lynus Barnes, K.J.R. Rosman, and Migdalia Diaz, "Lead Isotopes in Some Japanese and Chinese Glasses," *Ars Orientalis,* vol. 11, 1979, pp. 87–109.

Brown, B. Floyd, Harry C. Burnett, W.T. Chase, Martha Goodway, Jerome Kruger, and Marcel Pourbaix, eds., *Corrosion and Metal Artifacts: A Dialogue Between Conservators and Archaeologists and Corrosion Scientists,* National Bureau of Standards Special Publication 479, Washington, D.C.: U.S. Department of Commerce, 1977.

Carpenter, H.C.H., "Preliminary Report on Chinese Bronzes," *Anyang Fa-chüeh-pao-kao,* pt. 4, 1933, pp. 677–79.

Chadwick, R., "The Effect of Composition and Constitution on the Working and on Some Physical Properties of the Tin Bronzes," *Journal of the Institute of Metals,* vol. 64, no. 1, 1939, pp. 332–78.

Chang Kwang-chih, *The Archaeology of Ancient China,* 3rd. ed., New Haven and London: Yale University Press, 1977.

Chang Kwang-chih, "In Search of China's Beginnings: New Light on an Old Civilization," *American Scientist,* vol. 69, Mar.-Apr. 1981, pp. 148–60.

Chang Kwang-chih, *Shang Civilization,* New Haven and London: Yale University Press, 1980.

Chase, W.T., *Bronze Disease and Its Treatment,* exh. cat., Bangkok National Museum, 1975.

Chase, W.T., "Examination of Art Objects in the Freer Gallery Laboratory," *Ars Orientalis,* vol. 9, 1973, pp. 79–88.

Chase, W.T., "Solid Samples from Metallic Antiquities and Their Examination," in *Cultural Property and Analytical Chemistry,* Proceedings of The Second International Symposium on Conservation and Restoration of Cultural Property (Nov. 27–30, 1978), Tokyo: Tokyo National Research Institute of Cultural Properties, 1979, pp. 74–109.

Chase, W.T., and Ursula Martius Franklin, "Early Chinese Black Mirrors and Pattern-etched Weapons," *Ars Orientalis,* vol. 11, 1979, pp. 215–58.

Chase, W.T., and Thomas O. Ziebold, "Ternary Representations of Ancient Chinese Bronze Compositions," chap. 18 in *Archaeological Chemistry II,* ed. Giles F. Carter, ACS Advances in Chemistry Series 171, Washington, D.C.: American Chemical Society, 1978, pp. 293–334.

Clarke, Carl Dame, *Metal Casting of Sculpture,* Butler, Md.: Standard Arts Press, 1948.

Coghlan, H.H., *Notes on the Prehistoric Metallurgy of Copper and Bronze in the Old World,* Pitt Rivers Museum Occasional Papers on Technology, 4, Oxford: University Press, 1951.

Copper Development Association, *Standards Handbook, Cast Copper and Copper Alloy Products, Part 7—Alloy Data,* rev. ed., New York: C.D.A., 1978.

Craddock, Paul T., "The Copper Alloys of Tibet and Their Background," pp. 1–31 in *Aspects of Early Metallurgy,* ed. W.A. Oddy and W. Zwalf, British Museum Occasional Paper 15, London: British Museum, 1981.

Dian Zhanghu, "Brilliant Scientific Achievements of Chinese Ancient Bronze Casting by Using Modern Analysis," paper presented at the Beijing Archaeometallurgy Conference, 1981, 8 pp.

Donaldson, J.A., "The Use of Gold in Dentistry: An Historical Overview," pts. 1 and 2, *The Gold Bulletin,* vol. 13, no. 3, July 1980, pp. 117–24, and vol. 13, no. 4, Oct. 1980, pp. 161–65.

Fairbank, Wilma, "Piece-mold Craftsmanship and Shang Bronze Design," *Archives of the Chinese Art Society of America,* vol. 16, 1962, pp. 9–15.

Flemings, Merton C., *Solidification Processing,* New York: McGraw-Hill, 1974.

Feng Fugen, Wang Zhenjiang, Bai Rongjin, and Hua Jueming, "More Researches on the Casting of the Ssu Mu Wu *fang ding,*" *Kaogu,* 1981, no. 2, pp. 177–82.

Fong Wen, ed., *The Great Bronze Age of China, An Exhibition from the People's Republic of China,* New York: Metropolitan Museum and Alfred A. Knopf, 1980.

Franklin, Ursula, "The Three Contradictions in Early Chinese Metallurgy: An Attempt at Their Resolution," paper presented at the Beijing Archaeometallurgy Conference, 1981, 25 pp.

Gale, Esson M., trans., *Discourses on Salt and Iron,* Sinica Leidensia, vol. 2, Leiden: E.J. Brill Ltd., 1931.

Gettens, Rutherford J., "Some Observations Concerning the Lustrous Surface on Ancient Eastern Bronze Mirrors," *Technical Studies in the Field of the Fine Arts,* vol. 3, 1934, pp. 29–37.

Gettens, Rutherford John, *The Freer Chinese Bronzes, Volume II, Technical Studies,* Freer Gallery of Art Oriental Studies, no. 7, Washington, D.C.: Smithsonian Institution, Freer Gallery of Art, 1969.

Gibbons, Donald F., and Katharine C. Ruhl, "The Metallurgical Technique of the 'Silver Plate with Figures,' Gupta Period," *Ars Orientalis,* vol. 11, 1979, pp. 177–82.

Gibbons, Donald F., Katharine C. Ruhl, and Dorothy G. Shepherd, "Techniques of Silversmithing in the Hormizd II Plate," *Ars Orientalis,* vol. 11, 1979, pp. 163–76.

Griswold, A.B., " Bronze Casting in Siam," *Bulletin de l'ecole Francaise d'Extreme Orient,* vol. 46, fasc. 2, 1954, pp. 635–39.

Han Rubin, Sun Shuyun, and Ye Xingfu, "The Formation of Brass During Prehistoric Smelting," paper presented at the Beijing Archaeometallurgy Conference, 1981, 6 pp.

Hanson, D., and W.T. Pell-Walpole, *Chill-cast Tin Bronzes,* London: Edward Arnold & Co., 1951.

Ho Ping-ti, *The Cradle of the East,* Hong Kong and Chicago: Chinese University of Hong Kong and University of Chicago Press, 1975.

Hsü Cho-yun, *Ancient China in Transition: An Analysis of Social Mobility,* 722–222 B.C., Stanford, Calif.: Stanford University Press, 1965.

Hua Jueming, "Ancient Bronze Smelting, Casting, and Early Iron Casting in China," paper presented at the Beijing Archaeometallurgy Conference, 1981, 9 pp.

Hua Jueming, "The Origin and Evolution of the Lost-wax Process in China," paper presented at the Beijing Archaeometallurgy Conference, 1981, 9 pp.

Hua Jueming, et. al., "Study of the Casting Technique of Bronzes from Lady Hao's Tomb" (in Chinese), *Papers on Chinese Archaeology,* no. 1, 1981, pp. 244–72.

Hunt, L.B., "The Long History of Lost Wax Casting: Over Five Thousand Years of Art and Craftsmanship," *The Gold Bulle-*

tin, vol. 13, no. 2, 1980, pp. 63–79.

Institute of Archaeology, Chinese Academy of Social Sciences, *Yinxu Fu Hao Mu* [Tomb of Lady Hao at Yinxu in Anyang], Beijing: Cultural Relics Publishing House, 1980.

Institute of Archaeology, Chinese Academy of Social Sciences, and the Hopei Committee for the Preservation of Archaeological Monuments, Hopei Province, *Mancheng Fajue Baogao* [Excavation of the Han Tombs at Mancheng], Beijing: Cultural Relics Publishing House, 1980.

Jenyns, R. Soame, and William Watson, *Chinese Art, the Minor Arts,* vol. 2, New York: Universe Books, 1963.

Johnson, A.B., and B. Francis, *Durability of Metals from Archaeological Objects, Metal Meteorites, and Native Metals,* Report PNL-3198 (UC-70) prepared for the U.S. Department of Energy under contract EY-76-C-06-1830, 2nd ed., Richland, Wash.: Batelle Memorial Institute Pacific Northwest Laboratory, 1980.

Keyser, Barbara W., "Decor Replication in Two Late Chou Bronze Chien," *Ars Orientalis,* vol. 11, 1979, pp. 127–62.

Knauth, Percy, and the Editors of Time-Life Books, *The Metalsmiths,* The Emergence of Man Series, New York: Time, 1974.

Li Ching-hua (The Honan Bureau of Culture Archaeological Team), "The Casting Process of the Han Dynasty Iron Ploughshares As Indicated by the Pottery Moulds and Cores Unearthed from the Remains of Wan Ch'eng at Nanyang, Honan Province" (in Chinese), *Wenwu,* 1965, no.7, pp. 1–11.

Li Xueqin, *The Wonder of Chinese Bronzes,* Beijing: Foreign Languages Press, 1980.

Liang Shu-ch'uan and Chang Kan-nan, "The Chemical Composition of Some Early Chinese Bronzes," *Journal of the Chinese Chemical Society,* vol. 17, no. 1, 1950, pp. 9–17.

Ling Yeqin, "The Chinese Traditional Lost Wax Casting Process," paper presented at the Beijing Archaeometallurgy Conference, 1981, 12 pp.

Loehr, Max, "The Bronze Styles of the Anyang Period (1300–1028 B.C.)," *Archives of the Chinese Art Society of America,* vol. 8, 1953, pp. 42–53.

Loehr, Max, *Chinese Bronze Age Weapons,* The Werner Jannings Collection in the Chinese National Palace Museum, Peking, Ann Arbor: University of Michigan Press, 1956.

Maryon, Herbert, "The Mildenhall Treasure: Some Technical Problems, Parts I and II," *Man,* vol. 48, Mar. and Apr. 1948, pp. 25–27 and 38–41.

Matsuda, Tsutomu, "On the Quenching and Tempering of Brass, Bronze and 'Aluminum-Bronze,' " *Journal of the Institute of Metals,* vol. 39, no. 1, 1928, pp. 67–109.

Melikian-Chirvani, Assadullah Souren, "The White Bronzes of Early Islamic Iran," *Metropolitan Museum Journal,* vol. 9, 1974, pp. 123–53.

Meyers, Pieter, "Technical Study," chap. 6 in *Silver Vessels of the Sasanian Period,* vol. 1, Regal Imagery, by Prudence O. Harper and Pieter Meyers, Metropolitan Museum of Art, New York, 1981.

Meyers, Pieter and Lore Holmes, "Technical Studies of Ancient Chinese Bronzes: Some Observations," elsewhere in this volume.

Needham, Joseph, *The Development of Iron and Steel Technology in China,* The Newcomen Society, 1964, Cambridge University Press, 1975.

Needham, Joseph, *Science and Civilization in China,* vol. 4, Physics and Physical Technology, pt. 1: Physics, Cambridge University Press, 1962.

Pettinato, Giovanni, *The Archives of Ebla: An Empire Inscribed in Clay,* Garden City, N.Y.: Doubleday and Co., 1981.

Pope, John A., "An Analysis of Shang White Pottery," *Far Eastern Ceramic Bulletin,* vol. 1, no. 6, June 1949, pp. 49–54.

Pope, John Alexander, Rutherford John Gettens, James Cahill, and Noel Barnard, *The Freer Chinese Bronzes, vol. 1, Catalogue,* Freer Gallery of Art Oriental Studies, no. 7, Washington, D.C.: Smithsonian Institution, Freer Gallery of Art, 1967.

Rich, Jack C., *The Materials and Methods of Sculpture,* New York: Oxford University Press, 1947.

Riederer, Josef, "Metallanalysen chinesescher Spiegel" [Metal analyses of Chinese mirrors], *Berliner Beiträge zur Archäeometrie,* vol. 2, 1977, pp. 6–16.

Romanoff, William, F.L. Ridell, and G.P. Halliwell, "Copper-base Foundry Alloys," chap. 24, pp. 508–34 in *Copper, The Science and Technology of the Metal, Its Alloys and Compounds,* ed. Allison Butts, ACS Monograph Series, no. 122, New York: Reinhold, 1954.

Savage, Elaine I., and Cyril Stanley Smith, "The Techniques of the Japanese Tsuba-Maker," *Ars Orientalis,* vol. 11, 1979, pp. 291–328.

Smith, Cyril Stanley, "Bronze Technology in the East: A Metallurgical Study of Early Thai Bronzes, with Some Speculations on the Cultural Transmission of Technology," in *Changing Perspectives in the History of Science: Essays in Honour of Joseph Needham,* ed. Mikulas Teich and Robert Young, London: Heinemann, pp. 21–32.

Smithells, Colin J., *Metals Reference Book,* vol. 3, 4th ed., New York: Plenum Press, 1967.

Solymos, Fred, *Brass and Bronze Ingot and Casting Alloys,* chart, Columbia, Pa: Colonial Metals Co., 1975 (?).

Soper, Alexander C., "Early, Middle, and Late Shang: A Note," *Artibus Asiae,* vol. 28, no. 1, 1966, pp. 5–38.

Stephen, Barbara, "Early Chinese Bronzes in the Royal Ontario Museum," *Oriental Art,* n.s., vol. 8, no. 2, 1962, pp. 63–67.

Stewart, James J., "A Description of the *So-gata* Casting Process with Respect to Iron Tea-Kettles." n.p., n.d.

Stewart, James J., *A Series of Bronze Vessels Using a Traditional Japanese Piece Molding Process,* B.A. thesis for the Division of Arts, Reed College, 1976.

Sung Ying-hsing, *Tiangong Kaiwu (T'ien-kung K'ai-wu),* Chinese Technology in the Seventeenth Century, trans. E-tu Zen Sun and Shiou-chuan Sun, University Park, Pa., and London: Pennsylvania State University Press, 1966.

Tichane, Robert, *Those Celadon Blues,* Painted Post, N.Y.: The New York State Institute for Glaze Research, 1979.

Tylecote, R.F., *A History of Metallurgy,* London: The Metals Society, 1976.

Untracht, Oppi, *Metal Techniques for Craftsmen,* Garden City, N.Y.: Doubleday & Co., 1968.

Vandenbelt, John Melvin, *Chemical Analysis of a Suite of Old Chinese Bronze Mirrors,* thesis for the Degree of Master of Arts, Boston University Graduate School, 1936.

Wan Chia-pao, "The Casting and Inlaying Methods of a Bronze Chien-Basin from Northern Honan" (in Chinese), *The Bulletin of the Department of Archaeology and Anthropology,* National Taiwan University, no. 41, Apr. 1980, pp. 14–39.

Wan Chia-pao, "The Casting and Technical Development of Anyang Bronze Vessels," pp. 12–53 (English summary, pp. 133–44) in *Archaeologia Sinica,* n.s., no. 5, *Studies of Fifty-three Ritual Bronzes,* Nankang: Academia Sinica, 1972.

Wan Chia-pao, "On the Technics of Bronzes from Yin Ruin and Its Related Problems," *Soochow University Journal of Chinese Art History,* vol. 5, July 1975, pp. 1–48.

Wan Chia-pao, "The Process of Casting the *ku*-beaker," pp. 1–44 (English summary, pp. 119–22) in *Archaeologia Sinica,* n.s., no. 1, *Studies of the Bronze ku-beaker,* Nankang: Academia Sinica, 1964.

Wan Chia-pao, "The Process of Casting the *chüeh*-cup," pp. 1–29 (English summary, pp. 123–27) in *Archaeologia Sinica,* n.s., no. 2, *Studies of the Bronze* chüeh-*cup,* Nankang: Academia Sinica, 1966.

Wan Chia-pao, "The Process of Casting the *chia*-vessel," pp. 1–40 (English summary, pp. 91–94) in *Archaeologia Sinica,* n.s., no. 3, *Studies of the Bronze* chia-*vessel,* Nankang: Academia Sinica, 1968.

Wan Chia-pao, "The Process of Casting the *ting*-cauldron," pp. 1–33 (English summary, pp. 97–113) in *Archaeologia Sinica,* n.s., no. 4, *Studies of the Bronze* ting-*cauldron,* Nankang: Academia Sinica, 1970.

Wheeler, Tamara Stech, and Robert Maddin, "The Techniques of the Early Thai Metalsmith," *Expedition,* vol. 18, no. 4, 1976, pp. 38–47.

Young, Ronald D., and Robert A. Fennell, *Methods for Modern Sculptors,* San Rafael, Calif.: Sculpt-Nouveau, 1980.

Zhang Wanzhong, "Houma Dung Zhou Taufan di Zaoxing Gongyi" [The manufacture of the Eastern Zhou ceramic molds found at Houma, Shanxi], *Wenwu,* nos. 4 and 5, 1962, pp. 6, 7, and 37–42.

Zhang Xuezheng, Sun Shuyun, Han Rubin, and Hu Wenlong, "Early Copper and Bronzes (2800–1600 B.C.) in Gansu," paper presented at the Beijing Archaeometallurgy Conference, 1981, 13 pp..

Technical Studies of Ancient Chinese Bronzes: Some Observations

Pieter Meyers
Senior Research Chemist

Los Angeles County Museum of Art

Lore L. Holmes
Research Associate

Metropolitan Museum of Art

DURING THE LAST THREE DECADES considerable progress has been made in understanding the procedures for casting ancient Chinese ceremonial vessels. It is due predominantly to the studies of Karlbeck, Shi Zhangru, Barnard, and Gettens that techniques of the Chinese foundries of the Shang and Zhou dynasties have become reasonably well understood. Examinations of surviving mold fragments and bronze vessels have convincingly demonstrated that the Chinese foundry used exclusively the piece-mold or section-mold casting process.[1]

The development of metal technology in China is unlike that in any other part of the world. Little is known about the initial stages because only very few metal artifacts from the beginning of China's Bronze Age have been unearthed so far. The earliest vessels known, such as those from the Erlitou culture,[2] represent an already advanced state of metallurgy and metalworking. These and other objects were made by a complicated piece-mold technique using an alloy of copper and tin or a ternary alloy of copper, tin, and lead. No clear evidence exists of shaping by hammering, while the lost-wax technique was probably not employed until the late Spring and Autumn period (sixth-fifth century B.C.). The achievements of the ancient Chinese foundry using the piece-mold casting technique are truly remarkable, as is witnessed by the large number of ceremonial vessels, many of which are of great complexity and exhibit a high-quality craftsmanship.

It is generally agreed that piece-mold casting involved four operations:

(1) The manufacture of a model, probably made of ceramic materials. The model defines the shape and size of the vessel to be cast; decoration may have been applied to the model.

(2) The production of a series of mold impressions from the model in flexible ceramic material; decoration may have been applied to the mold sections.

(3) The assembly of the mold. The mold assembly consisted of the various hardened or fired mold sections, a core (possibly the model reduced in size by scraping away the outside surface), with the space between the mold and core fixed by means of a series of bronze spacers.

(4) The pouring of a molten alloy of copper, tin, and lead into the hollow space of the mold assembly. After it has cooled, and the mold and core broken away, the bronze is finished by cleaning and polishing away surface irregularities and some of the mold marks.

Although there is general agreement on the use of the piece-mold casting technique, much uncertainty still exists on various details of specific procedures. For example, the use of a model for certain vessels has been questioned,[3] while there is considerable ambiguity about how and at what stage decoration was applied: Was the decoration drawn on the model or on the mold, or perhaps partly on the model and partly on the mold?[4] Joining techniques, particularly in the Zhou bronzes, are not well understood. It is not known when the concept of solder became known to the bronze caster. More general questions remain unanswered as well. It has not yet been possible to establish a detailed chronological development in casting technology. Differences in casting techniques between various centers of bronze production cannot yet be recognized. These and many other questions can only be answered after detailed technical studies are made of ceremonial vessels, much larger in number than those that have so far been published. It is especially important that such studies be undertaken routinely on excavated bronzes by our colleagues in the People's Republic of China. Only vessels of accurately known date and provenance can serve as true "standards" for our observations.

Understanding of the development of bronze casting technology may also be of considerable significance for the art historian. During the Bronze Age of China, more than in any other civilization, the technology played a most important role in the production of ritual vessels—not only in providing metal alloys and basic casting procedures but also in affecting the shapes and forms of vessels and determining to a large extent their decorative patterns and the extent and level of relief. Therefore, stylistic developments were very closely linked to the progress in technology. In a society as free from external influences as that of China, stylistic developments can only be properly explained if the possibilities and limitations of the technology are fully recognized. This requires a detailed knowledge of all stages in the bronze casting procedures that can only be acquired through systematic investigations.

Technical studies alone, however, can never achieve a complete reconstruction of the technology of ancient China. Their results are most meaningful only when they are integrated with art historical and archaeological evidence.

The following observations, suggestions, and speculations on certain aspects of the bronze casting procedure are predominantly the result of a systematic technical study carried out by the authors on Chinese bronzes from the Arthur M. Sackler Collections.[5] In this partially completed investigation, one hundred twenty vessels from the Shang and early Western Zhou periods have been studied. Each of the vessels has been carefully examined visually and by using a binocular microscope. X-ray powder diffraction techniques have been employed to identify mineral components, and when needed, metallographic studies were carried out on available samples. X-ray radiographs, made of all objects studied, provided important information on details of the casting procedures and on ancient and modern repairs. Elemental analyses of drilled metal samples were carried out at Brookhaven National Laboratory; atomic absorption spectrometry was employed for the determination of the major components copper, lead, tin, and iron, while neutron activation analysis was used for the determination of minor and trace elements: arsenic, antimony, zinc, cobalt, nickel, silver, mercury, and gold. Lead isotope ratios are being processed by mass spectrometry at the National Bureau of Standards.

The Use of a Model and Evidence for Decoration Applied to the Model

Most descriptions of the Chinese piece-mold casting procedure include as the first step the preparation of a model, presumably one made of clay. There is, however, no direct evidence for the use of a model; no complete or partial ceramic models from the Shang or Western Zhou periods have ever been unearthed in China. Furthermore, the manufacture of certain types of vessels is feasible without a model, as has been demonstrated for example by Chase and by Smith.[6] However, the evidence collected in our study indicates that a large majority of vessels examined required a model in their production process.

A jia of pre-Anyang date carries literally the imprint of a ceramic model. This relatively simple and crudely made vessel, shown in Figure 1, reveals a faint design on parts of its interior wall (Figure 2). The presence of this design can only satisfactorily be explained as resulting from a core that consisted of the upper part of a decorated model, its surface scraped down but not deep enough to remove all decoration. The use of a scraped-down model as a casting core has been widely accepted, even though there was no direct evidence that this practice did take place. This jia provides the first direct evidence of the use of a scraped-down model. It is apparent that the model for a different vessel was used since the decoration pattern on the interior is not seen on the exterior surface.

The jue shown in Figure 3 is another vessel that provides evidence for the existence of a decorated model and therefore for the procedure: preparation of a decorated model, from which were fabricated mold sections with "negative" decoration, that served in turn to define the shape of the cast bronze. A detail of the decorative band seen in Figure 4 shows that in certain parts there is no decoration on the bronze. It is significant that these flat areas with missing decoration are at the same level as the top surface of the decorated areas. The possibility that the molten metal did not flow in the decorative pattern of the mold during casting must be excluded, since it would have caused the areas with missing decoration to be at a level below the actual surface. Most likely the cast metal surface reflected accurately what was on the mold sections. Areas with missing decoration in the mold sections would almost certainly have been the result of an inaccurate registration or incomplete transfer of the design at the time when mold impressions were made of the (decorated) model. Why the bronze caster allowed the use of an imperfect mold is an interesting question but beyond the scope of this essay.[7]

If the two vessels described above provide accidental proof for the use of decorated models in particular cases, the following will present more general evidence and will define the extent of decorating on a model versus decorating on mold sections. A careful study of the decoration on Shang or Western Zhou bronzes such as the jia of Figure 5 shows that the design elements are mostly linear, i.e., achieved predominantly by drawing lines. The lines could have been applied either to the model or the mold sections, in either case presumably on clay. The difference between the two methods is that on the model the decorating is done in the "positive," identical to that seen on the bronze vessel, while decoration of the mold sections requires a "negative" pattern with intaglio lines on the mold sections corresponding to raised lines on the bronze.

1 GREAT BRONZE AGE OF CHINA

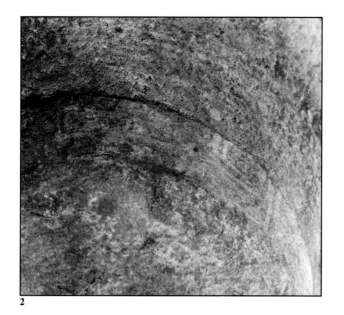

2

4

3

5

Figures

1. *Jia,* bronze, 14th century B.C., Arthur M. Sackler Collections, New York, V 319.

2. Detail of the interior wall of *jia,* V 319. The faintly visible decoration indicates that the core used in the casting process of this vessel consisted of the upper part of a decorated model, its surface scraped down, but not enough to remove all decoration.

3. *Jue,* bronze, 12th-11th century B.C., Arthur M. Sackler Collections, New York, V 249.

4. Detail of decorative band on body of *jue,* V 249. The absence of decoration is believed to result from incomplete transfer of the design when mold impressions were taken from the decorated model.

5. *Jia,* bronze, 12th century B.C., Arthur M. Sackler Collections, New York, V 325.

127

To distinguish between the two possibilities it is most helpful to compare the bronze surface with accurate impressions of it. Such impressions duplicate as closely as possible the actual decorated surfaces of the mold sections originally used for casting the bronze. The material chosen to make these impressions is a synthetic product, "Polyform," used predominantly for making seal impressions. By comparing side by side a specific area of a bronze (Figure 6) with its impression (Figure 7), it is often possible to decide whether the decoration was made on the model (positive) or on the mold sections (negative). Line widths,

undercut lines, and uneven line depths—all potential characteristic features—were closely examined, but the presence of small angular protrusions that result when two intaglio lines meet turned out to be the most convincing indicator. Such characteristic sharp and angular segments, such as those indicated by arrows in Figure 6, occur frequently in the corners of the swirls in the *leiwen* designs. It is easily seen that these protrusions are logically formed when the design is drawn on the model ("positive," as in Figure 6); to produce the matching "negative" design on the mold sections would require extensive carving and modeling

6

in addition to line drawings. Clearly, designs like the one on this *jia,* were made on the model.[8]

The *yu* shown in Figure 8 may serve as another example. A detail of its decorated upper register is shown in Figure 9, with the impression of this area in Figure 10. Angular protrusions in the *leiwen* indicate that at least this part of the decoration was made on the model. Careful comparison of the positive and negative images provides convincing evidence that the dragons, in relatively high relief, were also made on the model. It can be observed, for example, that the design on the dragons could be achieved as a simply

drawn pattern of lines when made on the model, but to produce this design on the mold sections would be so complicated as to make it an unlikely procedure.

With the exception of those with thread relief decoration, nearly all vessels examined would seem to have required fully decorated models. The designs for vessels with thread relief decoration, mostly in Loehr's Style I, were unquestionably applied in the mold sections.[9] There is in fact no evidence that models were employed in the manufacture of these objects, although for technical reasons the use of models seems likely.

7

9

10

8

Figures

6. Detail of design of *jia,* V 325.

7. Impression made of area shown in fig. 6. A comparison of the decoration seen in fig. 6, which is comparable to the decoration that would have been on the model, with that in figure 7, representative of the decoration on the mold, leads to the conclusion that all decoration was applied to the model. This conclusion is predominantly based on the presence of angular protrusions, such as those indicated by arrows, that could only have been formed when the design had been prepared on the model.

8. *Yu,* bronze, 12th-11th century B.C., Arthur M. Sackler Collections, New York, V 384.

9. Detail of upper band of decoration on *yu,* V 384.

10. Impression made of area shown in fig. 9. Comparison of the "positive" (fig. 9) and "negative" images (fig. 10) of the decoration, representing the designs on the model and mold sections, respectively, indicates that the entire design had been applied to the model.

129

One of the few vessels in the Sackler Collections with a substantial part of its design made in the mold sections is a *pou,* shown in Figure 11. The designs on the shoulder and on the foot were applied on the model. This conclusion is based on evidence similar to that described for the *jia* in Figure 5 and the *yu* in Figure 8. The design covering the lower two-thirds of the bronze vessel has different characteristics. For example, a number of vertical lines appear in this region of the vessel, visible in the detail shown in Figure 12. The first line on the left is a mold line; the others, indicated by arrows, are lines in relief interrupted only by the relief elements of the design itself. The impres-

sion of this area, shown in Figure 13, provides an explanation: The vertical lines were drawn in the mold sections as guides to assist the craftsman in applying an evenly spaced geometric pattern and *leiwen* decoration.[10] The characteristics of the design elements, observed by comparing the positive and negative images, are entirely consistent with the theory that this decoration was executed on the mold sections.

Decorated models seem to have been employed consistently in the production of ceremonial bronzes, starting with vessels with Loehr's Style II decorations.[11] Decorating on the mold sections took place for Style I and other vessels with thread relief design,

11

only occasionally on other vessels, and was otherwise restricted to small adjustments, repairs, and relatively minor additions to the decoration such as circles[12] and possibly extremities like the eyes of *taotie* faces and dragons. The consistent use of fully decorated models implies that the Shang craftsman at an early stage had mastered the skill of making mold impressions from models, without losing even the finest details while using only three or four and only occasionally six vertical mold divisions. To do this successfully, the mold material must have been sufficiently flexible to allow it to be withdrawn, even from models with high relief decoration such as seen in Loehr's

Style V vessels. The realization that nearly all decoration was conceived and executed in the "positive," and that decorations were routinely transferred from model to mold to bronze without loss of detail, may be of considerable value in understanding the development of bronze casting technology and decorative patterns.

Problems and Solutions in the Casting Procedure

Many bronze vessels carry the evidence of the problems that were encountered in casting. Casting flaws or failures were mostly due to trapped air and

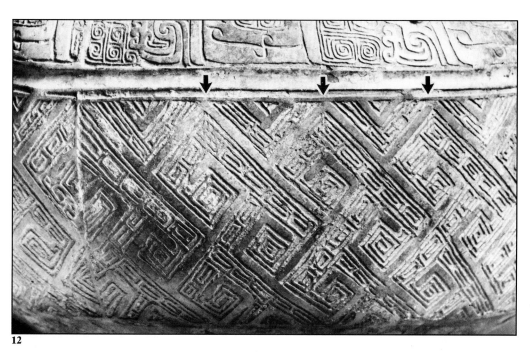

12

13

Figures

11. *Pou,* bronze, 13th century B.C., Arthur M. Sackler Collections, New York, V 380.

12. Detail of decoration on lower section of *pou,* V 380.

13. Impression made of area shown in fig. 12. Comparison of design characteristics in the "positive" and "negative" images of the decoration shows that this part of the decoration was made in the mold sections. The most characteristic features are the vertical lines (see arrows) which can be identified as guide lines drawn in the mold sections to assist in the execution of the design.

131

degassing of the molten alloy. The steps taken by the bronze caster to avoid or minimize these problems can often be reconstructed from careful examinations of the bronze vessels. It can be demonstrated that most vessel types were cast upside down. This casting position allowed pouring channels, gates, and risers to be attached to the legs and caused fewer problems than other possible mold orientations. However, casting flaws and failures still occurred, especially in the legs and in the bottom of the vessel where air and gases were likely to be trapped.

One of the most straightforward solutions to allow the escape of trapped air from the bottom was to provide vent holes in the foot core. This method was used for a large southern *zun,* shown in Figure 14. The underside of the bottom shows two metal extremities, indicating that small holes were pierced in the foot core in which trapped air could harmlessly be collected during casting (Figure 15).

A more common technique to facilitate the escape of trapped air in the porous core material was to score the foot core. This produced the often observed

14

fish net or criss-cross patterns, and occasionally more artistic patterns (Figure 16). Other explanations have been offered for the fish net patterns: that they resulted from the use of threads or strings to suspend the foot core, or that the lines in the foot core prevented slippage and insured the proper register of the mold sections.[13] Since the observed patterns were apparently always made by incisions on the foot core, not by strings, and since such an incised pattern would do little to secure the core in place or to align it in the mold assembly, it is unlikely that the incisions made

in the foot core were meant for anything else but to let trapped air escape.

Casting problems or failures occurred most often in the legs of vessels, especially those of *ding* and *fang ding* containers. The many ancient repairs on vessel legs bear witness to these problems. A number of variations in the casting process have been observed, each meant to reduce the risk of casting failure. Probably the earliest method was to cast partly hollow legs by extending the core into the legs. Another possibility to minimize casting failure was to cast each

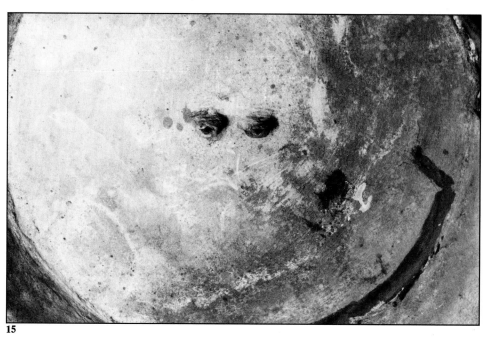
15

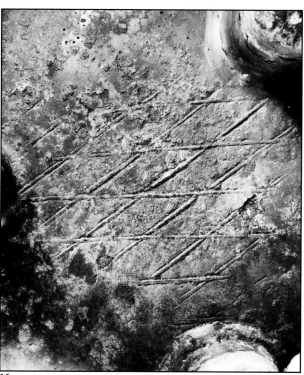
16

Figures

14. *Zun,* bronze, 13th century B.C., Arthur M. Sackler Collections, New York, V 286.

15. View of the underside bottom of *zun,* V 286, showing two extremities formed during the casting when metal flowed into holes pierced into the footcore for the purpose of venting trapped air.

16. Underside of *ding,* bronze, 12th-11th century B.C., Arthur M. Sackler Collections, New York, V 376. Criss-cross pattern was incised in foot core to let trapped air escape during casting.

leg integrally with the vessel, using a separate ceramic core in each leg, held in place by spacers or core extensions on the inner surface of each leg. Other methods involved separate casting operations for the legs and the vessel; legs were cast on to an already completed vessel, or they were pre-cast, generally around a ceramic core, and incorporated in the mold assembly prior to the casting of the vessel. Another technique, not previously reported, involved the use of copper leg cores. Each of three ding vessels of the Anyang period, one of which is shown in Figure 17, appears to have legs cast of solid metal (Figure 18). However, close examination of the X-ray radiographs reveals that the legs were cast around a metal core (Figure 19). Elemental analyses of samples from these metal cores, reported in Table 1, show that the core consisted of unalloyed copper. This is the first evidence for the use of pure copper in the manufacture of Shang bronzes.

The use of copper as a casting core may indicate that the Shang bronze caster had advanced knowledge of melting points of copper and bronze alloys, because a copper core has a melting point considerably higher than that of the alloy cast around it. This would significantly reduce the risk of casting failures. Whether or not the use of copper cores was limited to a specific period or to specific production centers is uncertain. If that were the case, the presence of such cores could be helpful in provenance studies. More research is needed to answer this question.

Clues to the provenance of a vessel may lie in another specific detail of the casting process, the manner in which ceramic cores were secured in the mold assembly of certain guang and gui vessels. X-ray radiographs of handles from three different vessels, all attributed to the early Western Zhou (or pre-conquest Zhou periods),[14] show that these handles were cast around a ceramic core that was kept in place during the casting by means of pairs of pyramid-shaped ceramic core extensions. One of these vessels is shown in Figure 20 with the X-ray radiograph of its handle, reproduced in Figure 21. The small square radiograph images of these core extensions can clearly be seen.

The observations and conclusions described above include only those results of the current investigation that relate in a general manner to piece-mold casting technology. The results of the analytical program are tentative, yet promising. Elemental compositions of the metal alloys have shown considerable potential for provenance studies. Analytical studies of core material appear to be less useful. Determinations of lead-isotope ratios will be completed soon; they are expected to contribute to the grouping of objects of common origin. Based on elemental compositions, lead isotope ratios, and other characteristics, it may ultimately be possible to establish the provenance of vessels that were not excavated under controlled conditions. This requires systematic examinations and analytical programs carried out on excavated and dated materials. Obviously, this can only be achieved through collaboration with our colleagues in the People's Republic of China who are studying their collections.[15]

17

18

Table 1: Elemental Composition of Samples from Legs of Three *ding* Vessels

Object Inv. No.	Sample Site	Concentration in percent				Concentration in micrograms per gram (ppm)								Total %
		Cu	Sn	Pb	Fe	Zn	Au	Ag	Hg	As	Sb	Co	Ni	
V 89	a	83.8	9.5	3.3	0.089	54	11.2	1190	6.6	860	116	28.0	92	97
	b	98.8	0.31	0.95	0.044	115	2.8	330	12.8	540	38	8.7	62	100
V 125	a	85.7	11.1	1.21	0.54	93	16.6	250	11.4	2200	77	160.0	2800	99
	b	96.4	<0.1	0.61	1.24	128	11.0	260	13.1	540	65	65.0	280	98
V 337	a	80.8	12.7	2.3	0.031	34	31.0	520	7.7	1320	220	18.8	79	96
	b	98.4	0.14	<0.05	0.122	76	44.0	164	15.5	144	35	16.3	n.d.	99

a – from outside wall of leg
b – from interior of leg
n.d. – not determined

Sample size: 50–60 mg. obtained by drilling.

Method of Analysis: 1. For major components copper, tin, lead, and iron: atomic absorption spectrophotometry on aqueous solutions containing 10 mg. bronze.
2. For trace elements zinc, gold, silver, mercury, arsenic, antimony, cobalt, nickel: instrumental neutron activation analysis on 20 mg. bronze.

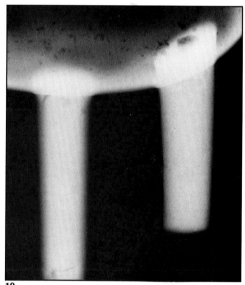

19

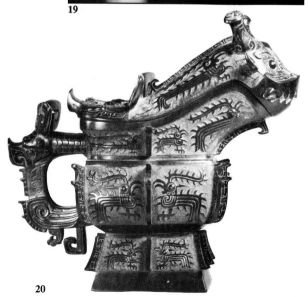

20

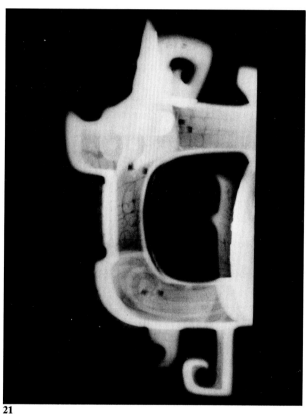

21

Figures

17. *Ding,* bronze, 13th-11th century B.C., Arthur M. Sackler Collections, New York, V 125.

18. X-ray radiograph of *ding,* V 125.

19. Detail of X-ray radiograph of *ding,* V 125. Legs are cast around a solid metal core, analyzed as unalloyed copper.

20. *Guang,* bronze, 11th century B.C., Arthur M. Sackler Collections, Princeton, V 307.

21. X-ray radiograph of handle of *guang,* V 307, showing three pairs of square images. They are caused by pyramid-shaped extensions from the ceramic core that served to keep the core in position while casting was taking place.

135

Notes

1. O. Karlbeck, "Anyang Moulds," *Bulletin of the Museum of Far Eastern Antiquities,* no. 7, 1935, pp. 39–60.
   Shih Chang-ju (Shi Zhangru), "Yin Tai ti Chu T'ung Kung-yi," *Bulletin of the Academia Sinica,* Taiwan, vol. 26, 1955, pp. 95–129.
   Noel Barnard, *Bronze Casting and Bronze Alloys in Ancient China,* Monumenta Serica Monograph XIV, Canberra: Australian National University and Monumenta Serica, 1961.
   Noel Barnard and Sato Tamotsu, *Metallurgical Remains of Ancient China,* Tokyo: Nichiosha, 1975.
   R.J. Gettens, *The Freer Chinese Bronzes, II, Technical Studies,* Washington: Smithsonian Institution 4706, 1969.

2. For example, see the *jue,* color pl. 1 in: Wen Fong, ed., *The Great Bronze Age of China: An Exhibition from the People's Republic of China,* exh. cat., Metropolitan Museum of Art, New York, 1980, p. 79.

3. See contribution of W.T. Chase, elsewhere in this volume.

4. Gettens, *Freer Chinese Bronzes,* pp. 57–60.

5. A multi-volume catalogue of the Chinese bronzes of the Arthur M. Sackler Collections is currently in preparation. Robert W. Bagley, *Shang Ritual Bronzes in the Arthur M. Sackler Collections, Vol. 1 of Ancient Chinese Bronzes in the Arthur M. Sackler Collections,* Harvard University Press, Cambridge, Massachusetts, will include full descriptions of the following objects illustrated in this article. The objects are identified by inventory number (V) and catalogue number, respectively: *jia,* V 319, cat. no. 3; *jue,* V 249, cat. no. 20; *jia,* V 325, cat. no. 6; *yu,* V 384, cat. no. 99; *pou,* V 380, cat. no. 53; *zun,* V 286, cat. no. 43; *ding,* V 376, cat. no. 86; *ding,* V 125, cat. no. 83. One of the vessels, a *guang,* V 307, cat. no. not yet determined, will be included in: Jessica Rawson, *Western Zhou Ritual Bronzes in the Arthur M. Sackler Collections, Vol. 2 of Ancient Chinese Bronzes in the Arthur M. Sackler Collections,* Harvard University Press, Cambridge, Massachusetts, in preparation.

6. See contribution of W.T. Chase, elsewhere in this volume. Cyril S. Smith, "Metallurgical Footnotes to the History of Art," *Proceedings of the American Philosophical Society, 116,* no. 2, 1972, pp. 107–12.

7. The phenomenon of missing decoration is not unique. During a recent visit to the People's Republic of China, one of the authors (Pieter Meyers) noticed two more examples, both *jue* vessels—one in the Museum of Luoyang, the other in the Historical Museum, Beijing—with large plain areas in the decorative band.

8. A particularly clear example of a design made on the model is shown in: Fong, *Bronze Age of China,* p. 226, pl. 53. Angular protrusions, line shapes, uneven line depths in this detailed photograph of a *yu* indicate that this design was made in the "positive," i.e., the model.

9. Max Loehr, "The Bronze Styles of the Anyang Period (1300–1028 B.C.)," *Archives of the Chinese Art Society of America,* vol. 7, 1953, pp. 42–53. For examples of Style I vessels see: Fong, *Bronze Age of China,* p. 84, pl. 4, and pp. 92–95, pl. 11.

10. There are in total 21 vertical lines on this vessel. Of these, 3 are easily identified as mold lines; the other 18 are guide lines, 6 in each mold section.

11. This conclusion differs from the description of casting procedures given by Bagley in: Fong, *Bronze Age of China,* pp. 70–73, 98–102, and 182. Bagley in his description of the development of decorative styles as a function of the progress in casting technology states that the decoration of Style II vessels took place in the mold sections. Our conclusion that, as a rule, the design was applied on the model starting with Style II decorations, appears to provide a better explanation for the relatively abrupt stylistic change from Style I to Style II and the gradual changes that were to follow later.

12. Circles were easily impressed in mold sections. See for examples: Fong, *Bronze Age of China,* p. 89, pl. 9; p. 135, pl. 13; and p. 143, pl. 17.

13. Gettens, *Freer Chinese Bronzes,* pp. 70–74.

14. Virginia C. Kane, oral communication, May 23–24, 1981.

15. We are most grateful to Dr. Arthur M. Sackler for his permission and encouragement to examine the Chinese bronzes from his collections. We would like to thank Lois Katz for her advice and suggestions. Without her enthusiastic support this project could not have been undertaken. The many long discussions with Robert W. Bagley have contributed significantly to our understanding of ancient Chinese bronzes. For this we are most grateful to him.
   All photography, except X-ray radiography, was performed by Otto E. Nelson. It is thanks to his skill that we are able to present a large amount of visual evidence.